Youth and the Extreme Right

Youth and the Extreme Right

Cas Mudde, editor

International Debate Education Association

New York, London & Amsterdam

Published by
The International Debate Education Association
105 East 22nd Street
New York, NY 10010

This book is published with the generous support of the Open Society Foundations.

Library of Congress Cataloging-in-Publication Data

Youth and the extreme right / Cas Mudde, editor.
    pages cm
 ISBN 978-1-61770-093-4
 1. Youth--Political activity. 2. Youth--Social conditions. 3. Right-wing extremists. I. Mudde, Cas.
 HQ799.2.P6Y656 2014
 305.235--dc23
                                    2013043351

 IDEBATE Press

Composition by Richard Johnson
Printed in the USA

Contents

Youth and the Extreme Right: Explanations, Issues, and Solutions

Most people associate the extreme right with young white males, often skinheads, an image strongly propagated by the media. Whether it is meetings of small neo-Nazi groups or large radical-right parties, media will focus their attention disproportionately on the most extreme elements within the crowd: young men, heavily tattooed, heads freshly shaven, with a fanatic stare and, preferably, their right arm in the air (to make the fascist salute). The young male skinhead is the international embodiment of the right-wing extremist, even though most right-wing extremists are not skinheads and most skinheads are not right-wing extremists.

Despite the fact that the media usually associate the extreme right with young males—that is, under the age of 30—there is very little academic research on the relationship between youth and the extreme right. While thousands of articles and books have recently been published on the extreme right, the vast majority of these academic sources focus almost exclusively on radical-right political parties and their voters (e.g., Bale 2012). Much less is known about extreme-right activists, including party members, whom mainstream social scientists find difficult to reach and study because of their closed and often hostile and violent nature (e.g., Blee 1998). Consequently, most studies of activists are based on a small sample of relatively prominent group members (e.g., Klandermans and Mayer 2006).

Although significant differences exist between various far-right activists, these activists have one factor in common: most develop their ideas during their youth, a finding consistent with decades of research on the early development of political attitudes (e.g., Greenberg 1970; Sears 1975). In fact, many first became active within the far right in their youth.

Given this important connection between youth and the extreme right, the dearth of studies on the topic creates important problems for both the understanding of and the response to the phenomenon. If we want to understand why people develop extreme-right attitudes, join extreme-right groups, or engage in extreme-right violence, we have to at least begin studying them during their youth. Moreover, we have to do so in an interdisciplinary way, as only through insights from various disciplines can we fully understand the extreme right in all its complexities.

This anthology brings together accessible articles on youth and the extreme right. The approach is truly multidisciplinary, bringing together essays from a variety of academic fields, including anthropology, political science, psychology, sociology, and social work. The texts address the situation in Europe and North America, but the broader processes can be observed outside of these particular geographical contexts. The selected texts are fairly representative of the English-language publications in the field.[1]

The main aim of the volume is to enable people to discuss the topic of the extreme right and youth, in all its facets, on the basis of factual information rather than common misperceptions. It also alerts readers to similarities with other youth cultures, ranging from soccer hooligans to street gangs, to enable practitioners to pull information from different (and partly more developed) fields of research and to learn from experiences with related youth groups.

The volume is divided into three thematic sections, addressing the main explanations of the rise of right-wing extremism among youth, the issues connected with it, and possible solutions. Each section opens with a short introduction and includes four articles. Although a few articles include some technical analyses, their main arguments and conclusions should be accessible to the average reader. The anthology ends with a short appendix of further resources, which includes additional academic texts, autobiographical books by (former) extreme-right activists, and movies that address the issue.

The rest of this introduction provides a broad overview of the literature on youth and the extreme right, following the broader structure of the book. In the first section we provide a concise overview of the extreme right, focusing in particular on youth groups. It first looks at the various ways in which the development of extreme-right attitudes and behaviors among youths is explained in the academic literature. The next section addresses two of the most important issues related to extreme-right issues: prejudice and violence. The final section deals with prevention and intervention, focusing on the many projects that have recently been implemented in a broad variety of Western democracies. The introduction concludes with a short summary and some suggestions to constructively address the sensitive topic of the extreme right with adolescents.

The Extreme Right

People participate in extreme-right activities in many ways, and youths are no exception to this general rule. However, there are some important differences in the ways in which youth and adults participate in politics in general, and the extreme right in particular. Simply stated, people can participate through political parties, social movement organizations, and subcultures (e.g., Minkenberg 2008; Mudde 2005).

Before we give a short overview of the extreme right, subdivided by type of organization, a few words on terminology would be helpful. This is not the place to reflect on the "war of words," the fierce academic and public debate over the correct terminology of the phenomenon of interest here (e.g., Mudde 1996), but it is important to clarify how we will use "extreme right." Most definitions of the term share several features: nationalism, authoritarianism, xenophobia, and anti-democracy. Some authors make a distinction between extreme and radical right, in which the first opposes the essence of democracy, namely popular sovereignty and majority rule, while the second accepts that essence but opposes key features of *liberal* democracy, namely pluralism and the protection of minority rights (e.g., Mudde 2007). Other authors point to differences in the primary identity of various extreme-right sub-ideologies, such as ethnic, racial, or religious identities (e.g., Minkenberg 2008).

To minimize confusion, we will use the term to include both extreme- and radical-right groups. Hence, the term captures both nationalist political parties that try to reform the political system through elections and parliamentary action, like the French National Front, and racist groups that reject elections and parliamentary democracy, like the National Social Movement in the United States. It also includes subcultures, or more often parts of subcultures, with relatively amorphous ideologies, such as football hooligans or skinheads. The various types of organizations have different relations to youths. Overall, the more formally structured an organization, the less attractive it is to young people, and the less important their roles within it are. This applies to all youths, not just those of the extreme right.

The most structured political organizations are political parties, which are key institutions in democracies around the globe. They are also the main democratic link between the people and the state. Of all forms of political participation, voting for political parties is the only one that a majority of people regularly engages in (Dalton 2008). Extreme-right parties contest elections in many democracies around the world, although these parties' electoral success differs significantly between countries and in time (e.g., Hainsworth 2008). Table 1 provides an overview of the main extreme-right parties in Europe, that is, those currently or recently represented in the national parliament.[2] The table includes the highest electoral percentage result since 1980, as well as the result in the last national parliamentary election of the selected extreme parties.

While millions of Europeans vote for extreme-right parties like the Austrian Freedom Party or the Movement for a Better Hungary (Jobbik), relatively few youths do. First of all, many young people are not allowed to vote, as they are younger than 18, the usual voting age. Second, the young people who are allowed to vote—that is, 18–25-year-olds—tend to vote much less than other age groups (e.g., Dalton 2008). Consequently, while voting is the main form of extreme-right participation for adults, it is not necessarily so for youths. That said, the young who do vote in countries like Austria and France vote disproportionately for extreme-right parties (Arzheimer 2012). However, "youth" is often defined as 18–35-year-olds, of which the main support comes from the 25–35-year-olds.

Table 1. Electoral results of parliamentary extreme-right parties in Europe, 1980–2013

Country result	Party	Highest result	Latest
		(%)	(%)
Austria	Alliance for the Future of Austria (BZÖ)	10.7 (2008)	10.7 (2008)
	Freedom Party of Austria (FPÖ)	26.9 (1999)	17.5 (2008)
Belgium	Flemish Interest (VB)	12.0 (2007)	7.8 (2010)
Bulgaria	National Union Attack (NSA)	9.4 (2009)	7.4 (2013)
Denmark	Danish People's Party (DFP)	13.8 (2007)	12.3 (2011)
Greece	Golden Dawn (CA)	7.0 (2012)	6.9 (2012)*
Hungary	Movement for a Better Hungary (Jobbik)	16.7 (2010)	16.7 (2010)
Italy	Northern League (LN)	10.1 (1996)	4.1 (2013)
Latvia	National Alliance (NA)	13.9 (2011)	13.9 (2011)
Netherlands	Party for Freedom (PVV)	15.5 (2010)	10.1 (2012)
Romania	Greater Romania Party (PRM)	19.5 (2000)	1.5 (2012)
Russia	Liberal Democratic Party of Russia (LDPR)	23.0 (1993)	12.5 (2011)
Serbia	Serbian Radical Party (SRS)	29.5 (2008)	4.6 (2012)
Slovakia	Slovak National Party (SNS)	11.6 (2006)	4.6 (2012)
Sweden	Sweden Democrats (SD)	5.7 (2010)	5.7 (2010)
Switzerland	Swiss People's Party (SVP)	28.9 (2007)	26.6 (2011)

* Greece held national elections in May 2012 and June 2012. Golden Dawn got 7.0% in May and 6.9% in June.

Youths do not play a very important role within extreme-right parties either as leaders or as the base. As is the case with virtually all political parties, extreme-right parties are run by adults. While young supporters are often very active and visible in campaign activities, they generally do not have leadership roles. Exceptions include the Hungarian Jobbik and the Sweden Democrats, both of which have young leaders and a strong core of young activists. The little data we have on party membership show that youths are not a major base for extreme-right parties. This is undoubtedly in part because most extreme-right parties have no or poorly developed youth organizations. There are some notable exceptions, almost exclusively youth organizations of the few successful extreme-right parties, such as the Circle of Freedomite Youth in Austria, the Flemish Interest Youth in Belgium, and the Front National Youth in France. Some of the less successful extreme-right parties have youth organizations that are almost as visible as the party itself, or even more so. This is the case, for example, with the Young National Democrats, the youth wing of the German National Democratic Party, and the All-Polish Youth, the youth organization of the now largely defunct League of Polish Families.

Although young people play a fairly marginal role in political parties, they tend to be much more central in extreme-right social movement organizations. While the leaders are often (well) above 35, they tend to have a long history of activism within extreme-right youth organizations and are still able to attract a lot of youths. Prominent examples of extreme-right non-party organizations with a significant youth component are CasaPound in Italy, the National Revival of Poland, and the English Defence League in the United Kingdom (e.g., Bartlett et al. 2012; Bartlett and Littler 2011; Pankowski and Kornak 2005). Adolescents are even more prominent within neo-Nazi and white-supremacist groups, going back to the now banned German Action Front of National Socialists or the White Aryan Resistance in the United States, and the broad variety of more esoteric extreme-right *groupuscules*, from fairly intellectual student groups like the Group of Union and Defence to more violent street gangs like the Russian National Unity.

While most adults participate in extreme-right activity by voting for extreme-right parties, the majority of youths do so through a connection to extreme-right subcultures. In fact, for many this is their only extreme-right activity, and it remains limited to a short period of their youth. As in all subcultures, participation within extreme-right subcultures is a mostly transient phenomenon, a rite of passage for a specific group of (mostly lower educated, male, and white) youths. By far the most well-known extreme-right subculture is that of the skinheads, the quintessential right-wing extremists in the media (e.g., Brake 1974; Travis and Hardy 2012). It is important to note that skinheads developed as a primarily white working-class subculture in the England of the 1960s but with strong multicultural influences. Specific clothes and music, not a particular politics, defined the subculture. Skinheads drew inspiration from other urban subcultures of that time, including both the white Mod and the mostly West Caribbean reggae subcultures. Skinheads became increasingly associated with the extreme right in the 1970s through the activities of the British National Front (NF). This notwithstanding, in many countries the majority of skinheads are "traditional" skinheads (or skins) and are nonpolitical, while significant groups of antifascist skinheads, so-called redskins or SHARP (Skinheads Against Racial Prejudice), also exist in direct opposition to extreme-right skins.

Extreme-right skins, sometimes referred to as "boneheads" by antifascists, participate in an international subculture that spans almost the whole globe. After it developed in the United Kingdom, the subculture spread in the 1970s to other West European countries, as well as the (white-majority) former British colonies, such as Australia, Canada, and the United States (e.g., Hamm 1993). Today extreme-right skinheads can be found in such unlikely locations as Belarus, Mongolia, and even Israel (e.g., Lastouski 2008; Sela-Shayovitz 2011). While accurate numbers are hard to come by, and are quickly dated (e.g., ADL 1995), at the beginning of the twenty-first century the largest extreme-right skinhead communities can be found in postcommunist Eastern Europe—notably Poland, Russia, and Serbia (e.g., Mudde 2005; Worger 2012).

The extreme-right skinhead subculture combines fashion, music, and politics. It was indeed through music that skinheads were initially connected to the extreme right. Ian Stuart (Donaldson), the now-deceased leader of the rock band Skrewdriver, was both a skinhead icon and a prominent NF activist. Through his activism, later institutionalized through the international skinhead organization Blood & Honour (B&H was named after the motto of the Hitler Youth), extreme-right skinheads increasingly separated themselves from the broader skinhead movement and developed a highly political subculture with its own bands, festivals, and magazines (see Meleagrou-Hitchens and Standing 2010).

The music of extreme-right skinheads goes by several names. Initially it came out of the Rock Against Communism (RAC) movement, an NF response to the Rock against Racism movement of English antifascist organizations like the Anti-Nazi League. After the fall of communism, in the early-1990s the RAC label was used only sparsely, and terms like "white power music" and "white noise" became more popular (e.g., Shekhovtsov and Jackson 2012). Among opponents, including many within the broader nonpolitical skinhead movement, the label "hate rock" is used. White-power music developed into a major moneymaker for extreme-right (and other) entrepreneurs in the 1990s (Lööw 1998), before falling victim to the Internet, just as the mainstream music business did. Some of the most popular bands of the past decades are Bound for Glory (United States), Kolovrat (Russia), Landser (Germany), Macht und Ehre (Germany), No Remorse (UK), Orlik (Czech Republic), RaHoWa (Canada), and, of course, Skrewdriver. In addition, there is a specific type of white-power music, often referred to as National Socialist Black Metal, with bands like Burzum (Norway). National Socialist Black Metal is particularly popular in Northern Europe (Goodrick-Clarke 2002, chap. 10). While white-power music initially included mainly rock and punk, today it includes all genres, from country and folk to hip-hop and techno.

Experts believe that most adolescents enter the extreme-right subculture through music (e.g., Cotter 1999; François 2012). Extreme-right groups target particular youths with white-power music and socialize them in their ideology through concerts and other low-threshold activities. While this theory makes sense intuitively, there is precious little empirical evidence for it. Clearly many more youth listen to white-power music than attend concerts, let alone join the broader subculture or become militant in extreme-right groups. Moreover, the thesis that white-power music generates significant funding for extreme-right groups, as held true to some extent during the 1990s (Corte and Edwards 2008), also seems dated. In fact, although white-power music concerts and festivals continue to attract thousands of young people around the world, the money these events generate often harms extreme-right organizations at least as much as it benefits them—as can be seen in the endless infighting with the various national B&H groups.

Explanations: Macro, Meso, and Micro Levels

Young people who participate in extreme-right groups are not the only ones generally included under the heading of extreme-right youth. The term also refers to young people who hold extreme-right ideas but are not active in extreme-right groups. As with all ideologies, there are many more youths with extreme-right ideas than there are youths who participate in extreme-right groups or subcultures (Frindte et al. 1996). Moreover, extreme-right ideas are not limited to the stereotypical uneducated young males.

The question of why people develop extreme-right attitudes has puzzled scholars for almost a century now. The general literature on political socialization teaches us that people develop their main political attitudes during their youth and are influenced by a plethora of forces, from the micro (individual, such as personality), through the meso (personal environmental, such as schools), to the macro (national and global, such as capitalism). Once developed, these attitudes tend to endure and only change slowly over time or, incidentally, as a consequence of a personal or national trauma. Hence, it is mostly during people's youth, particularly in the teens, that extreme-right attitudes are developed.

In the 1950s, as social scientists tried to explain the rise of fascism, the most popular explanations focused on the family and the individual. In line with the then fashionable Freudian psychoanalysis, scholars believed that the answer to why people were attracted to the ideology lay in a specific "authoritarian personality," which was supposed to be the result of a particular authoritarian upbringing and family structure (e.g., Adorno et al. 1969). When the extreme right became more integrated into the study of mass politics in the 1960s, emphasis shifted to a more class-based analysis, in which extreme-right values were considered a form of "working-class authoritarianism," the political resentment of the "displaced strata" of society (Lipset 1960). Thus, explanations moved from the micro level to the meso and macro levels, from individual traits to social and societal phenomena.

Today most scholars see the extreme right as a pathological normalcy of Western democracies. They argue that in every modern democracy a small minority of the population holds antidemocratic views (Scheuch and Klingemann 1967). Only during an economic or political crisis will extreme-right attitudes spread across the population. This theory is combined with modernization theory, which argues that modernization processes create winners and losers, and the latter will identify the process as a crisis (Edelstein 2005). These so-called "losers of modernization" (or, in today's terminology, globalization) hold extreme-right values, as they are unable to cope with the stresses of the "crisis" of the modernization process (e.g., Berezin 2009).

Macro-level explanations dominate studies of the extreme right, whether they focus on radical-right political parties or extreme-right youth. One of the main variables that scholars concentrate on is unemployment, both at the national (macro) and the individual (micro) level. The belief that unemployment is correlated to extreme-right values is popular in the public debate, perpetuated through the stereotypical image of the right-wing extremist as an unemployed young male. The theory holds that unemployment leads to marginalization, which leads to political frustration and extremism. However, research has not established a clear connection between unemployment and marginalization among youths (see Bay and Blekesaune, this volume). At the very least, this relationship seems to be mediated through the way unemployment is culturally constructed. In countries where the unemployed are ostracized, young unemployed tend to develop more extremist attitudes than in countries where unemployment is more normalized.

The most significant push to studies of extreme-right youths was given by the rise of extreme-right (youth) violence in Germany in the 1990s. Many studies have emphasized the differences between the (former) East and West of Germany, with extreme-right values and violence much more widespread in the former East (e.g., Hagan et al. 1999; Heitmeyer 1992). Numerous explanations have been put forward, including modern versions of the now largely discredited authoritarian personality thesis. Most accounts, however, use a specific interpretation of modernization theory, in which the postcommunist transition caused winners and losers, including a significant part of the youth, who are deemed particularly susceptible to extreme-right attitudes (Kürti 1998).

Little research is available on the meso-level effects—that is, the environmental factors that explain extreme-right attitudes and behavior of youths. Some small-scale studies look at the possible effects of neighborhoods, parents, and schools, arguing that these meso-level factors are more relevant than macro-level factors like modernization (see Gabriel, this volume). An influential comparative study of East and West Berlin youth, conducted shortly after the German unification of 1990, concludes: "Schools and families are underappreciated sources of informal social control and resulting social capital that constrain right-wing extremism and related problems of young people during a period of rapid social change in the former East Germany" (Hagan et al. 1995, 1028).

A more recent study, again on East versus West German youth, finds that children who grow up in single-parent families or in families with parental unemployment are more likely to develop extreme-right attitudes, although this applies more to East Germans than West Germans and more to boys than girls (Siedler 2011). This is consistent with other (German) studies that find regional and gender differences in the extreme-right attitudes and behavior of adolescents. For example, one prominent study, also conducted during the German unification process, found that extreme-right boys were more influenced by ideology, while for extreme-right girls, the (perception of) threat of foreigners was more important (Watts 1996).

Similarly little research is available on the role of extreme-right groups in attracting and socializing youths. The American sociologist Randy Blazak (2001) looked into the recruitment strategies of Nazi-skins in the United States and found that they particularly target isolated and troubled white youths—a theme also developed in the famous movie American History X. French political scientist Stéphanie Dechezelles (in this volume) focused on the transmission of ideological frames within the more-structured radical-right political parties of Italy, in which family histories play an interesting but complex role.

While the theory of the authoritarian personality has been largely discredited (e.g., Brewster Smith 1997; Stone et al. 1993), this does not mean that young right-wing extremists could not have specific personal traits. For example, we do know that authoritarian attitudes go together with a variety of prejudices, both among adults and youths. Some studies have linked macro- and micro-level explanations, investigating the link between social stress and extreme-right attitudes among youths (Laufer et al. 2009). Others have looked specifically at small groups of young extreme-right (former) activists to tease out specific gender effects. For example, American sociologist Michael Kimmel (in this volume) studied activity in extreme-right groups in Scandinavia and found that racism functions as a "rite of passage" for adolescent males, rather than a strongly ideological choice. This could explain why most youths spend only relatively short periods within extreme-right groups, which tend to perform similar functions for identity- and thrill-seeking adolescents as do other (nonpolitical) subcultures.

The role of women in extreme-right groups has been one of the main foci of the work of American sociologist Kathleen Blee (1996). We know that girls and women are significantly underrepresented in extreme-right groups, from relatively moderate radical-right political parties to the most extreme, violent neo-Nazi groups (e.g., Mudde 2007, chap. 4). Moreover, many prominent women within extreme-right groups tend to be personally related to a prominent male in the same organization—the most prominent example is Marine Le Pen, leader of the French National Front and daughter of Jean-Marie Le Pen, the party's founder and longtime leader. The work of Blee and others shows the diverse range of personal-relational and ideological-political motivations of girls and women to join extreme-right groups as well as the creative ways in which they self-justify their activist role within a male-dominated ideology and organization (see also Hammann 2002; Rommelspacher 2001).

ISSUES: PREJUDICE AND VIOLENCE

All extreme-right ideologies include strong prejudices against so-called outsiders, who could be defined in a multitude of ways, including ethnic (e.g., immigrants), political (e.g., communists), racial (e.g., blacks), religious (e.g., Muslims), and sexual (e.g., LGTB). Identities are based on a strict in-group, out-group differentiation, in which the in-group is perceived as positive and the out-group(s) as negative and threatening. Studies have shown that nationalists perceive their in-group (the nation) as superior to others (e.g., Doosje et al. 2012). In sharp contrast, out-groups are stereotyped on the basis of some specific, often negative, traits (e.g., Brewer 1999; Tajfel 1982). For example, blacks are stereotyped as lazy, gays as promiscuous, Jews as conniving, and Roma as criminal (e.g., Mudde 2007). The out-group is perceived as homogeneous and hostile to the in-group, while the in-group is seen as more internally diverse.

At the beginning of the twentieth century the main out-groups of the Western extreme right were blacks and Jews. Extreme rightists of all persuasions shared a colonialist racism, infused by pseudoscientific studies of the day. The German National Socialists made racism central to their ideology, in which the white "Aryan" race was considered superior to all others, most notably the Jews. Anti-Semitism is still central to neo-Nazis around the world, but is less important to many other contemporary extreme-right groups. This might reflect the fact that anti-Semitic attitudes have decreased significantly in Western Europe, but remain prevalent in the eastern part of the continent (e.g., Bergmann 2008).

Some scholars have called Muslims the new Jews of Europe and Islamophobia the new anti-Semitism (e.g., Bunzl 2007). As a result of the debates over mass immigration and jihadist terrorism, Muslims are increasingly seen by many westerners as the main threat to their way of life. Although Islamophobic arguments are virtually mainstream in the media and politics these days, we know very little about how many (young) people are Islamophobic. The few studies on the topic show that negative attitudes toward Muslims are the consequence of a complex interplay of socioeconomic, sociopsychological, and contextual variables (see Bevelander and Otterbeck, this volume). While boys and girls share similar levels of Islamophobia, there are some interesting differences in what prevents them from being or becoming Islamophobic. For example, girls are less negative toward Muslims when they have a Muslim friend, but boys are not.

It is important to realize that today's adolescents grow up in societies very different from those of their parents and previous generations. While most European adults grew up in fairly monocultural environments, with only limited personal encounters with immigrants, many European young people grow up in a (struggling) multiethnic society. In fact, in many big cities, "native" youths grow up as a minority in their local neighborhoods and schools. This makes the issue of diversity and tolerance very different for them from what it was for previous generations. Previous generations were part of an ethnic majority at the national and local level, yet contemporary urban youths are part of the majority at the (abstract) national level, but a minority at the (concrete) local level. This creates a somewhat schizophrenic situation in both ethnic identities and ethnic power relations.

So far we do not know much about views of tolerance and intolerance among our young (see Harrell, this volume). This lack of knowledge is problematic, given that adolescents grow up in a society in which terms like "hate speech" and "tolerance" are constantly used, but seldom defined. Moreover, it is very likely that there are generational differences in the perceptions of such terms, given the fundamentally different experiences with ethnic diversity of those who preach (e.g., politicians, teachers) and those who are preached to (e.g., pupils, voters). For example, imagine a 50-year-old German teacher in a basic school in Kreuzberg, a highly multicultural area of Berlin. Having grown up in a time that society was still very homogeneous, the teacher will consider "natives" as the powerful majority who should be tolerant toward the ("Turkish") minority. But the pupils she teaches are growing up in an area where "native" Germans are a minority, and "Turkish" youth are the majority.

Most public accounts assume a direct link between extreme-right attitudes and political violence. Whipped up by sensationalist media accounts of neo-Nazis and skinheads, the general public assumes that every right-wing extremist is a potential perpetrator of violence. In fact, the vast majority of right-wing extremists are not violent, and the majority of extreme-right and racist violence is perpetrated by people who are not associated with extreme-right groups (e.g., Wahl 2003). As far as racist violence is concerned, the perpetrator is indeed the stereotypical lower-educated, white male. However, the key factor in the violence is alcohol, not ideology. This is not to say that there is no connection. Youths who are active within extreme-right groups, in particular neo-Nazi and extreme-right skinhead groups, are much more likely to get involved in racist violence (see Watts, this volume).

The relationship between extreme-right ideology and the propensity to violence is not exactly clear, however. While it is logical that a violent racist ideology like neo-Nazism would lead activists to engage in racist violence, it is equally plausible that such an ideology would attract potentially violent youths. Indeed, studies find that extreme-right activists are on average disproportionately violent, even compared to their direct equivalents (i.e., lower-educated young males). But studies also find that in much of such violence, ideology is irrelevant or secondary at best (see Lööw, this volume). Finally, some research points at another relationship between violence and the extreme right: many

extreme-right activists come from families with domestic abuse and environments characterized by aggression and oppression—not unlike members of (other) street gangs (e.g., Baron 1997).

Solutions: Prevention and Intervention

At least since the extreme-right violence in Germany of the early 1990s,
nongovernmental organizations and states have started to develop prevention
and intervention programs for right-wing extremists in general, and extreme-
right youths in particular. Most of these initiatives have been implemented in
Northern Europe, notably Norway, Sweden, and Germany, although there have
been attempts in Eastern Europe and North America too. Generally speaking,
prevention programs are geared toward the general population, often youths in
school, while intervention programs target specific extreme-right activists.

Prevention programs come in many shapes and forms, dependent on both
who implements them and whom they target (see Beelmann, this volume).
Many Western countries have implemented pro-multicultural and anti-
prejudice campaigns in the past decades, generally targeted at the whole
population. Adolescents are confronted with direct or indirect prevention
programs in school, through both the curriculum and specific activities, or
through social work (see Carlsson, this volume). Some of these programs
target extreme-right attitudes, while others try to prevent extreme-right
violence. One of the problems of these programs is that school teachers and
social workers are often not very knowledgeable about right-wing extremism
and act on the basis of the stereotypes perpetuated by the popular media (see
Miller-Idriss, this volume).

So-called exit programs were developed to help young activists leave the extreme right. Just as there are a wide variety of reasons why young people consider joining the extreme right, they consider leaving for a broad range of reasons
(Van der Valk and Wagenaar 2010). Personal conflicts between "comrades,"
disappointment with the leadership, and the often large gap between expectation and reality can create doubt and insecurity within right-wing extremists
(Rommelspacher 2006, 169). Similarly, a change in personal situation, such as
a new relationship or moving to a different town, can create a new perspective
on life in general. Most extreme-right activists exit the extreme right without
much thought or trouble. But some, particularly those who have been active for
a long time and have a criminal conviction related to their political activity,
have much to lose—most of their friends are in the movement and will break
all contact—and not necessarily much to gain given their stigmatized past. Exit

programs are meant to help young activists in making this transformation out of the extreme right and back into the mainstream of society.

The "exit" or intervention programs were started in Norway and have since been adopted in various other countries, although in very different forms (Bjørgo 2002a; Bollin et al. 2009). The main issue of contention is what role the state should play in the exit projects. States can provide important resources for the projects, but can also constitute a hurdle for extreme-right youth to get involved with the project, particularly if they have been involved in illegal activities. In addition, many NGOs involved in antiracist and antifascist work are deeply skeptical of the state, and particular state agencies like the police. Less contentious is the role of parents, who are often central to intervention programs of all kinds. In the original Norwegian Exit Project, parental networks were key to the intervention process (Bjørgo 2002b).

Experts also differ on who should initiate participation in such programs, the project workers or the right-wing extremists themselves (see Van der Valk, this volume). Some programs are more proactive, contacting and persuading youths to leave their extreme-right group, while others are more reactive, waiting to be approached by youth who already doubt their commitment. Both approaches seem to have advantages and disadvantages. The proactive approach works best with youths who have recently joined an extreme-right group. The longer adolescents participate in these often-closed groups, the more they become separated from people outside the group, which means that an exit would have more severe social consequences. Moreover, given the propensity to violence of extreme-right skinhead and neo-Nazi groups, a longer stay within these groups increases the chance of violent behavior and criminal conviction, which increases the costs of an exit even further.

Conclusions

People develop most of their political attitudes during their youth, particularly in their teens, and right-wing extremists are no exception. Because attitudes remain relatively stable over a lifetime, and actions during one's youth can influence the rest of one's life (think of youths being convicted for extreme-right violence), the topic of youth and the extreme right is crucial to the overall understanding of the extreme-right phenomenon.

Unfortunately, we don't know that much about how young people develop extreme-right attitudes or why they join extreme-right groups. We know that socialization is a complex process and that a broad variety of actors (including families, social organization, and schools) can influence youths. No one actor is exclusively responsible for "turning" a child or adolescent into a right-wing extremist. There are children of extreme-right leaders who become right-wing extremist themselves and others who do not (some even become antiracist). There are youths who respond positively to social pressure, such as pro-multicultural education, and others who rebel and will adopt a right-wing extremist position just to upset the establishment (e.g., their parents or teachers).

This lack of solid explanations of the relationship between youth and the extreme right should be a warning to everyone interested in understanding and fighting right-wing extremism. It is crucial to keep an open mind! We should not simply assume that every young person with ethnic prejudices is a potential extreme-right terrorist or that every young right-wing extremist comes from a broken family. We should not assume that our values are universally shared or that youths will internalize our message because we are "authority figures." Moreover, many adolescents grow up in very different ethnic environments from those of the adults that study or teach them.

Young people are growing up in ethnically diverse cities and towns, where ethnic identity is often highly relevant as a social marker. While maintaining their (i.e., their parents') ethnic identity is mostly embraced and even encouraged for ethnic minorities, as an important step in their integration into the host nation, a strong emphasis on ethnic identity of "natives" is often treated with suspicion and even outright condemnation. Young "natives" who stress their ethnic identity are seen as (potential) right-wing extremists and are warned of the dangers of (majority) intolerance and counseled about the responsibilities of (majority) tolerance. This is not only confusing, coming across as two-faced, but also ignores the ethnic realities of their lives: while "natives" continue to constitute the majorities and the powerful in all European countries, this is not necessarily the case in the cities and schools in which these youths grow up. Increasingly, in schools in the big European cities, "native" youths are (also) a minority!

To understand the relationship between youth and the extreme right it is important to be open-minded and reflect critically on personal experiences and old dogmas. This is truly a topic where it is crucial to listen to our subjects. Only by opening our minds to the youths, and to the complexities of their life experiences and choices, will we be able to gain a better understanding of what makes young people adopt extreme-right attitudes and join extreme-right groups. And it is only then, after we actually know what is going on, that we can start to effectively prevent and intervene.

NOTES

1. Unfortunately, the vast majority of scholarly work on the topic is done in German—in fact, there are more studies on Germany than on all other countries of the world combined! This is more a reflection of the sensitivity of the Germans to the problem than of the severity of the problem in Germany.

2. Extreme-right parties have also contested national elections outside Europe, including in Australia (One Nation Party), but have not been represented in the national parliament recently. The main possible exceptions are Israel Our Home (now part of Likud) and the Jewish Home in Israel, and the Indian People's Party (BJP) in India, although BJP's extreme-right status is contested in the literature (e.g., Andersen 1998).

REFERENCES

ADL. 1995. *The Skinhead International: A Worldwide Survey of Neo-Nazi Skinheads*. New York: Anti-Defamation League.

Adorno, T. W., Else Frenkel-Brunswik, Daniel J. Levinson, and R. Nevitt Sanford. 1969. *The Authoritarian Personality*. New York: W. W. Norton.

Andersen, Walter K. 1998. "Bharatiya Janata Party: Searching for the Hindu Nationalist Face." In *The New Politics of the Right: Neo-Populist Parties and Movements in Established Democracies*, edited by Hans-Georg Betz and Stefan Immerfall, 219–232. New York: St. Martin's.

Arzheimer, Kai. 2012. "Electoral Sociology—Who Votes for the Extreme Right and Why—and When?" In *The Extreme Right in Europe: Current Trends and Perspectives*, edited by Uwe Backes and Patrick Moreau, 35–50. Göttingen: Vandenhoeck & Ruprecht.

Bale, Tim. 2012. "Supplying the Insatiable Demand: Europe's Populist Radical Right." *Government & Opposition* 47, no. 2: 256–274.

Baron, Stephen W. 1997. "Canadian Male Street Skinheads: Street Gang or Street Terrorists?" *Canadian Journal of Political Science* 34, no. 2: 407–432.

Bartlett, James, Jonathan Birdwell, and Caterina Froio. 2012. *Populism in Europe: CasaPound*. London: Demos.

Bartlett, Jamie, and Mark Littler. 2011. *Inside the EDL*. London: Demos.

Berezin, Mabel. 2009. *Illiberal Politics in Neoliberal Times: Culture, Security and Populism in the New Europe*. New York: Cambridge University Press.

Bergmann, Wolfgang. 2008. "Anti-Semitic Attitudes in Europe: A Comparative Perspective." *Journal of Social Issues* 64, no. 2: 343–362.

Bjørgo, Tore. 2002a. *Exit Neo-Nazism: Reducing Recruitment and Promoting Disengagement from Racist Groups*. Oslo: Norwegian Institute of International Affairs.

———. 2002b. "Rassistische Gruppen: Die Anwerbung reduzieren und den Ausstieg fördern." *Journal für Konflikt- und Gewaltsforschung* 4, no. 1: 5–31.

Blazak, Randy. 2001. "White Boys to Terrorist Men: Target Recruitment of Nazi Skinheads." *American Behavioral Scientist* 44, no. 6: 982–1000.

Blee, Kathleen M. 1996. "Becoming a Racist: Women in Contemporary Ku Klux Klan and Neo-Nazi Groups." *Gender & Society* 10, no. 6: 680–702.

———. 1998. "White-Knuckle Research: Emotional Dynamics in Field Research with Racist Activists." *Qualitative Sociology* 21, no. 4: 381–399.

Bollin, Saskia, Corinne Sieber, Nina Studer, Ueli Mäder, and Wassilis Kassis. 2009. "Right-Wing Extremist Youth: Motivations for Exiting the Right-Wing Extremist Scene and Clique Structure." In *Right-Wing Extremism in Switzerland: National and International Perspectives*, edited by Marcel Alexander Niggli, 181–192. Baden-Baden: Nomos.

Brake, Mike. 1974. "The Skinheads: An English Working Class Subculture." *Youth Society* 6, no. 2: 172–200.

Brewer, Marilynn B. 2002. "The Psychology of Prejudice: Ingroup Love and Outgroup Hate?" *Journal of Social Issues* 55, no. 3: 429–444.

Brewster Smith, M. 1997. "*The Authoritarian Personality*: A Re-review 46 Years Later." *Political Psychology* 18, no. 1: 159–163.

Bunzl, Matti. 2007. *Antisemitism and Islamophobia: Hatreds Old and New in Europe*. Chicago: Prickly Paradigm.

Corte, Ugo, and Bob Edwards. 2008. "White Power Music and the Mobilization of Racist Social Movements." *Music & Arts in Action* 1, no. 1: 4–20.

Cotter, John M. 1999. "Sounds of Hate: White Power Rock and Roll and the Neo Nazi Skinhead Subculture." *Terrorism and Political Violence* 11, no. 2: 111–140.

Dalton, Russell J. 2008. *Citizen Politics: Public Opinion and Political Parties in Advanced Industrial Democracies*, 5th ed. Washington, DC: CQ Press.

Doosje, Bertjan, Kees van den Bos, Annemarie Loseman, Allard R. Feddes, and Liesbeth Mann. 2012. "'My In-Group Is Superior!': Susceptibility for Radical Right-Wing Attitudes and Behaviors in Dutch Youth." *Negotiation and Conflict Management Research* 5, no. 3: 253–268.

Edelstein, Wolfgang. 2005. "The Rise of a Right-Wing Culture Among German Youth: The Effects of Social Transformation, Identity Construction, and Context." In *Developmental Psychology and Social Change: Research, History, and Policy*, edited by David B. Pillemer and Sheldon Harold White, 314–351. Cambridge: Cambridge University Press.

François, Stéphane. 2012. "Musical and Political Subculture—a Review of Attempts at Entrism." In *The Extreme Right in Europe: Current Trends and Perspectives*, edited by Uwe Backes and Patrick Moreau, 409–418. Göttingen: Vandenhoeck & Ruprecht.

Frindte, Wolfgang, Friedrich Funke, and Sven Waldzus. 1996. "Xenophobia and Right-Wing Extremism in German Youth Groups: Some Evidence Against Unidimensional Misinterpretations." *International Journal of Intercultural Relations* 20, nos. 3/4: 463–478.

Goodrick-Clarke, Nicholas. 2002. *Black Sun: Aryan Cults, Esoteric Nazism, and the Politics of Identity*. New York: NYU Press.

Greenberg, Edward S., ed. 1970. *Political Socialization*. New York: Atherton.

Hagan, John, Hans Merkens, and Klaus Boehnke. 1995. "Delinquency and Disdain: Social Capital and the Control of Right-Wing Extremism Among East and West Berlin Youth." *American Journal of Sociology* 100, no. 4: 1028–1052.

Hagan, John, Susanne Rippl, Klaus Boehnke, and Hans Merkens. 1999. "The Interest in Evil: Hierarchic Self-Interest and Right-Wing Extremism Among East and West German Youth." *Social Science Research* 28, no. 2: 162–183.

Hamm, Mark S. 1993. *American Skinheads: The Criminology and Control of Hate Crime*. Westport, CT: Praeger.

Hammann, Kerstin. 2002. *Frauen im rechtsextremen Spektrum: Analysen und Prävention*. Frankfurt am Main: VAS.

Heitmeyer, Wilhelm. 1992. *Rechtsextremistische Orientierungen bei Jugendlichen: Empirische Ergebnisse und Erklärungsmuster einer Untersuchung zur politischen Sozialisation*. Weinheim: Juventa.

Klandermans, Bert, and Nonna Mayer, eds. 2006. *Extreme Right Activists in Europe: Through the Magnifying Glass*. London: Routledge.

Kürti, László. 1998. "The Emergence of Postcommunist Youth Identities in Eastern Europe: From Communist Youth, to Skinheads, to National Socialists and Beyond." In *Nation and Race: The Developing Euro-American Racist Subculture*, edited by Jeffrey Kaplan and Tore Bjørgo, 175–201. Boston: Northeastern University Press.

Lastouski, Aliaksei. 2008. "Ideas and Practices of the Skinhead Youth Counterculture in Belarus." *Political Sphere* 11:101–113.

Laufer, Avital, Mally Shechory, and Zahava Solomon. 2009. "The Association Between Right-Wing Political Ideology and Youth Distress." *Journal of Child Adolescence and Social Work* 26:1–13

Lipset, Seymour Martin. 1960. *Political Man*. London: Heinemann.

Lööw, Heléne. 1998. "White-Power Rock 'n' Roll: A Growing Industry." In *Nation and Race: The Developing Euro-American Racist Subculture*, edited by Jeffrey Kaplan and Tore Bjørgo, 267–281. Boston: Northeastern University Press.

Meleagrou-Hitchens, Alexander, and Edmund Standing. 2010. *Blood & Honour: Britain's Far-Right Militants*. London: Centre for Social Cohesion.

Minkenberg, Michael. 2008. *The Radical Right in Europe: An Overview*. Gütersloh: Verlag Bertelsmann Stiftung.

Mudde, Cas. 1996. "The War of Words: Defining the Extreme Right Party Family." *West European Politics* 19, no. 2: 225–248.

————, ed. 2005. *Racist Extremism in Central and Eastern Europe*. London: Routledge.

————. 2007. *Populist Radical Right Parties in Europe*. Cambridge: Cambridge University Press.

————. 2010. "The Populist Radical Right: A Pathological Normalcy." *West European Politics* 33, no. 6: 1167–1186.

Pankowski, Rafal, and Marcin Kornak. 2005. "Poland." In *Racist Extremism in Central and Eastern Europe*, edited by Cas Mudde, 156–183. London: Routledge.

Reich, Wilhelm. 1970. *The Mass Psychology of Fascism*. New York: Penguin.

Rommelspacher, Birgit. 2001. "Das Geschlechterverhältnis im Rechtsextremismus." In *Rechtsextremismus in der Bundesrepublik Deutschland: Ein Bilanz*, edited by Wilfried Schubarth and Richard Stöss, 199–219. Opladen: Leske + Budrich.

————. 2006. *Der Hass hat uns geeint. Junge Rechtsextreme und ihr Ausstieg aus der Szene*. Frankfurt: Campus.

Scheuch, Erwin K., and Hans Dieter Klingemann. 1967. "Theorie des Rechtsradikalismus in westlichen Industriegesellschaften." *Hamburger Jahrbuch für Wirtschafts- und Sozialpolitik* 12:11–19.

Sears, David O. 1975. "Political Socialization." In *Handbook of Political Science*, vol. 2, edited by Fred I. Greenstein and Nelson W. Polsby, 93–153. Reading, MA: Addison-Wesley.

Sela-Shayovitz, Revital. 2011. "Neo-Nazis and Moral Panic: The Emergence of Neo-Nazi Youth Gangs in Israel." *Crime Media Culture* 7, no. 1: 67–82.

Shekhovtsov, Anton, and Paul Jackson, eds. 2012. *White Power Music: Scenes of Extreme-Right Cultural Resistance*. Islington: Searchlight and RNM.

Siedler, Thomas. 2011. "Parental Unemployment and Young People's Extreme Right-Wing Party Affinity: Evidence from Panel Data." *Journal of the Royal Statistical Society* 174, no. 3: 737–758.

Stone, William F., Gerda Lederer, and Richard Christie, eds. 1993. *Strength and Weakness: The Authoritarian Personality Today*. New York: Springer.

Tajfel, Henri. 1982. "Social Relations of Intergroup Groups." *Annual Review of Psychology* 33:1–39.

Travis, Tiffini A., and Perry Harvey. 2012. *Skinheads: A Guide to an American Subculture*. Santa Barbara, CA: Greenwood.

Van der Valk, Ineke, and Willem Wagenaar. 2010. *Racism and Extremism Monitor; The Extreme Right: Entry and Exit*. Amsterdam: Anne Frank House.

Wahl, Klaus, ed. 2003. *Skinheads, Neonazis, Mitläufer: Täterstudien und Prävention*. Opladen: Leske + Budrich.

Watts, Meredith W. 1996. "Political Xenophobia in the Transition from Socialism: Threat, Racism and Ideology Among East German Youth." *Political Psychology* 17, no. 1: 97–126.

Worger, Peter. 2012. "A Mad Crowd: Skinhead Youth and the Rise of Nationalism in Post-Communist Russia." *Communist and Post-Communist Studies* 45, nos. 3–4: 269–278.

Part 1: Explanations

We open the anthology with four articles that try to explain the attraction of certain youth to extreme-right groups and ideas at the macro, meso, and micro levels. Macro-level analysis focuses on factors at the national and supranational level, such as state policies and globalization, which are believed to have significant effects on individuals. To explore this level, we include "Youth, Unemployment and Political Marginalisation" by Ann-Helén Bay and Morten Blekesaune, who investigate whether well-developed welfare states reduce political marginalization, and thus political extremism, among unemployed youth.

Meso-level explanations focus on the level between the state and the individual—the most direct social context of people. People develop their attitudes during their youth, when their direct environment has more influence on them than when they are adults. Of particular importance are the communities—families, schools, and youth groups—in which people spend most of their time. Thomas Gabriel, in "Parenting and Right-Wing Extremism," focuses on the role of parents in the development of racist attitudes among young people. Stéphanie Dechezelles, in "The Cultural Basis of Youth Involvement in Italian Extreme Right-Wing Organisations," looks at the important role of both families and radical-right groups in the political socialization of young Italian activists.

Micro-level explanations focus on specific characteristics of individuals that explain their vulnerability to extreme-right attitudes and groups. While some of these characteristics might be innate, others are nurtured, consequences of the macro- and meso-level factors discussed above. To explore this level, we focus in particular on the importance of gender. Because all studies show that right-wing extremists are disproportionately male, Michael Kimmel, in "Racism as Adolescent Male Rite of Passage," investigates whether joining an extreme-right group is a kind of ritual event for adolescent males.

As you read through the articles, think about the following questions:
 • Which conditions are structural, and therefore largely beyond your individual control? Given these structural conditions, what can families, schools, teachers do to prevent political extremism among youths?
 • What is the worldview of young people in far-right movements? How do they perceive you, and how does that impact your possibilities of

influencing them?

• Which young people are particularly vulnerable to become right-wing extremists?

• How do the various explanatory factors relate to the strong gender bias within extreme-right groups?

Youth, Unemployment and Political Marginalisation

by Ann-Helèn Bay and Morten Blekesaune*

The article investigates the impact of being unemployed on political marginalisation among young people. Are unemployed youth politically marginalised compared with employed youth? Is the impact of unemployment on political marginalisation related to the development of the welfare state? Based on Marshall's concept of social citizenry, and Esping-Andersen's theory of decommodification politics, the impact of unemployment on political marginalisation was expected to be least in the most-developed welfare states. In these countries, welfare policies were expected to counteract marginalisation among the unemployed. The analyses were based on the Eurobarometer survey *Young Europeans* from 1990. Three aspects of political marginalisation were investigated: political confidence, political interest and political extremism. Unemployed youth express less confidence in politics, they talk less about politics and they more frequently support revolutionary political ideas, compared with employed youth. The greatest difference in political confidence between unemployed and employed is found in Great Britain, while Italy represents a deviant case where the unemployed have more confidence than the employed. The development of the welfare state does not appear to be a crucial factor for political confidence among the unemployed.

INTRODUCTION

Paid employment is often presented as an important resource for the welfare of the population in a modern industrialised society. It represents the admission ticket to a number of consumer goods, and at the same time develops the individual's skills, ability and social standing. Unemployment, especially long-term unemployment, from this perspective can have serious consequences for the individual's level of living. Unemployment results in lower or even no income. This means that the individual must relinquish the possibility of participating in a number of activities, or to purchase goods, which cost money. At the same time one is excluded from that relationship and social company enjoyed by working colleagues. There is abroad opinion that the situation for unemployed youth is more serious than for their more adult counterparts. One risks the situation whereby youngsters are drawn into negative lifestyles.

In this article we shall restrict ourselves to the significance of unemployment for political socialisation and mobilisation of youth. Two research questions will be addressed:

1. Are unemployed youths politically marginalised compared with employed youths?

2. Is the impact of unemployment on political marginalisation related to the development of the welfare state?

Even though the question of political involvement and marginalisation is central to the theoretical discussion of the consequences of youth unemployment, few empirical studies have been made of political behaviour among unemployed youth. Those studies that have been undertaken have been much cited in international papers (Banks & Ullah, 1987; Furlong & Cartmel, 1997). Our study distinguishes itself from earlier studies in that it is extensive. Several of the earlier surveys had limitations that made it difficult to make generalisations. Some were exclusively concerned with the unemployed themselves (Jackson & Hanby, 1982; Breakwell, 1986; Carle, 1997, 1998). When there is no control group of youth in work, it is difficult to draw conclusions on the effects of unemployment. Other studies have been concerned with both the unemployed and the employed. However, these have been geographically delimited such that we are uncertain whether the findings reflect a general situation (Clark & Clissold, 1982; Clark, 1985; Banks & Ullah, 1987). Based on the Eurobarometer survey *Young Europeans* from 1990, we shall study the effect of unemployment among a sample of youth in EU countries. More specifically we will test three hypotheses:

- Unemployed youth have less confidence in the democratic institutions.
- Unemployed youth are less interested in politics.
- Unemployed youth are more politically extreme than working youth.

First, we will discuss the hypotheses.

POLITICAL CONFIDENCE

The question of public confidence in democracy and in the political institutions is a central theme in the study of political behaviour (Almond & Verba, 1963; Easton, 1965, 1975; Huntington, 1975; Norris, 1999). Representative democracy is based upon—and dependent upon—the fact that members of the electorate express confidence in their opinion. A general confidence may act as a discouragement to abrupt changes in regimes, simultaneous to providing a change in government with the necessary stability in circumstances such that reforms may be introduced (McAllister, 1999). Studies show a stable and high level of support for democratic government in Western countries (Norris, 1999). The proportion critical to the regime's 'performance' has, however, increased overtime. According to Norris, this opinion emerges through the 'disenchanted democrats' who express a lack of faith in politicians' ability and powers to act.

It is natural to assume that youths who experience unemployment, and particularly long-term unemployment, also build up a lack of faith in the authorities. They experience that the authorities lack the ability or will to solve their problems, and become politically disillusioned. Youth unemployment can thus contribute to undermining the legitimacy of the political leadership and the political parties in society. An objection can be made to this hypothesis—it is not certain that youth direct their frustration with their own situation towards the authorities. Frustration can equally be directed inwards towards themselves or towards employers and the labour market. Abrams (1990) maintains that if individuals experience their problems as personal, there is little chance that this will be of any consequence for the individual's political orientation. On the other hand, should these problems be of a structural character and/or associated to the group the individual belongs to, then there is a greater possibility for frustration coming to political expression.

POLITICAL INTEREST

Whether a person has confidence or a lack of confidence in the political system can be of significance for the individual's political participation and involvement (Hernes & Martinussen, 1980). Confidence is, however, not the sole factor determining the individual's political orientation. Both structural and institutional trends and aspects of the individual and his/her socio-economic situation, are elements affecting political participation (Dahl, 1961; Verba, Nie & Kim, 1978). Gainful employment can function as a political resource for the individual in several different ways (Martinussen, 1973). A workplace may offer political stimuli, both through those who contribute to stimulating political opinion and through political debate between colleagues. Gainful employment can provide the individual with the experience of communality with his/her colleagues, and which in turn can contribute to stimulating political activity directed towards improving the situation of his group. At the same time, work experience can contribute to giving the individual a sense of security and self-confidence, and thereby a belief that his/her own political viewpoints have a value and are of importance in politics.

Based on the thesis that work participation is a political resource for the individual, there is reason to expect that unemployed youth are less involved in politics than employed youth. But it is also possible to formulate a counter-thesis. In as much as unemployment is defined as a political issue, one may expect a form of collective response to unemployment that involves political participation (Banks & Ullah, 1987). Unemployment represents a mobilisation potential.

The main impression of the relatively few studies that are to be found on political involvement among unemployed youth is that there is a lack of political interest. Jackson and Hanby (1982) found significant political apathy and resignation in their study of unemployed young persons in Scotland. Breakwell's (1986) study of a small sample of unemployed youth in England also revealed little political involvement. Carle (1997) studied a sample of long-term (at least three months) unemployed youth in the Nordic countries. He found least political involvement among those who were long-term unemployed. None of these surveys incorporated a control group of youth that had not experienced unemployment. Banks and Ullah (1987) compared political attitudes and voting behaviour among employed and unemployed youth in a sample of young persons drawn from eleven urban regions in England. They found low political interest among youth in general, and lowest among the unemployed.

POLITICAL EXTREMISM

There is a general opinion that unemployed youth are recruited into politically extreme groups who do not go out of their way to use illegal and violent methods in order to achieve their ends. The concept of political marginalisation is closely allied to the concept of irregular political activity among the unemployed. Unemployment among youth has been particularly associated with the growth and support for right-wing extreme parties or groups (Cochrane & Billig, 1983).

Several have pointed out that support for both the extreme right and the extreme left is greatest among youth that reside in (urban) areas with a high level of unemployment and poor living standards. However, Roberts and Parsell (1990) argue that it is more likely that the unemployed are politically alienated, and express their alienation in vandalism and conflicts with the police.

Present studies do not provide any clear picture of the effects of unemployment on political extremism. Two studies from Australia concluded that unemployed youth, more so than employed persons, favoured direct political action and law-breaking (Clark & Clissold, 1982; Clark, 1985). The samples in these two surveys comprised both employed and unemployed youth between 15 and 20 years who had a working-class background. Breakwell (1986) studied a small sample of long-term unemployed youth in England. Many of these expressed support for violent action. For their part, Banks and Ullah (1987) found little support for extreme-right or extreme-left parties among employed and unemployed youth in their study. In his survey, Carle (1997) raised the question concerning participation in political actions such as illegal strikes and house occupation. Very few of the unemployed had participated in this form of political activity.

The Impact of the Welfare State

The general expectations are as already mentioned that unemployed youth are more politically marginalised compared with those employed: we expect that they have less confidence in the political authorities, that they are less interested in politics and that they are politically more extreme. In addition, we expect to find national variations in the effects of unemployment on political marginalisation. We expect that the development of the welfare state contributes to the impact of unemployment on political orientation and involvement. One reason for this we find in Marshall's concept of social citizenry, and in Esping-Andersen's ideas about decommodification policies.

In his classic article 'Citizenship and Social Class', Marshall (1950) maintains that social rights are a key element of the welfare state. According to Marshall, full citizenship yields three types of rights: civil, political and social. The social rights include, among other things, a certain minimum of financial security that should enable all inhabitants to realise their political and civil rights.

Esping-Andersen (1985, 1990), building upon Marshall's concept on social citizenry, characterizes modern welfare politics as decommodification. Decommodification politics weakens the individual's dependency on the market. It gives the inhabitants 'access to welfare independently of market exchange' (Esping-Andersen, 1985: 31). According to Esping-Andersen this is taken care of for the most part within the Scandinavian model of the welfare state, which is characterised by its broad availability on the basis of citizenship. The opposite of this is found in liberal welfare states where its application is at a low level and coverage is based on means testing. This model is found in the Anglo-Saxon countries. In between we find the so-called corporatist welfare states, where its usage is strongly associated with input on the labour market. This model is found in continental Europe, including Italy. Leibfried (1993) operates with a fourth category of rudimentary welfare states, which is found in southern Europe, in countries where the welfare services are little developed.

Suffice to say, based on Marshall's concept of social citizenry, and Esping-Andersen's theory of decommodification politics, there is reason to expect that the impact of unemployment on political involvement and integration is least in the most-developed welfare states. The welfare states in these countries counteract the trend whereby unemployment leads to marginalisation among the unemployed. The welfare state ensures that one may function as a citizen even though one does not have paid employment.

When applying this simple and general model on empirical data, one should also consider other factors contributing to national variations, which may make it difficult to test precise hypotheses. The level of unemployment generally, and of youth in particular, may also influence the relationship between youth unemployment and political marginalisation. Cultural differences, for example those associated with the protestant ethics, may also affect this relationship. The protestant duty-bound ethics draw a very positive picture of work. Work is generally regarded as something that meets human needs for stimulus and development. To be unemployed in societies influenced by protestant ethics, more so than in other societies, is to be seen as an outsider in society, both by those who are unemployed and by the community. In turn, this position could lead to political apathy and alienation, or to political attitudes extraneous to 'the establishment.' We also anticipate that political confidence increases with age, and that men have more confidence than women.

SAMPLE

The data were drawn from the Eurobarometer survey of Young Europeans in 1990 (Eurobarometer 34.2—Youth Sample).[1] The survey comprised youth in the age range 15–24 in the EU membership countries in1990, together with East Germany. The sample comprised 7,706 persons. We restricted our analyses to those who belong to the labour force, that is those in paid employment and those who were unemployed. Hence, students, housewives and those doing military service were excluded. The respondents reported employment and unemployment status, based on the question 'What is your present main occupation?' Employment was measured by the alternative 'Paid full-time or part-time employment.' Unemployment was measured by the alternative 'Unemployed and looking for work.' East

Germany and Luxembourg were excluded from the analysis. The latter was excluded as there were only two unemployed persons in the sample.

Political Confidence

Political confidence was measured by the question 'On the whole are you very satisfied, fairly satisfied, not very satisfied, not at all satisfied with the way democracy works in your country?' This is a classic question in the Eurobarometer to measure satisfaction on how democracy works (Fuchs, 1995). The question involves people's evaluation of politics, as compared, for example, to confidence in democracy as a general form of government (Norris, 1999).

Table 1 shows that the majority express satisfaction with the working of democracy in their own country. Simultaneously a relatively large proportion express dissatisfaction. A larger proportion of employed persons are satisfied than for those who are unemployed.

Table 1. Descriptive statistics of four questions about political attitudes in 11–12 European countries.
The countries with equal weighting. n = 2.784–3.368.

Questions	Alternatives	Employed	Unemployed
On the whole are you very satisfied...or not at all satisfied with the way democracy works in your country?	Very satisfied	7	6
	Fairly satisfied	56	44
	Not very satisfied	26	29
	Not at all satisfied	11	20
What sort of things interest you a lot? National politics?	Yes	12	9
	No	88	91
When you get together with friends, would you say you discuss politics...	Frequently	8	8
	Occasionally	50	41
	Never	41	51
Three attitudes towards society we live in...	Revolution	6	10
	Reforms	72	73
	Defence	22	17

Table 2 shows the results of a logistic regression analysis. In addition to the variable 'unemployed/employed', the variables 'age', 'gender' (men/women) and 'country' are included. (The country is a pure control variable and is not referred to in the table.) The analysis shows that the unemployed have less political confidence than the employed. Age and gender make no difference.

Table 2. Logistical regression of five political attitudes as a result of age, gender, and unemployment status and country (not shown). Binominal and ordinal models. Logit coefficients. The countries with equal weighting.

Explanatory variables:				
Dependent variables:	Age in years	Men = 1 Women = 0	Unemployed	N
Political confidence	-0.013	-0.012	-0.382*	2.784
Interest in national politics	0.165*	0.335*	-0.234	3.365
Discuss politics with friends	0.180*	0.357*	-0.278*	3.341
System changed by revolutionary action	0.008	0.248	-0.526*	3.368
System strongly defended	-0.002	0.203	-0.161	3.368
Note: *= p < 0.01 in two-tailed tests				

Political Interest

Two questions from the survey were used as a measure of political interest. One question asked the respondent 'What sort of things interest you a lot?' The list contained 12 themes, where national policy was one of these. The respondents could cross off several alternatives. The other question was concerned with how often the respondent discusses politics when he/she is together with friends, with the alternative replies: frequently, occasionally, never. The replies on the two questions were not particularly correlated and were therefore analysed separately.

Few are interested in politics among both those who are employed and the unemployed (Table 1). These results conform to previous surveys (Banks & Ullah, 1987). Even though there is a larger proportion who state an interest in politics among the employed than the unemployed, the level remains low for both groups. Neither does the measurement 'discuss politics with friends' show particularly large interest for politics. Interest is lowest among the unemployed.

The logistic regression (Table 2) shows that the unemployed discuss politics with their friends less frequently than the employed. The unemployed also tend to be less interested in national politics than the employed, but the difference is not statistically significant. Men and older youths are more interested in politics than women and younger persons.

Political Extremism

Political extremism was measured by the question where the respondent had to consider 'three basic kinds of attitudes towards the society we live in.' The alternatives comprised revolutionary action, reforms and strongly defend society against subversive forces.

In the literature significant discussion is concerned with the extent to which unemployment leads to radical political interests, sometimes labelled left-and right-wing extremism. In order to test this hypothesis we made two analyses; one where we emphasised the significance of unemployment for revolutionary ideas, and one where the unemployed were supposed to be more inclined to defend society against subversive forces.

The large majority are reformists, both among the employed and the unemployed (Table 1). There are few revolutionaries, slightly more among the unemployed than the employed. The situation is the opposite for those who would strongly defend society against subversive forces.

The regression analysis (Table 2) also shows that the unemployed are more frequently revolutionary than the employed. There is no difference between the employed and the unemployed in defending society against subversive forces.

Provisional Summary

The status as unemployed is first and foremost manifest in their lack of political confidence and in support of revolutionary ideas. Unemployed youths express their displeasure with the working of democracy in their own country more so than employed youth. This is the main impression of the analysis for the European sample in general. The unemployed also participate less in political discussions with their friends. There is no connection between status as unemployed and inclination to strongly defend society against subversive forces.

National Variations

Does the impact of unemployment on political marginalisation vary between the countries? Our hypothesis is that the effect of status as unemployed varies according to the development of the welfare state in the various countries. In order to examine whether there are national variations in the effect of status as unemployed we have specified interactions between country and the unemployment variable within the logistic regression models reported above. Table 3 shows the chi-squared statistics and their p-values for each of the five dependent variables for the different effects of the unemployment variables between the countries.

There are significant differences between the countries in one out of the five political attitude variables when comparing unemployed and employed youths. The difference is in political confidence. Along other political attitudes the unemployed are not generally more politically marginalised in some countries compared to others. However, it is interesting to note that the differences we do observe between the countries apply to the dependent variable, where we also find the greatest differences between employed and unemployed. Is the difference between the employed and the unemployed concerning political trust smaller in those countries with the most developed welfare services, as hypothesised? Figure 1 shows the confidence for employed and unemployed persons for each country.[2]

Table 3. Chi-squared and p-value of the associations between country and status as unemployed controlling for age and gender. Countries with equal weighting.

	Political Confidence	Interest in National Politics	Discuss Politics With Friends	Revolutionary	Conservative
Chi-squared	41.56 (10 d.f.)	7.23 (11 d.f.)	13.00 (11 d.f.)	8.31 (11 d.f.)	10.70 (11 d.f.)
P-value	0.00	0.780	0.293	0.685	0.469

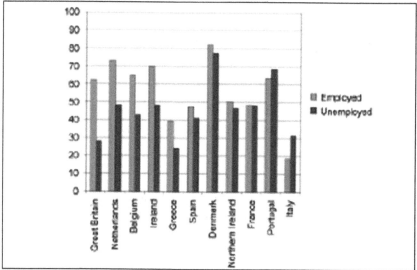

Figure 1. Evaluation of regime performance among young employed and unemployed in 11 European countries.

We find the greatest difference in political confidence between unemployed and employed youth in Great Britain, followed by The Netherlands, Belgium, Ireland and Greece. There are no significant differences in Spain, Denmark, Northern Ireland, France or Portugal. In Italy the unemployed have more political confidence than the employed.

Our hypothesis related to the development of the welfare state receives very little empirical support. Indeed, there are small differences between the employed and the unemployed in Denmark, which, in keeping with Esping-Andersen's typology, has the most developed welfare state. There are also small differences between the employed and the unemployed in Portugal, a country with a limited welfare state. The deviant result for Italy cannot be explained within our hypothesis on the development of the welfare state. The large difference between the employed and the unemployed in Great Britain does not support our hypothesis either, as Great Britain was classified as a relatively developed welfare state (Esping-Andersen, 1990). This finding does, however, support the previous finding made by Banks and Ullah (1987) of a larger level of political marginalisation among unemployed than among employed youth in Britain.

Previously we have indicated that the level of unemployment in the country may influence the relationship between unemployment and political marginalisation. However, this effect may work two ways:

1. High unemployment may increase the frustrations of the unemployed concerning politicians' efforts to reduce unemployment.

2. High unemployment may also give a sense of normality of being unemployed. One is not an outsider even though one does not have paid employment.

Let us compare the difference in political confidence between unemployed and employed youths with the level of youth unemployment in the country. Youth unemployment in the country is measured here on the basis of the proportion of the respondents reporting unemployment.[3]

Figure 2 does not reveal any clear association between the effects of unemployment and the level of unemployment in the country. Excluding the deviant finding for Italy, there is no association at all. Italy has the largest proportion of unemployed, simultaneously being the only country where the unemployed are significantly more politically confident than the employed. The difference between the employed and the unemployed is small in Denmark, Northern Ireland and France—countries with marked differences in the levels of unemployment. Ireland, Northern Ireland and Italy all have high unemployment, but deviant patterns between the employed and the unemployed youth.

SUMMARY AND DISCUSSION

In this article we have investigated whether unemployed youth are

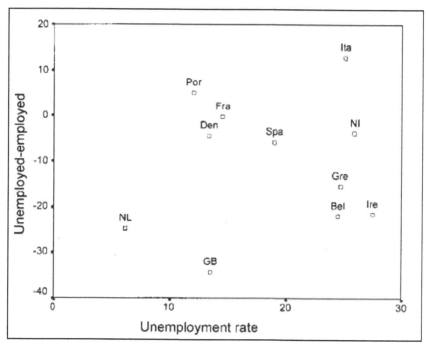

Figure 2. Evaluation of regime performance among unemployed youth minus evaluation of regime performance among employed youth and level of unemployment among the youth in the country.

politically marginalised compared with employed youth. We have looked at three aspects of political marginalisation: political confidence, political interest and political extremism. The results do not provide a basis for saying that the unemployed throughout are politically marginalised compared with the employed.

Regarding political interest measures such as interest in national politics, there is hardly any difference between the employed and the unemployed. On the other hand, the employed have a greater disposition to discuss politics with their friends. The general impression is first and foremost that European youth do not care much about politics. *That* is a greater challenge to European democracy than the fact that the unemployed are less interested than the little-interested employed youth.

Some of the earlier studies of political marginalisation among the unemployed have concluded that the unemployed tend to have more radical political attitudes. This conclusion was supported by our study concerning revolutionary political ideas. All in all there are, however, few revolutionaries both among the employed and the unemployed.

The unemployed distinguish themselves first and foremost in that they have less political confidence; they are less satisfied with how democracy works. It is tempting to interpret this finding as a result of being unemployed. They are disappointed about the authorities' efforts in respect of unemployment. The analysis of variations between the countries complicates this conclusion, however. Dissatisfaction among the unemployed regarding how democracy works compared to the views of the employed, is not generally larger in countries with high unemployment than those with a low level. This we would have expected, based on an explanation that the dissatisfaction of the unemployed is based on an evaluation of the efforts made by the authorities.

Great Britain and Italy form the extremes in respect of the relationship between status as unemployed and political confidence. The difference between the employed and the unemployed is greatest in Great Britain. The employed have greater propensity to be satisfied with how democracy works than the unemployed. On the other hand, Italy is the only country where the situation is the opposite; the unemployed are more satisfied than the employed, while at the same time Italy is among the highest in youth unemployment of the countries in the study.

One explanation of this difference can be in the selection process of being unemployed in these countries. The low level of confidence among the unemployed in Great Britain can be an expression of the fact that unemployment here is largely an 'underdog' phenomenon (Bynner & Ashford, 1994). Unemployment reproduces and reinforces what for the young is already a marginal social situation. This conclusion corresponds to previous studies of youth unemployment in Great Britain (Breakwell, 1986; Banks & Ullah, 1987). In Italy, where youth unemployment is among the highest in Europe (Julkunen, 1998), recruitment to unemployment is presumably broader than in Great Britain. The unemployed are not recruited from the lower strata of society alone.

The high unemployment in Italy also contributes to a normalising of the situation of being unemployed. One is no longer an outsider in society. The basis for a lack of political confidence is thus less. But perhaps equally important: political distrust is a majority attitude in Italy. Several studies show that Italy comes out worst in Europe when considering confidence in and an evaluation of the democratic institutions (Listhaug, 1995; Klingemann, 1999). Bluntly stated, it can be maintained that it is those who are *satisfied* who form the deviant group in Italy.

The comparison between Great Britain and Italy indicates that a number of factors affect how unemployment influences political confidence. Access to paid employment is not sufficient in itself to prevent political indifference, apathy and distrust among youth. Neither does the development of the welfare state, as it has been elaborated by Esping-Andersen, appear to be a crucial factor.

NOTES

1. Data was made available by Norwegian Social Science Data Services in Oslo. NSD is not responsible for the use of the data material.

2. The figures are based on the model person in the regression model (a woman aged 20 years) being fairly or very satisfied with the way democracy works in the country. The choice of this model person makes no difference since neither gender nor age has any impact on political confidence (Table 2).

3. As a proportion of those in the labour market. It is difficult to find comparable data for youth unemployment in official statistics. One advantage with the measure applied is that the instrument is the same for all countries. A drawback is that it is based on small samples.

REFERENCES

Abrams D (1990). *Political identity. Relative deprivation, social identity and the case of Scottish Nationalism.* ESCR 16–19 Initiative Occasional Papers, No. 24. London, City University.

Almond GA, Verba S (1963). *The civic culture: political attitudes and democracy in five nations.* Princeton, NJ, Princeton University Press.

Banks MH, Ullah P (1987). Political attitudes and voting among unemployed and employed youth. *Journal of Adolescence* 10: 201–216.

Breakwell G (1986). Political and attributional responses of the young short-term unemployed. *Political Psychology* 7: 265–278.

Bynner J, Ashford S (1994). Politics and participation: Some antecedents of young people's attitudes to the political system and political activity. *European Journal of Social Psychology* 24: 223–236.

Carle J (1997). Politiskt engagemang (Political involvement). In: Carle J, Julkunen I eds. *Arbetslöshetens villkor—om ungdom, arbetslöshet och marginalisering i 1990—talets Norden.* [The conditions of unemployment—on youth, unemployment and marginalisation in Europe in the 1990s]. København, Nord 1997: 19.

Carle J (1998). Political involvement among the youth. In: Julkunen I, Carle J, eds. *Young and unemployed in Scandinavia—a Nordic comparative study.* Copenhagen, Nord 1998: 14.

Clark AW (1985). The effects of unemployment on political attitude. *Australian and New Zealand Journal of Sociology* 21: 100–108.

Clark AW, Clissold, MP (1982). Correlates of adaptation among unemployed and employed young men. *Psychological Reports* 50: 887–893.

Cochrane R, Billig M (1983). Youth and politics in the 80s. *Youth and Policy* 2: 31–34.

Dahl R (1961). *Who governs?* New Haven and London, Yale University Press.

Easton D (1965). *A framework for political analysis.* Englewood Cliffs, NJ, Prentice-Hall.

Easton D (1975). A reassessment of the concept of political support. *British Journal of Political Science* 5: 435–457.

Esping-Andersen G (1985). *Politics against markets.* Princeton, NJ, Princeton University Press.

Esping-Andersen G (1990). *The three worlds of welfare capitalism.* Cambridge, Polity Press.

Fuchs D (1995). Support for the democratic system. In: Klingemann H-D, Fuchs D, eds. *Citizens and the State.* Oxford, Oxford University Press.

Furlong A, Cartmel F (1997). *Young people and social change. Individualisation and risk in late modernity.* Buckingham, Philadelphia, Open University Press.

Hernes G, Martinussen W (1980). *Levekårsundersøkelsen. Demokrati og politiske ressurser* [The level of living study. Democracies and political resources]. NOU 1980: 7.

Huntington SP (1975). The democratic distemper. *Public Interest* 41: 9–38.

Jackson MP, Hanby V (1982). *The British work creation programme.* Aldershot, Gower.

Julkunen I (1998). Active labour-market policy and integration. In: Julkunen I, Carle J, eds. *Young and unemployed in Scandinavia a Nordic comparative study.* Copenhagen, Nord 1998: 14.

Klingemann HD (1999). Mapping political support in the1990s: A global analysis. In: Norris P, ed. *Critical citizens. Global support for democratic governance.* Oxford, Oxford University Press.

Leibfried S (1993). Towards a European welfare state? In: Jones C, ed. *New perspectives on the welfare state in Europe.* London, Routledge.

Listhaug O (1995). The dynamics of trust in politicians. In: Klingemann H-D, Fuchs D, eds. *Citizens and the State.* Oxford, Oxford University Press.

Martinussen W (1973). *Fjerndemokratiet* [The distant democracy]. Oslo, Gyldendal Norsk Forlag.

Marshall TH (1950). *Citizenship and social class.* Cambridge, Cambridge University Press.

McAllister I (1999). The economic performance of governments. In: Norris P, ed. *Critical citizens. Global support for democratic governance.* Oxford, Oxford University Press.

Norris P (1999). Introduction: The growth of critical citizens? In: Norris P, ed. *Critical citizens. Global support fordemocratic governance.* Oxford, Oxford University Press.

Roberts K, Parsell G (1990). *The political orientations, interestsand activities of Britain's 16 to 18 year olds in the late1980s.* ESRC 16–19 Initiative Occasional Papers, No. 26. London, City University.

Verba S, Nie NH, Kim JO (1978). *Participation and political equality.* Cambridge, Cambridge University Press.

*Ann-Helén Bay is director of the Institute for Social Research in Oslo, Norway.

Morten Blekesaune is professor of sociology at the University of Agder in Norway.

Bay, Ann-Helén, and Morten Blekesaune. "Youth, Unemployment and Political Marginalisation." *International Journal of Social Welfare* 11 (2002): 132–139.

Parenting and Right-Wing Extremism: An Analysis of the Biographical Genesis of Racism Among Young People

by Thomas Gabriel*

This contribution discusses the influence of the family and the immediate social environment on the development of racist attitudes and behaviours among young people. The specific focus of the study was to scrutinize the influencing factors that lead to development of racist attitudes and behavioural dispositions among young people in an interactive and generative dimension. Surprisingly, and despite theoretical expectations, the findings show that social marginality, usually interpreted as the result economic and social change, plays only a minor role. Far more influential are deprivation or disintegration as a result of domestic violence and parental conflicts, and the consequences of both within the family system. The findings imply a critique of the German-speaking discourse, both theoretical and practical, that has tried to explain right-wing extremism by pointing to the consequences of social change in modern societies. The findings also show how closely the genesis of right-wing extremism can be linked to culture and tradition, even in a country that has long and strong democratic history.

INTRODUCTION

Research into right-wing and xenophobic attitudes, and acts of violence, has a long history. The classic study of the "Authoritarian Personality" was fuelled by an interest in explaining the origins of German fascism (Adorno et al. 1950). It seems practically indisputable that cultural codes that are handed down historically (such as anti-Semitism, nationalism, and racism), create an environment in which aggressive xenophobia can develop and grow. During the last decade, against the backdrop of the violent events in eastern Germany during the 1990s, the German-language discourse has become increasingly focused on violent youths. That has moved the focus toward issues such as youth delinquency, the reactions of youth welfare services, and the judiciary system.

In making adolescent criminal activity the central focus, one overlooks that comparable attitudes can be found, at the level of racist patterns of interpretation, among both adolescents and adults. This is supported by findings of the European Monitoring Centre on Racism and Xenophobia. At the end of the 1990s, and across all 15 EU member states at the time, 33 percent of those interviewed defined themselves as "quite racist" or "very racist" (Westin 2003). Numerous studies (including the German Allbus and Sinus studies) have pointed out the social normality of nationalistic attitudes, and in particular of ethnocentric viewpoints, in Western democracies. These findings underscore that the attitudes and opinions in question are not located at the fringe but instead have far more mainstream appeal.

On the other hand, the results of macro-sociological studies cannot explain the actual processes of transmitting attitudes and values that come about during the process of socialization and education. The relevant behaviour patterns seem to be actualized on an extremely small scale, not at a macro-level but at most at the level of social meso-systems. Empirical findings also show that it is the primary groups, in particular, the right-wing perpetrator's family and the perpetrator's immediate social group, which are relevant for explaining the genesis of right-wing radical motives and actions.

DEFINITIONS

The relationship between violence committed by young offenders, racism, and right-wing extremism first requires terminological differentiation. Unfortunately, there are a lack of terms that are clearly defined, usable, comparable, comprehensive and free of ambiguity. The same is true of related terms, such as "hostility towards foreigners" or "ethnocentrism." Obvious inaccuracies in terminology can also be found even in specialized publications on these subjects. Frequently, the terms being used are simply not defined at all (Butterwegge 2000, Ganter 1998, Zick 1997).

When trying to narrow down the terms, one needs to first consider the patterns of interpretation and behaviour vis-à-vis 'strangers.' Based on an assumption that there is a close link between stereotype, prejudice and discrimination, one often finds a simple conclusion drawn: it is enough to know the prejudices exist on an interpretational and attitudinal level in order to explain, or even predict, discrimination on a behavioural level. This is usually stated without benefit of detailed explanation. Such arguments ignore marked differences in terminology, and complex empirical connections thereby escape more profound analysis.

It bears repeating, though it has been said many times before, that there can be profound differences between expressed attitudes and actually demonstrated behaviour. A particular difficulty arises from the fact that the debate frequently relates to attitudes, orientations and value systems (Fend 1994). These need not be immediately relevant for behaviour or may not even adequately describe it. Some studies show high correlations between attitudes and behaviour, others find only very weak relationships. The results are inconsistent and hence inconclusive (Winkler 2002, Dovidio et al. 1996, Eckes and Six 1994), and the same applies to the relationship between prejudice and discriminatory behaviour. Not everyone who admits to prejudices toward 'strangers' in an interview necessarily behaves in a discriminatory manner toward them, and a person may discriminate against a group of persons even if their expressed attitude toward them in general may not be demonstrably negative (Ganter 1998).

Reasons for these uneven findings can be found in the terms of action theory, which argues that actions consist of a multitude of "conditioning moments." The motivational orientation, the subjective knowledge about social appropriateness, the perception of the situation in which the action takes place, and the anticipation of potential consequences of the action all play an important part (Giddens 1995, Esser 1996). Prejudice (and stereotype) can permeate the subjective "situational definition" and activate behavioural dispositions, thereby providing a basis for discrimination. In addition, the reflexive controls material interests exert on the actions are also of decisive importance, as are the anticipated rewards or sanctions important attachment figures or groups provide. Some studies show that a close connection between prejudice and discrimination may only come about under very special circumstances (Ajzen 1993, Esser 1996, Fazio 1990). Hence, no one-dimensional conclusions should be drawn about the connection between opinions and attitudes and actual discriminatory acts.

Although there is a debate as to what the definition of right-wing extremism legitimately encompasses, there is wide academic consensus that right-wing extremism is essentially anti-democratic, in that it stands contrary to human rights traditions and democratic constitutions. Ethnocentricity, often in the form of overt racism and nationalism, is at the core of an ideology that claims superiority to other values in democratic societies. The values of universal human rights (of individual liberty, equality, respect for human dignity) are despised, rejected, or denied—as are fundamental rights like freedom of speech, thought, conscience and religion.

Right-wing extremism is directed against democratic political values, including pluralism, and parliamentary systems. Its adherents principally advocate inequality and an aggressive nationalism that breeds resentment against groups regarded as ethnically foreign—which often leads to an advocacy of pure racism. However, at the level of the individual right-wing extremist, not all such features and attitudes need contradict democratic political values to match the definition (Altermatt and Kriesi 1995, 18).

One may already speak of ethnic marginalization when beliefs about the relatively stable particularities of certain ethnic groups, based on origin and culture, manifest themselves. Racism describes a special type of ethnic marginalization that is characterized by prioritizing seemingly stable biological differences between human beings. Especially in the Anglo-Saxon and French linguistic communities, but in German discourse as well, the difference is frequently neglected or blurred by the use of neologisms such as "neo-racism" or "differential racism." An important cause for this lies in the fact that it is very difficult to draw the boundaries between ethnic and racist marginalization in empirical analysis. Nevertheless, the term "racism" should be reserved for attitudes, modes of behaviour and ideologies which refer to the construction of misrepresentations about genetic differences and thus hierarchical levels between ethnic groups. Ethnocentrism is used as part of the terminology of social science, defining a phenomenon which is basically characterized by a tendency to regard the thinking patterns, behaviour and other claimed characteristics attributed to one's own group as a "natural" standard with which to compare and judge "strangers." The idealized evaluation of one's own group goes hand in hand with a negative opinion of the group(s) of strangers. The glorification of one's own group and the defamation of groups of strangers are by no means based on actual facts or even on the real existence of the perceived group of strangers; simple virtual concepts suffice (Heyder and Schmidt 2002; LeVine and Campbell 1972). While ethnic marginalization can include comparatively "harmless" ideas about the existence of ethnic difference, the term "ethnocentrism" clearly signifies a one-sided orientation, both concerning one's attitudes and behaviour in favor of one's own group, and in conjunction with it, a distancing, feelings of antipathy, and discrimination against the "strangers" (Rieker 2002; Heyder and Schmidt 2002).

As already mentioned, a basic difficulty arises from these terminological connections. It is not at all necessary for attitudes, orientations and values to have an immediate relevance for behaviour or actions. Likewise, they may be insufficient as explanations for actual behaviour.

Depending on family background and social environment, the strength of an adolescent's ego, or in other words, the ability to balance social demands and

individual needs that is essential for coping in a civil society, can vary significantly. On a continuum, the attitudes and demeanour (or mindset) could range
from an individual's ability to resist racist assaults to a capacity to commit acts of
racist violence in which—in an extreme case—they could see themselves as the
"executive body" of their parents or their environment. The notion of 'family'
thus needs to be analyzed as a structural and functional construct, to obtain an
idea of its potential and influence.

The central indicator of the family is the bond between two or more linked
generations, sharing a parent-child relationship. In this regard, the generational
relationships can be said to be a specific characteristic of the family. Relevant
here are studies by Welzer et al. (2002) and Jensen (2000) which deal with
the question of transmitting a sense of responsibility for the Nazi era and the
Holocaust across the generations, as expressed in family memory and family
narratives in Germany. In Switzerland, it is not a question of transmitting cul-
pability and historical consciousness, but instead the transmitting of racism and
right-wing extremism through the generations.

The central issue here is the formation of a generational memory, a subject
that intrigued Karl Mannheim already in the 1930s (Assmann 2002; Erdfelder
2002). Mannheim (1964) described a significant multi-generational aspect of
the sociology of biography by defining tradition as the transmitting of inherited
life attitudes, sentiments and attitudes to the new, next generation. That . . .
which is consciously taught can be of only limited quantity and significance,
by contrast. His theoretical speculations are relevant here because they point
to the complex inter-generational dynamic in the transmitting of attitudes and
values that goes beyond the intentional influence of parenting and education.
One of the questions to be asked, therefore, is why some young people are susceptible to right-wing extremist ideologies, or participate in violent acts of aggression, while others who live under similar economic and social conditions,
do not have these tendencies.

THE SWISS STUDY

Our research project, conducted at the University of Zurich, began with the
hypothesis that the primary groups, the family and the immediate social environment, play a decisive role in explaining the genesis of racist attitudes and
behavioural dispositions. Yet, the processes of parenting and socialisation are
products of active, subjective interaction and thus needed to be reconstructed
as such within the framework of the research project. The study aimed to determine the influencing factors leading to the development of racist attitudes and

behavioural dispositions among young people in an interactive and generative dimension. Since these influences can reinforce, relativise or cancel each other out, the only way to handle these issues is by a highly intensive and detailed analysis of selective biographical processes. In this context, it was of special interest to uncover the biographies' "development paths" and "junctions" (Rieker 2002), which would enable one to hermeneutically reconstruct and understand the genesis and intensifying of racist interpretation and behaviour patterns. This method is supported by more recent findings which unanimously warn against any tendency to rely on the results of socialisation while neglecting that the acquisition of social disposition is a process which is highly individual in character. An appropriate way to approach the central issues here is therefore one which is qualitative and reconstructs the biographical development of adolescent subjects by means of in-depth empirical case studies (N=26), including interviews with parents and significant attachment figures.

The case selection concentrated on juvenile actors in the area of right-wing extremism. This seemed particularly suited with regard to the biographical causes of racism, right-wing extremism and violent behaviour of young people because it circumvents the above-mentioned problem of connections between interpretation and attitudes on the one hand, and manifest behaviour patterns on the other. In conjunction with a multi-generational perspective, the aim was to gain more insight into the familial conditions which create racism-motivated violence among young people. This reconstructive perspective could allow us to draw conclusions as to the biographical genesis of racist interpretation and action patterns. In the few existing studies on the subject of parenting that are relevant, right-wing extremism and racism were only examined with respect to the quality of the parent-child relationship from the subjective view of the adolescents. This could be one reason for individual contradictions, since the subjective "truth" about the relationship to one's parents is always also a product of one's successful integration (Gabriel 2001, 91). The multi-generational analyses made it possible to pinpoint the quality of interpersonal familial relationships on an inter-subjective level; this has thus far been neglected. In order to be able to describe the conditional factors in intra-familial processes more precisely and, especially where interfering conditions are concerned, engage in a more exact analysis, a combination of case-reconstructive procedure (Kraimer 2000, Fatke 1997) and educational biography research (Krüger 1997) was used as methodology. In the research framework, this is linked to a multi-generational approach with which a more in-depth analysis of the complex effects of intra-familial processes in their biographical significance became possible.

Findings

The adolescents and families researched by our study are no 'modernisation losers." On the contrary: there is a large degree of 'normality' among the 26 youths and families studied, both in their life scripts and their life-worlds. In fact, we found attributes reflecting a high level of social integration in a large proportion of our sample. Surprisingly, social marginality, which is usually interpreted as the result of economic and social changes, plays only a minor role, despite theoretical expectations. Instead, deprivation or disintegration is the result of domestic violence, parental conflicts and their consequences within the family system.

The high number of youths in the sample who have an affinity to violence and who are organised either politically or in sub-cultural groups indicates that the right-wing adolescents who participated in this study not only have a politically right-wing attitude, but also a disposition to act accordingly. This precludes the explanation that the case selection might be responsible for the high measure of familial normality. Even the few adolescents who are politically or sub-culturally inactive have a significant disposition to act based on their racist and right-wing extremist thought patterns and world-views.

The influences on the adolescents' course of development that were studied did not include a direct if-then causality. However, dispositions of a biographical origin become analytically subsumable, allowing us to reconstruct affiliation to right-wing groups and organisations as well as right-wing interpretation and action patterns and their plausible development clusters. Even if a young person's contact to the right-wing scene is based on coincidence and structures of opportunity ('my mate took me along'), the significance connected with it is by no means coincidental but has been acquired biographically, as a disposition. Intra-familial efficiency factors constitute an important mediating factor of social-structural measures of influence of a young person's environment. By looking at the meso-level of social systems, an analysis on the macro-level of social development can thus be supplemented as necessary. Violent and xenophobic actions on the part of adolescents seem to be caused to a large degree by the social environment as well as by the family, its culture and history. In the biographies that were studied, the following three development clusters or paths of development could be shown to be empirically present.

A. Dissociation by Over-Adaptation—Radicalisation of the Values and Standards of the Social Environment of Origin

This development cluster is characterised by the fact that politically right-wing attitudes and behavioural dispositions are already found in the adolescents' parents, grandparents and other close attachment figures, as well as in their cultural environment. The fear of foreign infiltration, the drawing of national demarcation lines, the attribution of cultural characteristics and devalorisation are political issues within the family and part of the family's culture and history. The adolescents see themselves as an executive power in a widely accepted culture and sociality. Their political statements and actions earn them recognition and acceptance. There is, however, no unilateral transmission from one generation to the next, but rather a discourse about values and traditions of the elders. Unlike Development Clusters II and III, there is no direct link between being right-wing and coping with family conflicts or socialisation conditions experienced as difficult. Instead, there is a connection in this development cluster to 'non-extremist' or 'hidden extremist' tendencies. On the level of biographical development, there are traces of influence that lead directly to the centre of society and culture.

B. Violence, Disregard and the Search for Recognition

The biographies of the adolescents in this development cluster are characterised throughout by the violation of their physical, psychic and social integrity in the context of growing up in their respective families. What they experience, as well as how they try to deal with it, constitutes a central topic of their biographies and is connected to the familial and inter-generational issues as well as the adolescents' right-wing extremist patterns of interpretation and behaviour. The intra-familial experience of physical powerlessness, and both social and personal disregard, entail a fundamental lack of relationships of recognition with their primary attachment figures. Youths in this cluster have in common how they experienced violence in connection with their fathers. Their interactions within the family circle are characterised by conflicted reactions to their person, often experienced by the adolescents as contingent, or as something they cannot anticipate. This loss, or rather, this lack of habitualised recognition conditions, has an effect on the ability and disposition for empathy generated through socialisation, and thus also on the possibility to recognise and acknowledge other human beings in social contexts. Such effects can be shown in the deregulated way in which these adolescents commit violent acts, as well as in their uncertainty vis-à-vis social relationships. In the process of right-wing group rituals, this biographically acquired disposition is condensed into a habitus.

C. Non-Perception and the Search for Experience, Visibility and Difference

This development cluster is not characterised by the experience of physical violence, open and aggressive disregard, or contingent actions by the primary attachment figures of the adolescents' immediate family. As in Development Cluster II, the absence of communication and direct experience and thus lack of recognition conditions again has an effect that is biographically relevant. This manifests itself in social uncertainty on the part of the adolescents, albeit in a weaker form where identity-relevant confidence is concerned. The central characteristic is a lack of interaction and communication in the family circle, which are mutually perceived as relevant and meaningful, and as significant from a subjective perspective. The phenomenology related to this is multi-layered, ranging from rigid authoritarian patterns of behaviour to mutual ignorance, spatial and temporal absence (by parents or children), inauthentic parenting behaviour and the belief in an unrealistic ideal of how an adolescent should be that has nothing in common with reality. The common ground consists of a lack of significant adults who are visible, and can thus be experienced, through their interaction and affective sympathy for the adolescent. Attempts to obtain visibility by means of the deliberate provocation of family issues or inter-generational topics either elicit no reaction at all or affect-regulated contact (the youths are tested/diagnosed, agreements are drawn up), or it results in explicit 'non-perception' as a form of punishment. Achieving visibility through difference and by breaking through the isolation by means of an affiliation (right-wing group, virtual home, ideology) is of significance as an experiential space, in particular for the affiliated adolescents in this category.

Final Remarks

The study found no evidence that "right-wing" actors come from "socially disadvantaged groups." Apparently, they come from all social strata, though mainly from lower middle-class families. They clearly don't suffer from social exclusion or social deprivation. This is quite surprising, as the German-language discourse on right-wing extremism is dominated by the studies of Wilhelm Heitmeyer (1987, 1992) that explain right-wing extremism as a consequence of modernity, caused by social and economic changes. His theory locates the problem at the edge of society, and is linked to a group of young people suffering from deprivation and lack of integration. In his definition, the perpetrators are "modernisation losers." Beside this problematic moral implication, his view on right-wing extremism was adopted by politics, juvenile courts and social work in a very uncritical manner.

Results presented here clearly support the assumption that violent and discriminatory actions are strongly influenced by the social environment and the family. There are parents with similar attitudes and parental reactions which lead to an intensification, but also a strong "culture of non-attention" in the families. This also marks the hermeneutic gap, and a search for meaning even when there is no significant interaction. Such parental ignorance also has an effect on the biographies of right-wing actors. The transmission hypothesis, that political extremism is handed down from one generation to the other, seems to be far too simple (Kracke et al. 1993). Mono-causal explanations are unacceptable, especially since it must be assumed that there is interference between the individual factors. In the generational context of the family, the contextual attitudes of the adults take on an importance for the adolescent who picks up on parental values but also examines them in an interactive process. Significant here is the emotional-affective climate in the intra-familial context which manifests itself in family narratives, in the quality of familial attachment, parenting styles and in the moral dimension of conflict resolution. The contextual and structural influences on the socialization process (e.g., fundamentalist and authoritarian dispositions, orientations and attitudes) must not be thought linear; they can reinforce each other but they can also put each other in perspective or cancel each other out.

Generalizing attributions are as problematic as probabilistically determined generalizations about individual biographies. It is true that influencing factors exist which can be uncovered by research, and there are thus probabilities favouring a tendency for adolescents to assume and act on xenophobic value judgments and behaviour patterns.

These results demonstrate that macro-sociological explanations of right-wing extremism alone are too narrow, in particular since interference by individual factors can be shown to exist in biographical and familial development processes. At the same time, generalising attributions are just as problematic as probabilistically determined generalisations about right-wing adolescents. Research can uncover influencing factors which enable us to find probabilities that may make it easier for adolescents to adopt and operate within values and behavioural patterns that are hostile towards foreigners. However, even if we accept that socio-structural conditions have considerable influence, a large measure of autonomy remains. This not only applies to the individual biographies but also to the development of individual family systems.

REFERENCES

Adorno, T. W., Frenkel-Brunswik, E., Levinson, D. J. and Sanford, R. N. 1950 The Authoritarian Personality, New York: Harper.

Altermatt U. and Kriesi H. 1995 Rechtsextremismus in der Schweiz. Organisationen und Radikalisierung in den 1980er und 1990er Jahren, Zürich: Verlag NZZ.

Ajzen, I. 1993 'Attitude Theory and the Attitude-Behavior Relation,' in D. Krebs and P. Schmidt (eds) New Directions in Attitude Measurement, Berlin and New York: de Gruyter.

Assmann, A. 2002 'Vier Formen des Gedächtnisses,' Erwägen, Wissen, Ethik 13: 183–190.

Butterwegge, C. and Lohmann, G. 2000 Jugend, Rechtsextremismus und Gewalt, Opladen: Leske + Budrich.

Boehnke, K., Fuß, D. and Hagan, J. (eds) 2002 Jugendgewalt und Rechtsextremismus—Soziologische und psychologische Analysen in internationaler Perspektive, Weinheim und München: Juventa.

Dovidio, J. F., Brigham, J.C., Johnson, B.T. and Gaertner, S. L. 1996 'Stereotyping, Prejudice, and Discrimination: Another Look,' in C. N. Macrae and C. Stangor and M. Hewstone (eds) Foundations of Stereotypes and Stereotyping. New York/London: The Guilford Press.

Eckes, T. and Six B. 1994 'Fakten und Fiktionen in der Einstellungs-Verhaltens-Forschung: Eine Meta-Analyse,' Zeitschrift für Sozialpsychologie 25: 253–271.

Erdfelder, E. 2002 'Auf dem Weg zu einer interdisziplinären Systematik des Gedächtnisses?', Erwägen, Wissen, Ethik 13: 197–200.

Esser, H. 1996 'Die Definition der Situation,' Kölner Zeitschrift für Soziologie und Sozialpsychologie 1: 1–34.

Fatke, R. 1997 'Fallstudien in der Erziehungswissenschaft,' in B. Friebertshäuser and A. Prengel (eds) Handbuch qualitative Forschungsmethoden in der Erziehungswissenschaft, Weinheim und München: Juventa.

Fazio, R. H. 1990 'Multiple Processes by which Attitudes Guide Behavior: The MODE Model as an Integrative Framework,' in M. P. Zanna (ed.) Advances in Experimental Social Psychology 23, San Diego: Academic Press.

Fend, H. 1994 'Ausländerfeindlich-nationalistische Weltbilder und Aggressionsbereitschaft bei Jugendlichen in Deutschland und der Schweiz—kontextuelle und personale Antecendenzbedingungen,' Zeitschrift für Soziologie der Erziehung und Sozialisation 14: 131–162.

Gabriel, T. 2001 Forschung zur Heimerziehung. Eine vergleichende Bilanzierung in Grossbritannien und Deutschland, Weinheim und München: Juventa.

Ganter, S. 1998 Ursachen und Formen der Fremdenfeindlichkeit in der Bundesrepublik Deutschland, Bonn: Electronic edition.

Giddens A. 1995 Die Konstitution der Gesellschaft, Frankfurt/M.: Campus.

Heyder, A. and Schmidt, P. 2002 'Autoritarismus und Ethnozentrismus in Deutschland: Ein Phänomen der Jugend oder der Alten?', in: K. Boehnke, D. Fuß and J. Hagan (eds) Jugendgewalt und Rechtsextremismus—Soziologische und psychologische Analysen in internationaler Perspektive, Weinheim und München: Juventa.

Heitmeyer, W. 1987 Rechtsextremistische Orientierungen bei Jugendlichen, Weinheim und München: Juventa.

Heitmeyer, W. 1992 Die Bielefelder Rechtsextremismus-Studie. Erste Langzeituntersuchung zur politischen Sozialisation männlicher Jugendlicher, Weinheim und München: Juventa.

Jensen, O. 2000 Zur gemeinsamen Verfertigung von Text in der Forschungssituation [32 Absätze], Forum Qualitative Sozialforschung (http://qualitativeresearch.net/fqs/fqs-d/200inhalt-d.htm).

Kracke, B., Noack, P., Hofer M. and Klein-Allermann, E. 1993 'Die rechte Gesinnung: Familiale Bedingungen autoritärer Orientierungen ost- und westdeutscher Jugendlicher,' Zeitschrift für Pädagogik 39 (6): 971–988.

Kraimer, K. 2000 Die Fallrekonstruktion. Sinnverstehen in der sozialwissenschaftlichen Forschung, Frankfurt/M.: Suhrkamp.

Krüger, H. H. 1997 'Erziehungswissenschaftliche Biographieforschung,' in B. Friebertshäuser und A. Prengel (eds) Handbuch qualitative Forschungsmethoden in der Erziehungswissenschaft, Weinheim und München: Juventa.

LeVine, R. A. and Campbell, D. T. 1972 'Ethnocentrism: Theories of Conflict, Ethnic Attitudes, and Group Behavior,' New York: John Wiley.

Mannheim, K. 1964 'Das Problem der Generationen,' in K. H. Wolff (ed.) Wissenssoziologie, Berlin und Neuwied: Luchterhand.

Rieker, P. 2002 'Ethnozentrismus und Sozialisation. Zur Bedeutung von Beziehungserfahrungen für die Entwicklung verschiedenen Ausprägungen ethnozentristischer Orientierungen,' in K. Boehnke, D. Fuß and J, Hagan (eds) Jugendgewalt und Rechtsextremismus—Soziologische und psychologische Analysen in internationaler Perspektive, Weinheim und München: Juventa.

Welzer, H. (ed.) 2002 Das kommunikative Gedächtnis. Eine Theorie der Erinnerung, München: C. H. Beck.

Westin, C. 2003 'Racism and the Political Right: European Perspectives,' in P. H. Merkl and L. Weinberg (eds) Right-Wing Extremism in the Twenty-First Century London, London: Frank Cass Publishers.

Winkler, M. 2002 Gewaltbereitschaft, Fremdenfeindlichkeit und Rechtsextremismus: Bedeutung, Funktion und Leistung von Familien, Expertise für den Unterausschuss 3 des Landesjugendhilfeausschusses Thüringen, unpublished paper, Jena.

Zick, A. 1997 Vorurteile und Rassismus. Eine sozialpsychologische Analyse, Münster: Waxmann.

*Thomas Gabriel is professor in the Department of Social Work of the Zurich University of Applied Sciences in Switzerland.

Gabriel, Thomas. "Parenting and Right-Wing Extremism: An Analysis of the Biographical Genesis of Racism Among Young People." In *Right-Wing Extremism in Switzerland: National and International Perspectives*, edited by Marcel Alexander Niggli, 193–202. Baden-Baden: Nomos, 2009.

The Cultural Basis of Youth Involvement in Italian Extreme Right-Wing Organisations

by Stéphanie Dechezelles*

ABSTRACT Taking into account the cultural dimensions of extreme right-wing parties, this article attempts to open the 'secret box' of these organisations through a comparison of two groups of young Italian activists inside Alleanza Nazionale and Lega Nord. It is shown that these cultural frames are collectively constructed and composed of three main elements: an ideal model of society, a legendary narrative and a symbolic territory. But to understand why young activists appropriate such elements, it is worth examining the different ways in which party members experience their political involvement, their family socialisation and their social origins. The mechanism that allows individual appropriation of the above mentioned elements is driven by certain shared biographical, familial and social experiences. Thus, in the first case (AN) intimate (familiar) memory and political commemoration are inexorably associated and transmitted, whereas in the second case (LN) the topographical and historical inventions of the party organisation are in response to the poor 'family memory' of the young activists.

EXTREME RIGHT PARTIES IN CONTEMPORARY ITALY

Some significant changes occurred in the Italian party system during the early nineties. These were due to the slow but progressive disintegration of the electoral basis of the key parties which mainly characterised the so-called 'First Republic' (1948–1992) (the Second Republic is deemed to have begun in 1993 when the national and local electoral system was modified), and the strong delegitimisation of the political elites involved in a corrupted political and economic system ('Tangentopoli', i.e. 'Kickback City'). At that time, much of the political class was under investigation by the so-called 'mani pulite' ('clean hands') judges in Milan, who demanded a moralisation of national politics. In line with public opinion, this 'quest for morality' was adopted by many political leaders and officials–even by those who would later be accused of corruption. In particular, opposition forces and their leaders saw it as a good way to obtain the political power and democratic legitimacy which they had never had. 'Change' and the need for a 'new elite' became the watchwords. One of the first outcomes of these turbulent times was the electoral victory of the first short-lived coalition between the Right and the extreme Right, led by the much discussed media tycoon Silvio Berlusconi, in 1994. Berlusconi and his allies got back to power in 2001 and again in 2008. The initial Polo del Buon Governo e delle Libertà (1994) and then Casa delle Libertà (2001) were both pre-electoral alliances consisting of Forza Italia, some of the ex Christian Democrats, Alleanza Nazionale (AN) led by Gianfranco Fini, and the powerful Lega Nord (LN) led by Umberto Bossi. Apart from Berlusconi's controversial role, and the rise of his own party, the real 'shock' was represented by the electoral successes of two parties that some key scholars of Italian political life labelled as 'extreme right' (Ignazi, 2001): the heir of neo-fascism, the AN, which had always been excluded from governments since the first democratic elections of 1948, and the regionalist, anti-Southern and xenophobic LN.

Officially created at the time of Tangentopoli (after the Fiuggi congress in 1995), the AN represents the 'nationalist pole' of the domestic right-wing parties, and its direct roots are in the neo-fascist Movimento Sociale Italiano (MSI). After having controversially decided to abandon the positive reference to Benito Mussolini's Fascism (against the wishes of most of the leaders and members), the AN leader Gianfranco Fini managed to increase the share of the vote of the party throughout Italy—although, like the MSI, the Southern regions (Mezzogiorno) remain its electoral stronghold. The ideological turn of the party, together with Berlusconi's assistance, has helped the AN to emerge from the darkness since 1994. As a consequence, the party has increasingly been classified as a 'post-fascist' party by some social scientists. At the latest national elections of April 2008 the AN even fused with Forza Italia in a new party named Popolo delle Libertà, whose precise organisational transformation is still unknown, but which seems more a conservative than a fascist party. Despite these changes, the AN should still be considered as a 'far' right party because of its ideological references, the political orientation of its members and voters and its positions on immigration (see the so-called Bossi–Fini law on immigration of 2002, for example) or more recently on Italy's Roma population. To sum up, its nature is controversial and contains not only conservative but also extreme right features (Chiarini & Maraffi, 2001).

The creation of the LN followed another path. The LN was born in 1990–1991, with a regionalist, anti-statist and anti-Southerner stance. It appeared when several regional leagues previously created during the 1980s in the north of the country decided to form a federation under the leadership of Umberto Bossi (Diamanti, 1993). After its growing electoral success in the northern provinces the party of Bossi, also known as the 'Senatùr' (the dialect pronunciation of 'Senatore') has progressively become a movement for independence of the Padania, the imaginary state located in northern Italy, mostly in the Po valley (Gold, 2003), and, like other similar European extreme right parties, has quickly adopted a radical rejection of immigration, Islam, the EU and homosexuals.

As Ignazi has shown, the LN has now left its position as a regionalist protest party to adopt an extreme right-wing platform, particularly in its authoritarian and anti- immigrant rhetoric, whereas the AN seems to have shifted towards the ideological centre and reinvented itself as a conservative party (Ignazi, 2005). However, in spite of these contradictory ideological shifts, the AN and LN belong to the broad family of European radical/extremist right organizations, because of their specific positions on moral values, law and order and immigration (Eatwell & Mudde, 2004; Dechezelles, 2006b).

THE CULTURAL BASES OF POLITICAL INVOLVEMENT

Despite the necessary compromises and the recent transformations of the political contest (Katz & Mair, 1994), the political parties and their members still retain several impermeable cultural and ideological specificities. As both mediators and actors in democratic political life, parties are among the main suppliers of collective identities for both voters and, especially, activists. These identities are also revealed through the discourses developed by activists about their political organisation and also through the party literature and various (internal and external) documents: this can be translated as the activist culture.

A sociological definition of the culture of a political organisation is quite difficult. For both social actors and social scientists the notion of culture is controversial and must be used and defined as cautiously as possible.[1] In my analytical framework it is the product of social constructions of collective frameworks of meaning that are generated by institutions and appropriated by individuals (Berger & Luckmann, 1967). These are socially constructed and cannot be considered as an 'essence,' but nor can one ignore the effects they can have on the social actors. The approach that is developed in this article is grounded in a comprehensive sociology and anthropology of culture (Geertz, 1973). In such a perspective the culture of an organisation can be used as a tool to regulate exchanges, impose 'marks' and 'frameworks,' indicate what is forbidden and what is possible, good and bad, inside or outside, ritual or subversive, ordered and disordered, relative and absolute, important or accessory for the whole group (Johnston & Klandermans, 1995). They also identify challenges and specify the hierarchies of objects and people (Pizzorno, 1978).

The culture of any political organisation is made up of specific symbols, references, values, protest styles, rules and rhetorical lexis (Eliashop & Lichterman, 2003). In other words, the affection for certain causes, the entry into activism and the way the activists behave are based not only on certain ideological principles and articulated doctrines, but also on the construction of common and collective references which activists are exhorted to assimilate and appropriate. Understanding the culture of a militant group consists of examining not only the process of production and appropriation of a collective framework, but also how it is used in internal and external relations in order to construct similarity—identity—and to assert difference—otherness (Barth, 1969; Sawicki, 2001). Every collective identity is based on a double strategy of homogenization and differentiation: the creation of an inclusive and positive us that can be opposed to the irremediably different and negative them. However, it also involves paying attention to evolutions, transformations and tensions (Faucher-King, 2005), because cultures are far from being considered as abstract essences or peaceful social constructions. Political cultures are never peacefully accepted, but generate struggles between rival groups and individuals who seek to impose themselves or to modify some elements of this culture. They also lead to further conflicts between different movements or groups to control references or symbols. This means that cultures are neither homogeneous nor stable. On the contrary, they are clearly affected by the struggles and tensions between the *émetteurs* (intellectuals, political leaders) and the *récepteurs* (activists, elected representatives, sympathisers, voters).

Yet, youth organisations, and especially those of the extreme right, seem to defend their 'identities'—and the ways in which they are created and spread—much more than 'adult' organisations. Given this, detailed research on youth political organisations and their members should be central to understanding the parties to which they are linked and of which they might represent the future political elite. Indeed, cultural analysis of the parties allows one to (i) understand how they generate a group and shape the individuals according to their expectations, (ii) take into account the individual experiences of activism and the phenomena of generational heritage and, finally, (iii) partially comprehend the political and ideological reference points of future leaders.

This article essentially deals with activists (i.e. those who are defined as 'young' by the official party *statuto*, generally people between 14 and 30 years old) of the youth organisations of extreme right-wing parties in Italy: Azione Giovani (AG) and the Movimento Giovani Padani (MGP).[2] The former is the youth section of the AN while the latter is that of the LN. This study is also based on (1) data collected for a research project on the degrees of 'involvement' within the right-wing youth organisations and extreme right parties during the second Berlusconi government (2001–2006), (2) internal documents and pamphlets and (3) 60 interviews made in the northern regions of Veneto and Emilia-Romagna (Dechezelles, 2006a). The main argument of this article is that the appropriation of a youth movement culture depends on two main mechanisms: (a) the interiorisation of the three identification elements produced by the 'group' (an ideal society, a legendary narrative and a symbolical territory) and (b) common or shared family stories or individual experiences (which make the appropriation of collective cultural references easier).

The Ideal Society

The culture of all Italian extreme right youth organisations includes a teleological project concerning the ideal society, which is made up of hierarchies, codes (behaviour, clothes and vocabulary) and specific forms of sociability. As for many other extreme right movements, the ideal society for young AN activists is the family. In such a context the links between individuals are domestic and they consider themselves as faithful and obedient members of the same dynasty. The biological lexical field is often used to describe the links which all activists (the members, the cells, the flesh) have to maintain with the organisation (the nucleus, the stem, the body). The young are then exhorted to follow a given 'discipline' and a strict hierarchical 'order.' Abnegation and self-sacrifice are therefore erected as fundamental values. As a consequence, all activities that provoke 'virile sentiments' are strongly promoted, especially fly-posting at night or leaflet distribution. Indeed, these can eventually help cultivate strong self-esteem and solidarity during times of 'hardship.' Due to the low frequency of violent confrontations between political groups in contemporary Italy, the epic tales of physical struggles during the 1960s–1980s gives status to the 'elders,' which the young are encouraged to respect. They must also be educationally prepared both for street combat (i.e. physical education) and intellectual struggle (i.e. doctrinal education). This also helps us to understand why the 'formation' of the AN youth includes studying the biography, methods, 'agonistic struggles' and epic 'actions' of fascist leaders (e.g. Léon Degrelle and Corneliu Zelea Codreanu) and movements (the Italian Squadristi, Romanian Archangel Michael Company and Belgian Rexism), and also the actions of the MSI's young activists. Great importance is also attached to Julius Evola's radical philosophy. It is worth noting that Evola is considered one of the main ideologues of the extreme right in Europe and his books also represent doctrinal references for some new and 'non-fascist' movements, including the MGP and LN.

Another fundamental reference for young AN activists is Tolkien's writings (especially the trilogy *The Lord of the Rings*). Having been ghettoised for many decades, young AN activists identify themselves with the innocent Hobbits, who are also perceived, just like them, to be the only people capable of saving the world from 'evil forces.' This omnipresent identification with Tolkien's mythology harks back to the 1970s when the young leaders of the Fronte della Gioventù (the MSI youth organisation), such as Marco Tarchi, introduced the ideology of the French Nouvelle Droite in order to 'revitalise' Italian neo-fascism (Germinario, 2002). Giorgio, an interviewee who joined the Fronte della Gioventù in the late 1980s, explained how Tolkien, inspired by the Scandinavian sagas in which all human feelings are represented (bravery, cowardice, cupidity, anger), is useful in providing an interpretative framework and a model for activists:

> Tolkien, with his adventure books like *The Lord of the Rings* and *The Hobbit*, has been considered by the Italian extreme right as an example to follow and as a world which we should reproduce in our private existences as well as in our political activity.

In the case of the MGP the group perceives itself through the symbolic representation of an emotional community. Just as in other recent European extreme right parties, the young activists explain that their real conversion to and involvement in the party followed some 'conductive event' (Ihl, 2002). This event was often an electoral meeting or a partisan social gathering they attended for the first time, where they were intrigued by the leader's speech (Zanoni, 2001, pp. 82–83). For the LN these 'strong emotions' are valorised because they prove that the 'chosen' people/activists are not the hated 'professional politicians' but, on the contrary, are pure and passionate. As they are strongly attracted to the 'emotional elements' of political involvement, the young LN activists abandon the usual ideological writings for a sort of 'affective evangelisation,' which is supposed to be more intuitive and faith-worthy. They also tend to prefer poetical means of expression, as do several other regionalist and independence movements (e.g. Occitan, Corsican and Irish): there are frequent quotations from poems by famous authors, Umberto Bossi or members of Arte Nord (the Padan poets association) in the documents of the LN youth organisation. They also participate in the actual organisation of events on dialectal languages or local literature. Some of them have contributed to the Movimento Giovani Padani novel, which aspires to be the glorifying saga of the brave knights of the Lega Nord (Capitanio, 2003). Unlike the proud collective self-representation of the AN young militants, the LN young activists seem to share a common negative stigmata: they say they feel constrained to say nothing about their involvement for fear of ridicule or rejection. During the various interviews they also explained that they feel relatively distressed when they expose themselves outside the protecting group. For this reason they also attempt, through poetry or other means, to invert the negative labels linked to their party and to build a 'sublime portrait.'

THE LEGENDARY NARRATIVE

The 'ideal society' of all right-wing extremist cultures is closely linked to a legendary tale about 'origins' and 'roots' (Coakley, 2004). If young AN activists are not unique in evoking and celebrating the story of their own party, the importance of these activities in the socialisation and the formation of activists is much greater than in other organisations. Nostalgia for fascism and for the heroic times—when the party and its members were marginalised—is central: even such memories of suffering are perceived as propitious and erected as a collective value (Tarchi, 1995). In particular, the 'good activist' is the one who constantly pays tribute to the legendary Great Men of the party. Involvement in the group requires collective remembrance of remarkable events and past facts in order to guarantee their transmission and perpetuation. For example, Azione Giovani (AG) promotes the publication of books in which events are ritualised in order to allow the reader to perceive himself as the heir to a golden age. The AG also organises collective excursions to the Duce's grave (in Predappio, his native village in Romagna), distributes posters that invite people not to forget and produces leaflets for several fascist and neo-fascist anniversaries. Due to their frequent elective responsibilities in the secondary education system, young AN activists are used to denouncing in their schools the so-called 'lies' or 'factious interpretations' in historical textbooks.

The customary lists of 'their' martyrs and 'their' dead also incite activist groups to hate the 'enemy' (from the anti-Fascist resister to the anti-global militant) and to demand some sort of 'compensation.'[3] In particular, the internal literature regularly tells the story of young neo-fascist activists who were involved in the Movimento Sociale Italiano and who died in riots with young extreme left activists. There is also a continuing glorification of the young nationalists who mobilised at Trieste in 1953, Budapest in 1956 and Prague in 1968, as well as the Dalmatian and Istrian Italians who were brutally killed in deep swallow-holes (foibe) in the Kras region by Yugoslav communist forces at the end of the Second World War. These victims are used to justify commemorative gatherings. This is the case of Treviso, where many AG activists go every year with other associations linked to the AN or to local skinhead groups. In the same way, young activists are actively involved in local campaigns to have streets or public squares named in honour of 'their' heroes or the 'victims of communist barbarism.' Despite Gianfranco Fini's attempts to distance the party from its fascist and neo-fascists roots, it also seems that it is exactly this glorification of the 'heroic memory' of the MSI which influences and convinces young people to join it (Ignazi, 1994, p. 89). Moreover, in such a context it is not surprising that a fascist (and Nazi) symbol, the burning torch, is used as the AG logo (Cheles, 1995). The torch represents a past which never dies but is reproduced by every generation.

Young LN activists express their fear of an 'occult' political world from which they feel excluded by seeking mythical origins in an invented past (Hobsbawm & Ranger, 1993), specifically by seeking supposed Celtic roots in opposition to the supposed Roman roots of the Southern people. The party leader, Umberto Bossi, is seen as a talented prophet who will make possible the liberation of the people of Padania. Hence, he can purify and regenerate the imagined Padania from violence and, in the long-term, from the 'voracious' Roman and Italian state. In this historical revisionist context Italy is in fact perceived as the dreadful product of two irremediably different entities: the kingdom of Piedmont–Sardinia and the kingdom of the Two Sicilies; Padania is instead portrayed as the only 'eternal nation.' In such a perspective, if Italy is the 'disgusting' land, Padania is the 'burning torch' for activists. Similarly, LN mythology considers the period when Celti and Protoveneti lived in northern Italy as the golden age which must be fundamentally 'restored.' The Po valley, with its hard working populations oppressed by *Roma ladrona* (the thief Rome) is, therefore, compared with a paradise which activists have to liberate from the oppressors. The invented 'barbaric heritage' is also useful to legitimate the ongoing economic differences between the north and south of the country, by basing them on biological differences between peoples or on a revisionist historical reading (Huysseume, 2004). For this reason Movimento Giovani Padani activists seek to denounce all iniquitous domination and colonisations led by the Italian state—from the constitutional monarchy to the fascist dictatorship and the post-war democratic republic. As in the case of the Basque 'nationalists,' this political discourse of 'oppression' seeks to convert their external image of being 'rich and selfish' into one of victims whose cultural and linguistic heritage is under threat.

The iconography of the MGP uses sublime medieval symbols (knights, armour, battles) that are historically 'twisted' or confused in an attempt to mobilise memories of the Lombard League of the free northern towns that were opposed to Frederic of Hohenstaufen (12th century), as well as William Wallace, the Scottish leader who challenged the king of England, Edward the 1st

(13th century).[4] The federal leaders and the local sections of the party encourage young activists to join all 'Celtic' movements or events organised by the Lega: cultural associations, seminars on Celtic history and civilisation, bagpipe sessions, old sports (crossbow shooting) and fancy-dress balls and Celtic concerts. These activities are also proposed during the two annual party meetings (at Pontida in June and Venice in September), when young men can also prove their strength (tossing the caber, jumping over bonfires). These demonstrations also serve as a means of transmission for radical and racist theories through conferences and the sale of books, introducing some of the classical extreme right references to the LN youth organisation, such as Ernst Jünger and Julius Evola.

Far from being just a folkloric form of partisan mystification, all these invented frameworks lead youth activists to perceive themselves as the heirs of heroic ancestors and, moreover, to perpetuate the reproduction of a certain historical memory. In such a context the constant reminders of past struggles and martyrs has an essential pedagogical purpose: to build 'responsibility links' between these ancestors and the contemporary party.

THE SYMBOLIC TERRITORY

The 'territories of identification' of extreme right youth organisations do not correspond to the 'administrative' Italian provinces and regions. Young activists essentially refer to a 'national' territory: Italia for AG, Padania for the Movimento Giovani Padani, which is a symbolic, imagined, hoped for or artificially constructed space. This invented *topos* allows us to analyse the political culture through the lens of particular spatial references. Along with the cult of Imperial Rome, which is borrowed from the mythology of the fascist regime, it appears that young AN activists are encouraged to refer to certain closed spaces. These are simultaneously considered as places for excluded, marginalised or outlawed people and at the same time as fortresses or bastions in which neo-fascists can be protected. Indeed, since the collapse of fascism the two neo-fascist youth organisations (the Fronte della Gioventù and AG) have developed a rhetoric of 'confinement' and marginalisation. The use of the word 'ghetto' is in fact recurrent in the propaganda of these youth organisations. This metaphoric image of the ghetto essentially evokes the situation of the Italian Social Republic (1943–1945), when the northern part of Italy was also controlled by the Nazis and where the Resistance was very efficient (Germinario, 2005, p. 20; Mammone, 2005), but also the exclusion of the MSI from every governmental coalition from 1948 until 1993. This lexical field refers to a space of forced reclusion, or to a secret place, but it is also a synonym of 'vermin.' Indeed, it is the rat that these organisations have chosen as their symbol for many years.[5]

In a hostile external political environment young AN activists seek refuge in party sections which are perceived as veritable sanctuaries. The local section represents a safe place, where everyone feels free to express his/her feelings. One can find here the intimate context among the young *camerati*. *Camerata*, also used by inter-war fascists, is etymologically derived from *camera*, 'room,' and evokes intimacy and the sharing of a common, secret space. This also explains why meetings and social evenings inside the local sections are just as fundamental as public demonstrations in the formation of the young activist. All young activists interviewed claimed to spend a lot of time inside party buildings and to feel good in their warm collective atmosphere.

As previously suggested, the young LN activists defend and oppose their *Eldorado*, their bucolic space Padania to a discredited country, Italy, and an immoral supranational space, Europe. This became a key element within the identity strategy led by *padanist* ideologues such as Gilberto Oneto and Giancarlo Pagliarini—a strategy pursued since the 1990s and particularly after the first Berlusconi government in 1994. The high point of this strategy was reached in September 1996, when Bossi invited the 'northern inhabitants' to come to the banks of the Po in Venice and support the proclamation of the 'independence of the free republic of Padania.' Being a rhetorical invention, Padania has no precise boundaries, no unifying language and no ethnic homogeneity. It had never before been mobilized by protest movements or regionalist parties before the LN. This explains the LN's efforts to create supposed 'natural' frontiers for Padania (from the Alps to the Apennines and from the Tyrrhenian sea to the Adriatic). Historically and geographically these claims are completely inconsistent—but this affects the imagined partisan world, internal literature and activists (see also Dematteo, 2003, p. 152). This absence of precise historical and geographical references is echoed in the way the young activists present the story of their organisation. Thus, in the already mentioned MGP novel there are no precise details of time or space. On the contrary, they use expressions like 'once upon a time,' 'nowhere,' 'everywhere' and 'here as elsewhere,' and they have invented their own calendar which starts from 15 September 1996, the day Bossi declared the liberation of Padania in Venice (Capitanio, 2003, pp. 7–13).

This legendary narrative and territory obviously needs an opponent to build its own identity. The 'enemy' is found in the rest of the Italian peninsula, and especially in the southern regions, the so-called despicable *Terronia*. The construction of an imagined country/space is thus essentially rooted in the racist 'rejection' of the population of the South. They are portrayed as a distillation of all the negative human features (e.g. laziness, fraud, ignorance) against which to set the virtues of *Padans* (e.g. courage, honesty). During the Venice LN meeting in September 2005 the MGP sold T-shirts on which was stamped a split peninsula: the north, the 'socially liberated' Padania, and the south, the 'united Terronia.' The latter is depicted as a sewer attracting rafts, full of clandestine immigrants. For the last 10 years the biggest enemy for Padan people has been the clandestine (and supposedly Muslim) immigrant.

In order to promote their 'invented' territory young members are also encouraged to promote and take pictures of *ciulade*. These are graffiti which are painted on buildings or roads in northern Italy and demand the liberation of Padania.[6] In social terms young LN activists are often strongly attached to their local 'land.' Most of them live in houses or farms inherited from their grandparents, their social origins are more often linked to farming and agriculture than the national average and they often study for diplomas which are relevant to the territory (e.g. land survey or agriculture).

An ideal society, legendary narrative and symbolic territory are, therefore, the fundamental elements of the culture of extreme right youth organisations in Italy. Nevertheless, in order to understand how cultures are appropriated by individuals it is useful to analyse their social origins and shared experiences.

Shared Common Experience as a (Pre) Condition for the Appropriation of a Partisan Culture

For a better understanding of the relationship between an organisation and its members it is necessary to examine the connection between the partisan culture and individual biographical experiences. In the AN the adulation of a glorious historical heritage is closely linked with family stories and backgrounds. Indeed, the veneration of 'party ancestors' is rooted in the remembrance of heroic relatives who perpetuate 'traditions' that are familial, but also political, because of their ideological involvement or opinions. Thus Benito, the AG provincial secretary of Forlì, described his fascist pedigree and the memory of his childhood, which he associated with the involvement of his father in the MSI:

> I remember that when I was a child, I was six or seven years old, my father brought me to the MSI for the fascist Epiphanies. I remember the bags full of toys and the torch [logo] of the MSI.

In a similar vein, Enrico (a sympathiser whose father often voted for the MSI or AN) pointed out that his grandfather participated in the actual construction of fascist sites in Africa (Ethiopia) and that his political orientation was 'something that is transmitted from father to son, from one generation to another.' The process of political identification is based on the indexation of the family story onto national history, and vice versa. Consequently, the veneration of Fascism and the MSI coincides with and is equivalent to the homage that is paid to members of one's own family—as suggested, this works both ways. Politics is in fact considered a 'family issue' which young activists must pass on. This also gives activists the chance to identify with and refer to close or familiar figures.

Fascist *Podestà* or ex activists of the MSI or the Fronte della Gioventù thus represent family heroes to be venerated and imitated. For some young activists the first link between their families, fascist tradition and extreme right political involvement is to be found in their own names: some are called Benito (Mussolini's first name), but also Alessandro (the first name of Mussolini's father), Giorgio (the old MSI leader, Giorgio Almirante) or even Galeazzo (as in Galeazzo Ciano, Mussolini's son-in-law). These indelible 'marks' confirm that young AN activists are in the 'right place' within an extreme right-wing political organisation and that they are fully involved in the perpetuation of a familial engagement and a collective story.

The historical and familial 'proximity' to certain past events/figures therefore allows the young activists to place themselves in a direct line of historical continuity with a certain (political) history. Gianluca (the local leader in Ravenna) explained that he decided to join the youth party organisation when he came across a gathering of young Fronte della Gioventù activists in his home town. They invited him to watch a film about the victims of the *foibe*. His grandfather died in such circumstances and he explained that this was the reason behind his choice to start an activist career. Elena is the daughter of an ex-member of the MSI, her mother is a member of the AN, her sister is also a young activist in the AG. She is also the granddaughter and grand-niece of fascist volunteers in the Spanish Civil War. During the interview she spoke a lot about her family's past involvement and above all about her great-uncle Costantino. He was a volunteer in Spain and then instructor of the first Ethiopian military school of the Italian army:

> I didn't talk about the [neo-fascist] party with him but we talked about uniform, duty, patriotism, fidelity and coherence., I can describe my uncle with these five words. And these five words became my political programme. . . . To become part of the MSI for me was as natural as being part of my family.

In many different respects the 'small story' of the family matches the 'big history' of the fatherland, and this can explain how the young AN activists easily appropriate a party culture emphasising the memory of past times. They are the living evidence that the (political and biological) dynastic thread is not broken. Past involvement thus survives through these young people.

There are very few details of 'familial' for the Movimento Giovani Padani. In addition to this 'volatile memory,' we can also perceive a sort of modesty with respect to intimate (familial) memory. Unlike the young AN activists, who gave many details and seemed proud to know them, it is hard to collect material to reconstruct the 'histories' of young *leghisti*. When asked: 'Could you speak about your family story?', Valerio, as secretary of the MGP in Piacenza, answered:

> I don't know if I have one. . . . So, my grandparents . . . I have known only one of them. My grandmother . . . died more than ten years ago and the others died of illness when they were very young and . . . what else could I tell you?

The LN activists also differ from those of the AN in that they consider both their ancestors and themselves as having endured governments and policies over which they could have no say. Even if they are members of a governmental party, they still consider they are at the margins of political life in Italy. They consider there is nothing heroic in their partisan (and familial) engagement. Their discourse often includes expressions denoting exclusion or marginalisation. Rather than any previous family involvement in politics, what they usually share is a common rejection of 'politics.' During the interviews this came out more clearly than biographical details about their familial history. As Meri, provincial leader in Belluno in Veneto, noted:

> my grandmother often used to talk to me about the fascists. But she told me that the Partisans were not much better. She remembered some precise events when the [anti-fascist] partisans got into every house to steal things and that they were very hard with German soldiers . . . she told me that once they also killed a young local woman, one of them, because she had danced with some German soldiers.

Similarly, Mara, a regional councillor in Vicenza in Veneto, recalled one of her uncles who disappeared during the Russian campaign: 'he never came back . . . . He was my mother's brother, from whom we received only a very few censored letters . . . there it is, but let's talk about something else.'

The few memorial 'souvenirs' of the young LN activists often describe a world made up of 'little people,' victims of abuses of power or fraud at the hands of southern Italians, gypsies and immigrants. In such a vein, they pay tribute to these ordinary people, 'their people' against 'the others'—their people 'without histories' against the 'official history.' Unlike the case of young AN activists, in the Movimento Giovani Padani there is thus no trace of 'pride': suffering, amnesia and death seem to be the watchwords. For example, Marco (an ex local leader in Rovigo) recalled two members of his family in the following terms:

> My grandfather . . . I never met him because he died when I was two months old. He was a servant. . . . He participated in the Libyan war, in 1938, no in 1940, 1937–1938 I think. . . . It was first and foremost a war where nobody knew who they were fighting and without knowing why. These were little things my grandfather told my grandmother and she repeated them to my mother. For example, he said they fought in disgraceful conditions, without shoes, without ammunition. . . . My grand-uncle was in the Russian expedition in 1940–1942 and he never came back. He sent postcards up until the end of 1942 but after that we don't know anything about him. Even when the USSR archives opened, we did research on him but nothing was found. I don't know what happened to him.

The ordinary sense of history of the MGP activists is thus actualised in the consciousness of an irreversible contrast between the past and the present and the necessity to invent a legendary history. They seem to have no other opportunity than to appeal to an indistinct history and geography which is a projection of their family member's experiences.

Conclusions

It is uncommon to take into account the cultural dimension of extreme right-wing parties and the different ways in which party members experience their political involvement. The aim of this article was to open the 'secret box' of these organisations through a comparison of the activist cultures of two groups of young Italian activists (the AN and LN). Each culture is a constructed artefact composed of three main elements: an ideal model of society, a legendary narrative and a fictional land. The mechanism that allows individual appropriation of the above mentioned elements lies in certain shared biographical and familial experiences.

In the first case (AN), intimate (familial) memory and political commemoration are inexorably associated and passed down. In the second case (LN), the poor 'family memory' has its corollary in the topographical inventions of the party organisation. Finally, the process of appropriation of a common political culture is also rooted in shared social, professional and educational origins or experiences.

This also leads to a better understanding of the differences, similarities, political transfers and conflicts between the two parties. This is especially the case with recent political developments, where the AN leadership seeks to manage the tension between the legitimate 'democratic' strategy which led to the *Popolo delle Libertà* coalition with Silvio Berlusconi and an activist base which had been socialised with the myth of the 'purity of origins.' The LN also constantly radicalises its position in order to woo Berlusconi's electorate in northern Italy.

Unlike what is regularly believed about these extreme right-wing parties, the article also shows how the type of political involvement they promote is not 'new,' but is firmly rooted in old forms of activism (e.g. sacrifice for the cause, a collective imagination, the struggle for a 'nation' or a community, glorification of past or present leaders). Due to the very good electoral results of the two parties in the 2008 election and their participation in the third Berlusconi government, these activist and ideological continuities could at times turn into problematic and dissonant features, as shown in the past (Dechezelles, 2007).

NOTES

1. The expression 'political culture' is not used in the sense employed by proponents of the 'civic culture' or the 'political development' approaches. Further, it is not equivalent to the 'opinions' or 'attitudes' that survey researches usually seek to measure.

2. Both the AG and the MGP have specific student organisations: Azione Studentesca and Azione Universitaria, and Movimento Studentesco Padano Federale and Movimento Universitario Padano, respectively. It is worth pointing out that this study is based on interviews with young members from all these groups.

3. A similar approach can be observed for the youth movement of the French Front National (Crépon, 2006, p. 79).

4. The iconography of the MGP (websites, leaflets, posters and logos of the local sections or regional federations) uses many images from the movie *Braveheart*, in which William Wallace is the hero. Several times Umberto Bossi declared that it was his favourite film.

5. Marco Tarchi, ex national leader of the Fronte della Gioventù, founded a radical and satirical magazine, *La Voce della Fogna* (*The Voice of the Sewer*) whose symbol was a black rat. The latter previously also appeared in the iconography of some small French extreme right groups in the 1950s.

6. The MGP website (http://www.giovanipadani.it) has a section entirely dedicated to photographs of the *ciulade* which are sent by local party activists.

REFERENCES

Barth, F. (1969) *Ethnic Groups and Boundaries: the Social Organization of Culture Difference* (Boston, MA: Little Brown).

Berger, P. & Luckmann, T. (1967) *The Social Construction of Reality: A Treatise in the Sociology of Knowledge* (New York: Anchor Books).

Capitanio, M. (Ed.) (2003) *Tutto Nacque all'Improvviso, non Certo per Caso* (Milan: Lega Nord).

Cheles, L. (1995) "Nostalgia dell'avvenire." The propaganda of the Italian Far Right between Tradition and Innovation, in: L. Cheles, R. Ferguson & M. Vaughan (Eds) *The Far Right in Western and Eastern Europe*, pp. 41–90 (London: Longman).

Chiarini, R. & Maraffi, M. (Eds) (2001) *La Destra allo Specchio* (Venice: Marsilio).

Coakley, J. (2004) Mobilizing the past: nationalist images of history, *Nationalism and Ethnic Politics*, 10(4), pp. 531–560.

Crépon, S. (2006) *La Nouvelle Extrême Droite: Enquête sur les Jeunes Militants du FN* (Paris: l'Harmattan).

Dechezelles, S. (2006a) Comment peut-on être militant? Sociologie des cultures politiques et des (dés)engagements. Les jeunes militants d'Alleanza Nazionale, Lega Nord et Forza Italia face au pouvoir, Ph.D. dissertation, Sciences Po Bordeaux.

Dechezelles, S. (2006b) Visages et usages de l'"extrême droite' en Italie. Pour une analyse relationnelle et non substantialiste de la catégorie 'extrême droite,' *Revue Internationale de Politique Comparée*, 12(4), pp. 451–467.

Dechezelles, S. (2007) Entre révolution et gestion. L'engagement des jeunes militant(e)s de la Ligue du Nord et d'Alliance Nationale face à l'expérience du pouvoir en Italie, in: P. Delwit & P. Poirier (Eds) *Extrême Droite et Pouvoir en Europe*, pp. 225–246 (Brussels: Éditions de l'Université de Bruxelles).

Dematteo, L. (2003) La stigmatisation de l'idiotie montagnarde et son détournement par la Lega Nord, in: O. Ihl, J. Chêne, E. Vial & G. Waterlot (Eds) *La Tentation Populiste en Europe*, pp. 146–158 (Paris: la Découverte).

Diamanti, I. (1993) *La Lega. Geografia, Storia e Sociologia di un Nuovo Soggetto Politico* (Rome: Donzelli).

Eatwell, R. & Mudde, C. (2004) *Western Democracies and the New Extreme Right Challenge* (London: Routledge).

Eliashop, N. & Lichterman, P. (2003) Culture in interaction, *American Journal of Sociology*, 108(4), pp. 735–794.

Faucher-King, F. (2005) *Changing Parties. An Anthropology of British Political Party Conferences* (Basingstoke, UK: Palgrave Macmillan).

Geertz, C. (1973) *The Interpretation of Cultures* (New York: Basic Books).

Germinario, F. (2002) *La Destra degli Dei. Alain de Benoist e la Cultura Politica della Nouvelle Droite* (Turin: Bollati Boringhieri).

Germinario, F. (2005) *Da Salò al Governo. Immaginario e Cultura Politica della Destra Italiana* (Turin: Bollati Boringhieri).

Gold, T. W. (2003) *The Lega Nord and Contemporary Politics in Italy* (Basingstoke, UK: Palgrave Macmillan).

Hobsbawm, E. & Ranger, T. (Eds) (1993) *The Invention of Tradition* (Cambridge, UK: Cambridge University Press).

Huysseume, M. (2004) *Modernità e Secessione. Le Scienze Sociali e il Discorso della Lega Nord* (Rome: Carocci).

Ignazi, P. (1994) *Postfascisti? Dal Movimento Sociale Italiano ad Alleanza Nazionale* (Bologna: Il Mulino).

Ignazi, P. (2001) Les partis d'extrême droite: les fruits inachevés de la société postindustrielle, in: P. Perrineau (Ed.) *Les Croisés de la Société Fermée. L'Europe des Extrêmes Droites*, pp. 369–384 (La Tour d'Aigues, France: Edition de l'Aube).

Ignazi, P. (2005) The extreme right: legitimation and evolution on the Italian right: social and ideological pepositioning of Alleanza Nazionale and the Lega Nord, *South European Politics and Society*, 10(2), pp. 333–349.

Ihl, O. (2002) Socialisation et événements politiques, *Revue Française de Science Politique*, 52(2/3), pp. 125–144.

Johnston, H. & Klandermans, B. (1995) The cultural analysis of social movements, in: H. Johnston & B. Klandermans (Eds) *Social Movements and Culture* (Minneapolis, MN: University of Minnesota Press).

Katz, R. & Mair, P. (Eds) (1994) *How Parties Organize. Change and Adaptation in Party Organizations in Western Democracies* (London: Sage).

Mammone, A. (2005) Gli orfani del Duce. I fascisti dal 1943 al 1946, *Italia Contemporanea*, 239/240, pp. 249–274.

Pizzorno, A. (1978) Political exchange and collective identity in industrial conflict, in: C. Crouch & A. Pizzorno (Eds) *The Resurgence of Class Conflict in Western Europe Since 1968*, pp. 277–298 (New York: Holmes & Meier).

Sawicki, F. (2001) Les partis politiques comme entreprises culturelles, in: D. Cefaï (Ed.) *Cultures Politiques*, pp. 191–211 (Paris: PUF).

Tarchi, M. (1995) *Cinquant'anni di Nostalgia. La Nestra Italiana dopo il Fascismo* (Milan: Rizzoli).

Zanoni, P. (2001) *Bossi e la Rivoluzione Tradita* (Venice: Editoria Universitaria).

*Stéphanie Dechezelles is assistant professor in the Political Studies Institute of Aix-en-Provence in France.

Dechezelles, Stéphanie. "The Cultural Basis of Youth Involvement in Italian Extreme Right-Wing Organisations." *Journal of Contemporary European Studies* 16, no. 3 (2008): 363–375.

Reprinted by permission of the publisher (Taylor & Francis Ltd., http://www.tandf.co.uk/journals).

Racism as Adolescent Male Rite of Passage: Ex-Nazis in Scandinavia

*by Michael Kimmel**

In-depth interviews with ex-neo-Nazis in Scandinavia reveal a profile of the extreme right that is both strikingly similar to and significantly different from the profile of their counterparts in the United States. Drawn from clients at EXIT, a state-funded organization based in Sweden, these interviews reveal that the extreme right draws adherents from a declining lower middle class background, small towns, and metropolitan suburbs, and from divorced families. Their mean age is in the mid-teens to late-teens, and their commitment to specific ideological tenets is low. Their entry and exit have less political and more developmental and situational origins than the Americans'. Detailed interviews suggest that participation on the extreme right is, for some Scandinavian adolescents, more a masculine [rite] of passage than evidence of a firm commitment to racialized ideologies.

Andrew[1] is a relatively small boy, with short, streaked dyed-blond hair tucked under a black baseball cap. His eyes are bright and blue, and his round prepubescent face gives an almost androgynous sweetness to his features. He wears a black hooded sweatshirt that says, in English, "Go Fuck Yourself" and a black nylon bomber jacket over that. He sits, slouched, his buttocks barely touching the edge of the seat as he strains to lean back as far as the chair will allow. His arms are crossed over his chest in an edgy mix of defiance and resignation as he describes to me what first brought him into the Nazi movement, what he believes, and how he left the movement several months ago. Andrew is thirteen years old.

David is a bit older; he's seventeen, and he "jumped" out of the Nazi movement two years ago. He's bigger and pudgier, with two studs in his right eyebrow and a labret (piercing) just below his lower lip. His smile reveals a serious overbite and his glasses are a bit smudged and crooked. Each of his forearms is tattooed; one is of Bart Simpson, smiling demonically, his shorts around his ankles as he moons the viewer.

Andrew and David are two of the more than 350 ex-Nazis who have come through the Swedish program called EXIT. Founded in 1998 by Kent Lindahl, himself a former Nazi, the program is designed to help members of Nazi and skinhead organizations leave the movement and reclaim their lives. EXIT has also established offices and groups in Norway and Denmark.

In this article, I describe the gender dynamics of entrance and exit for neo-Nazis in Scandinavia. By using materials from EXIT and interviewing clients, I argue that participation in neo-Nazi skinhead groups has more to do with adolescent demonstrations of masculinity than it does with political ideology. Participation is more a first step toward adult manhood than the first step to a full-fledged adult life as a Nazi zealot. To its participants, racism is a rite of passage.

This article is based on archival and online materials published by neo-Nazi groups and in-depth interviews with members of these groups in Sweden, Norway, and Denmark.[2] I explore several related themes.

1. What is the appeal of neo-Nazi groups to young men in these societies?

2. What are the dynamics of entry into the movement?

3. How do they experience their masculinity within these organizations?

4. What are the ritual, embodied practices of demonstrating and proving masculinity?

5. What is the role of ideology in their membership?

6. What are the gendered dynamics of leaving the organization?

Before turning to the specific groups, here are a few words of methodological caution. Material gathered through interviews should always be buttressed by other sorts of data, because interviews rely on retrospective analysis. Memory is often self-serving, and the narratives of one's childhood offered by ex-participants in the movement may say more about their current positioning as "outside" the movement than they say about entry into and experience inside the movement. However, given that I am equally concerned with the experiences of "exit," these interviews provide useful, if uncorroborated, narratives of that process.

David's Story

David is from Uppsala. His father worked as a foreman in a warehouse of a pharmaceutical company; his mother is on disability. His stepfather works in a photocopy shop. At seventeen years old, he has dropped out of school, but plans now to return. Chubby, academically disinterested, and feeling marginal, David was a target for bullies in primary school. By 6th grade, though, he and many of his classmates were increasingly drawn into neo-Nazi ideology and affect, and they began to wear the clothing, offer the various salutes, and identify as Nazis. He had a few friends who were into Blood and Honour or the National Youth (NU). "We spent all our time drinking and fighting," he explains, which was the primary draw for him as well.

In 7th grade, his school was so alarmed by the number of kids who were getting interested in Nazism that the administrators called in a member of EXIT to give a presentation. But the life of a Nazi was too much fun. He'd go to meetings of more than 100 and sometimes upwards of 200 kids—with a pretty even gender split. "The meetings would become parties, and then everyone would go out afterwards. The girls used to start the fights, provoking some immigrants or something, but then they'd run away, leaving me to clean it up. But it was OK, and there were plenty of girls."

David felt that the Nazis "had the right idea about unifying the country and unifying the people." He sees Sweden as divided and the politicians as corrupt. He wants them to act; to bring Sweden together again. He targeted immigrants "because we hate them. They have no reason to be here. They keep saying they don't like Sweden. So what are they doing here?"

Arrested three times, but never convicted, David had his share of injuries, but none serious. Gradually, he began to feel that movement participation was losing its fun. "I began to think that the people I was hanging out with were not living up to the ideals of the movement, weren't living up to what they were saying. They were drinking and smoking and one of the leaders was actually dating a Thai woman! And it started to get boring, always going to the same parties with the same people." Although he also continued to drink and smoke, David began to drift away. He came to EXIT one year ago and for a while lived in a safe house. "They said they were going to kill me," he said of his former comrades. He has gone back to school, now has a regular girlfriend, and is about to take his first holiday with her. "I just want to have a good life," he says.

ANDREW'S STORY

Andrew is from Värmdö, a working-class Stockholm suburb. His father is in construction and his mother is a housewife who formerly worked as a kindergarten teacher. Andrew also felt marginalized—in 3rd grade. By 4th grade, he had discovered white power music, like Screwdriver, and that was his point of entry into the white power movement. He spent his time going to parties, putting up posters, drinking, and driving around in a car with several other kids, yelling obscenities at immigrants. Unlike all the others, Andrew says he was not the target of bullies. "Not at all," he states calmly and flatly. "I was the bully."

"I liked the fighting and the attention," he says of being part of the movement. He doesn't see himself as a Swedish nationalist. When asked what it means to be Swedish he said, "Dunno. I'm white." Being a Nazi "means I'm part of something, part of a group. It gives me a chance to express my hate."

Still living at home, Andrew has lots of conflicts with his parents about his beliefs. His mother has a friend who is Jewish and was in a concentration camp. "She's OK, I guess," he says. "My mom likes her. It's OK." But it isn't so "OK" with his mother, who has taken down the Nazi flag he hung in his room and burned it, along with his rather small-size storm-trooper uniform.

Ironically, although Andrew had been the bully in his school, as a visible and visibly small Nazi, he has now become the target for others. He is constantly harassed and beat up by violent anti-Nazi groups—"which is really just other kids my age who hate just like I do." "I drink all the time," he says casually. Addicted to the videogame "Counterstrike," Andrew now says he likes gaming more than fighting. This past summer, he "jumped." The group's leader, twenty years old, was furious and threatened him. "But my mother's boyfriend knows some Hell's Angels, and I just told him [the leader of the group] that if he messes with me, I'll tell my mom's boyfriend. Now he's incredibly nice to me, and said, 'Cool, whatever.' He even offers to drive me home from school." Andrew hopes to become a fireman.

THE EXTREME RIGHT IN SCANDINAVIA

Andrew and David are fairly typical of the young men and boys who join the neo-Nazi movement throughout Scandinavia. Most are between sixteen and twenty years old (Fangen 1999b, 362), but some are considerably younger. Most come from lower middle class families; their fathers are painters, carpenters, bricklayers, and road-maintenance workers. Some come from small family farms or their fathers own one-man businesses, are small capitalists or self-employed tradesmen (Fangen 1998b, 36). These occupations have been dramatically affected by the global economic restructuring in recent decades. (See also Fangen 1998a, 1999c, 2000; Bjørgo 1998; Loow 1994.)

White supremacists in the Nordic countries have made a significant impact on those normally tolerant social democracies. Norwegian groups such as Boot-boys, NS 88, the Norsk Arisk Ungdomsfron (NAUF), Varg, and the Vikings, the Green Jacket Movement (Gronjakkerne) and the Danish National Socialist Movement (DNSB) in Denmark, and the Vitt Ariskt Motstand (VAM, or White Aryan Resistance), Kreatrivistens Kyrka (Church of the Creator, COTC), and Riksfronten (National Front) in Sweden have exerted an impact beyond their modest numbers. They are frequently discussed in the media, and newspapers flock to cover events and demonstrations; they are also the subject of constant governmental concern and the object of significant police interest. While some of these groups have disappeared (VAM disbanded in 1994), the most readily identifiable group today is Blood and Honour, a spin-off of the notorious British skinhead group that is an amalgam of right-wing zealots and drunken soccer hooligans spoiling for a fight. The Nationell Ungdom (National Youth Movement) and National Socialist Party are also important groups in Sweden.

Norwegian groups number a few hundred, while Swedish groups may barely top 3,000 adherents, with perhaps double that number in supporters and general sympathizers. The Salem march in the southern suburbs of Stockholm on December 11 draws between 1,000 and 1,200 annually in the largest annual demonstration of the movement. The Danish National Socialist Party may be the largest and certainly the most mainstream political organization on the extreme right in Scandinavia. A "respectable" amalgam of traditional Nazism with occasional nods to street hooliganism and skinhead neo-Nazis, they run candidates in local elections, publish a national e-newspaper, *The Fatherland*, and have set up a local radio station called Radio Oasis (www.radiooasen.dk/english.htm).

Most of the groups meet formally irregularly, but have specific ritual dates for meetings, such as Hitler's birthday. But because these groups serve social needs at least as much as they address political questions, they meet informally almost every night, to drink, listen to music, and to go out looking for fights. They prowl through neighborhoods, frightening passersby, and occasionally angrily and violently confronting immigrants. They are especially eager to pick fights with groups of immigrants, and information about an immigrant gang's whereabouts is highly prized.

Social Background of the Participants

All the participants I interviewed initially through EXIT were male. There are often girls and women around the Nazi scene, but they were not seen by the boys I interviewed as integral to the group's central projects, which were enabling these guys to feel like real men. My informants described the girls' motives as similar to theirs—they enjoy the drinking and partying and fighting. And sometimes they were welcomed, especially at the parties. But sometimes they were simply, as David says, "nuisances." Skinhead events are almost entirely homosocial, such as drinking and listening to music before going out to party and fight. "We'd drink a lot and start screaming along with the music," says Edward, "and start hitting each other and slam dancing into each other. Then we'd go out, and a few girls would join us, and we'd go looking for fights."

The relegated status of women and girls among Scandinavian skinhead groups may differ from the more central and active role played by some women in American groups on the extreme right (Blee 2002). More young women may be attracted to Scandinavian groups than earlier research might have predicted. However, I saw no evidence whatsoever that girls and women play a major role in the activities of these neo-Nazi groups. They are girlfriends, partiers, and drinkers, and fun to have around. But their numbers are small, and their presence is relatively immaterial to young skinhead men. This difference may be attributed to the much younger ages of Scandinavian neo-Nazis than their counterparts in the U.S., with prepubescent Scandinavian girls more circumscribed in their evening activities. But mostly, the age of the Scandinavian neo-Nazi skinheads indicates that their "project" has more to do with proving adolescent masculinity than in spreading Nazi ideology. Their project, implied or explicit, is the restoration of masculinity, the retrieval of masculine entitlement. And while one might discern support among some women for such a restoration of traditional masculinity, compensatory masculinity projects almost always involve intense homosocial bonding as the basis for masculine validation. The presence of women would, as Edward put it, "pollute things."

Consistent with the general pattern of far-right members in Scandinavia, almost all of those I interviewed came from lower middle class backgrounds—skilled tradesmen, farmers, military, police, and construction trade, and many from divorced families. One or two had more working-class origins, but in highly skilled trades. And one father was a successful local politician and was solidly middle class. Their mothers are either housewives, or professional—nurses and teachers. A few work in the public sector. Several worked with their ex-husbands in small-scale businesses.

All these young men are themselves downwardly mobile; they work sporadically, have little or no control over their own labor or workplace, and none owns his own business. Youth unemployment has spiked, especially in Sweden, just as the numbers of asylum seekers has spiked, and with it attacks on centers for asylum seekers. These young men struggle, Fangen notes, to recover a class identity "that no longer has a material basis" (1999a, 192).

EXIT

The "clients" at EXIT, as they are known, range from between thirteen and twenty-three years; the average age is between sixteen and seventeen years. About twenty-five new young guys are actively participating at any one time and one new one comes to EXIT every week. They describe themselves as searchers who did not fit in with any of the available cliques in middle school. Often targeted by bullies, they describe their first flirtation with Nazism as a way to both express their growing sense of anger and entertain fantasies of revenge. "Being a Nazi in a country like Sweden is probably the worst thing you could be," said Lasse, an eighteen-year-old former skinhead. "And since I wanted to be bad—really bad—I decided to be a Nazi."

The staff at EXIT is composed of former Nazis. Robert, the current Coordinator, is twenty-five and from Stockholm. His father owns a hobby shop and his mother is an assistant in a home for the elderly. Trim, fit, and handsome, Robert looks hip and stylish and blends in easily with other young Swedish men. Pelle, an assistant at EXIT, is twenty-seven, from Nortalje, a summer resort city; his father is a local politician and his mother teaches nursing. A tall, muscular hulking presence, he wears what appears to be classically skinhead garb—baggy black cargo pants with a few graffiti-like names written on them, tucked into black combat boots, shaved head with unshaved sideburns, and a red t-shirt with gothic letters surrounding a bloody skull. He laughs about his appearance, explaining that the names on his pants are rave bands, the boots are canvas, not leather, and the t-shirt is actually from a paintball competition. Having been out of the movement for ten years, he feels he can finally return to the comfort of the clothing, with certain ironic twists, and knowing that unsuspecting sociologists might get the wrong idea at the beginning of interviews. Both Robert and Pelle speak in soft and calm voices, consider questions carefully, and reply thoughtfully in measured tones.

DYNAMICS OF ENTRY

In previous research, I described how young men of the extreme right experience their downsizing, outsourcing, or economic displacement in specifically gendered ways: they feel themselves to be emasculated (Kimmel 2006). This political-economic emasculation is accompanied by a more personal sense of emasculation: all but one of the Scandinavian participants (Andrew) I interviewed had been bullied in school. The only other interview-based study of EXIT, *Smaka Kanga* (literal translation: "Kiss the Boot!"), found that bullying was a common unifying theme among the participants (Arnstberg and Hallen 2000, 9). Typical is this client: "It was common knowledge that you could beat me up without risk. And my parents thought I should stay submissive. I didn't get the support I should have had. They did nothing" (EXIT 2000, 5).

Pelle and Robert, EXIT staffers, also described themselves as having been small, skinny, and easily targeted. Robert says now he was a "searcher," which is "a young kid looking for an identity, a place to fit in." "I felt like a nobody," he says, picked on by gangs of immigrants in his school and neighborhood. First, he hung out with some soccer thugs, later he got into death metal music. "Then the 'Viking wave' sort of hit Scandinavia in the early 90s, and I became really interested in Vikings, and I had a necklace of Thor's hammer. The Vikings were such strong men."

Insecure and lonely at twelve years old, Edward started hanging out with skinheads because he "moved to a new town, knew nobody, and needed friends." Equally lonely and utterly alienated from his distant father, Pelle met an older skinhead who took him under his wing and became a sort of mentor. Pelle was a "street hooligan" hanging out in street gangs, brawling and drinking with other gangs. "My group actually looked down on the neo-Nazis," he says, because "they weren't real fighters." "All the guys had an insecure role as a man," says Robert. "They were all asking 'who am I?' " Markus, eighteen, also an EXIT staffer, told it this way:

> As a child, I had friends, sometimes, but I was completely left out at times. I got beat up a lot, both at home and at school. And I was always told I was stupid. When I was 11, I started looking up to my stepbrother, he was 18 and he was a skinhead. He took care of me, he cared. Once, when I got beat up by five blokes (three Swedes and two immigrants), he started going on about "those bloody foreigners." Being only 11, I had no racist opinions but I was affected by what he said. And when I walked around with him, I suddenly got my revenge for everything that had happened to me. Everyone I was afraid of was suddenly afraid of me. It felt great. My stepbrother started giving me white supremacy records, a T-shirt with some nationalist slogan on it, and eventually a bomber jacket. I went straight from listening to boy bands to listening to white supremacy music. (Exit 2000, 3–4)

Already feeling marginalized and often targeted, the boys and men described themselves as "searchers" or "seekers," kids looking for a group with which to identify and where they would feel they belonged. "When you enter puberty, it's like you have to choose a branch," said one ex-Nazi. "You have to choose between being a Nazi, anti-Nazi, punk or hip-hopper—in today's society, you just can't choose to be neutral" (cited in Wahlstrom 2001, 13–14).

Of course, not all boys who have been bullied in school, or who have divorced parents, or distant and perhaps abusive fathers become neo-Nazis. Some drift into other identities, and some may even become violent *antiracists*, as their profiles often seem very similar. But that, in a way, underscores my argument that other dynamics, besides the lure of the ideology, bring these guys into the movement. Points of entry into the movement included social activities such as parties and drinking with other kids. Many also described relationships with older guys who were already in the movement, who served as mentors and guides. An older cousin or brother, or an older friend, is often the gateway to choosing Nazism over other forms of rebellion:

> Then I joined my cousin to go meet his skinhead friends, drink beer and listen to white supremacy music. And it just went on from there. The music got harder and harder. You'd sit there, not knowing you were a racist. You'd get your boots, your flight jacket and peel off your hair. (Exit 2000, 6)

For others, it was a sense of alienation from family and especially the desire to rebel against their fathers. "Grown-ups often forget an important component of Swedish racism, the emotional conviction," says Jonas Hallen (2000). "If you have been beaten, threatened, and stolen from, you won't listen to facts and numbers."

One must not underestimate the power of white power music on these young prepubescent boys decision to "go Nazi" instead of the variety of other rebellious identities on offer (see Loow 1998a, 1998b). Music by such bands as Skrewdriver, Arvingarna, and especially Ultima Thule offer angry, hardcore, punk-inspired, metal-inflected driving rock—almost deliberately amateurish, loud, and raucous, with a pounding simple beat and nearly indecipherable lyrics screamed out over the thundering rhythm section. Every song seems to be a contrived anthem. In short, just the sort of music that an enormous number of young boys find irresistible. "The music reinforces the feelings that I am righteous and outside of society," says one (cited in Arnstberg and Hallen 2000, 13). Johnny got his start in the movement at age eleven, "painting swastikas, drinking and listening to Ultima Thule and other white power bands." As the purveyor of the largest white power music website on the Internet proclaims, "music that is hard, music that awakens the warrior spirit in these white people, within these white youth, which stirs up barbarian rages in them—is healthy" (cited in Back 2002, 114). Their "concerts" also provide a sort of instant community, a place to meet friends, get drunk, slam dance, and take out all of one's frustrations and rage.

NAZISM AS EMBODIED GENDERED PRACTICE

Alienated young adolescent boys, searching for a masculine identity, targeted by school bullies, whose family ties are attenuated at best and diffident and abusive at worst—easily a recipe for adolescent rebellion. Indeed, many of the ex-Nazis in EXIT see their behavior exactly in these terms, more as efforts to secure a masculine identity and experience community than as commitment to ideology. A wide variety of affective styles—posture, clothing, drinking, fighting—were engaged with consciously masculinizing effects.

Edward, who joined VAM when he was twelve, was called a "babyskin" because he was prepubescent and had not begun shaving yet. "I felt like such a little boy," he said. "Before I joined, I felt like a nobody, I felt like a loser, I felt like, worthless," says Robert. "Their world offered me a world where I was better—just because I was white." Another remembered his time with VAM as commanding respect and even awe:

It was like joining the Baader Meinhof gang or something like that. Powerful as hell. And it was powerful just standing there with robber's mask and a banner [at a demonstration]. People were shouting at me but I was just standing there, like a statue. I felt invincible, like there was nothing that could break me down. (in Arnstberg and Hallen 2000, 23)

Another former skinhead recounted his experience of masculine transformation as he joined up:

When I was 14, I had been bullied a lot by classmates and others. By co-incidence, I got to know an older guy who was a skinhead. He was really cool, so I decided to become a skinhead myself, cutting off my hair, and donning a black Bomber jacket and Doc Martens boots. The next morning, I turned up at school in my new outfit. In the gate, I met one of my worst tormentors. When he saw me, he was stunned, pressing his back against the wall, with fear shining out of his eyes. I was stunned as well—by the powerful effect my new image had on him and others. Being that intimidating—boy, that was a great feeling! (Cited in Bjørgo 1997, 234)

For Pelle, it was a "pure power trip":

I really wanted to fight and the best way to start a fight is to say "Sieg Heil." I wanted to fight, to release all that anger and hatred. I think it was a good way for me to rebel against my father, he is a legitimate politician, and the worst thing a legitimate politician's son could be is a Nazi.

In the end, Pelle said, "I held the opinions to get the more personal feelings I wanted."

The cultural practices of white power culture were also masculinizing. White power music was both "visceral and emotional," says Robert. Drinking also made them feel like real men. All the guys I interviewed described drinking between twenty and thirty beers, listening to white power music, or watching certain videos (*Romper Stomper* or *Clockwork Orange*) to get them ready to go out and look for fights. "By the time we'd downed twenty beers and watched the movies, we'd be banging into each other, butting our heads together, and screaming," recalls Pelle.

On the other hand, many of these rituals were also deeply intimate and caring. Pelle describes how the skinheads in his group would shave each other's heads as they bonded for "war," and how their physical affection during and after fights was the source of the most physical intimacy he had ever had to that point. "I was hugged very seldom as a kid," he remembers. "I guess now looking back, some of the things we did would look pretty gay."

Becoming a soccer supporter was also a dominant theme. In Scandinavia, as in Britain, being a "fan" is different from American adherence to a sports team, no matter how passionate. For some British and Scandinavian fans, fandom is the occasion for indulging in massive quantities of alcohol and engaging in serious brawling. In one survey, half of all Swedish Nazis were serious soccer hooligans (Arnstberg and Hallen 2000, 7). All of the guys I interviewed were avid soccer fans and were making the transition from soccer hooliganism to simple fandom.

THE ROLE OF IDEOLOGY

Thus far, I have described the points of entry into Nazism as embedded within a developmental psychological trajectory of response to marginalization and the effort to establish and sustain a hypermasculine identity as a hedge against feelings of psychological emasculation. I have said nothing about the ideology—the role of anti-Semitism, racism, nativism, and xenophobia. Such an omission is deliberate.

Among the ex-Nazis of EXIT, white supremacist ideology played a relatively minor role, both while they were in the movement and today. Being a boy, growing up to be a man, these were important in their developmental process, and occasionally the ideology would serve as a sort of theoretical prop for their masculinity. On the other hand, racist ideology served to underscore the taken-for-granted aspect of their entitlement. "We believed we were superior," says Robert, "that we had the right to beat up other people because we were white."

EXIT's promotional material underscores the minimal role of political ideology and instead emphasizes the developmental trajectory for young boys:

> Political opinions have little to do with it, but many of them have been abused early on in their lives. They have felt unwanted or pushed aside, sometimes by "friends" and teachers, sometimes by ethnic youngsters and occasionally by their own parents. They are used to being picked upon, and find themselves at the bottom of their social hierarchy. (Exit 2000, 3)

Only one of fifteen neo-Nazis interviewed by Arnstberg and Hallen denied the Holocaust or used any other catch phrases from National Socialism; in my interviews, none of the young men did. In fact, those who expressed any political opinions at all might just as well have been categorized as liberal or progressive, supporting a strong regulatory state to restrain greedy corporations and promote environmental stewardship.

Perhaps the only central component of ideology that seems consistent among members is "an idealized view of the male as a strong defender of the family and nation" (Exit 2000, 7). These young men maintain a fairly traditional understanding of male-female relations, especially in the absence of positive male role models in their development. They believe that wild, young immigrant boys have been foisted on their schools by a seemingly beneficent, but ultimately blighted government and they look on with dismay as "free" Swedish girls are attracted to immigrant boys, who, in turn, see them as "easy" or "tramps." Swedish boys are cowardly "wimps" who must unite to protect Swedish "girlhood" and reclaim the mantle of masculinity (see Arnstberg and Hallen 2000, 31). "Swedish men are such wimps," says Robert. "That's what we believed. They're soft, so easily pushed around. We looked up to the police, the military. We looked up to strength."

Nazism as a masculinizing project is also easily observed in the symbolism of the movement. In addition to Nazi paraphernalia, the single most common symbolic tropes among Scandinavian Nazis are references to Vikings. Viking men are admired because they lived in a closed community, were fierce warriors, feared and hated by those they conquered (Fangen 1999b, 36). They represent an untrammeled masculinity, an "armed brotherhood" of heroes and martyrs (Bjørgo 1997, 136). "The Vikings were real men, all right," explains Lars, now eighteen. "They were so strong and powerful, and they never gave up. They also knew who was boss in the family." "Vikings destroyed all those other cultures, conquering them and subjecting them," notes Thomas. "That's what we need to be: Vikings."

Another interesting symbol that unites many Scandinavian Nazis is the Confederate battle flag, the Stars and Bars. Outside of the American South, where it is celebrated as the hallmark of tradition and loyalty to the "lost cause," the Confederate flag is the universal symbol for racism. Scandinavian Nazis sport T-shirts, tattoos, and hats with Confederate insignias, and hang flags in their rooms or from their apartment windows.

EXIT STRATEGIES

How and why do Nazis leave the movement? What do their decisions tell us about masculinity validation as a motivation for participation in the first place? Ironically, the tolerance of Scandinavian societies may work against exit. All subjects in a 2000 study said they wish they had been stopped earlier, but the society of "niceism" facilitated their Nazism (Arnstberg and Hallen 2000, 29). But Nazis do leave, for various reasons. Some described the hypocrisy of the movement; one said:

> There is a very strong double standard: you should look after your body, not drink, and live soundly, but then you live like a pig anyway. I think this was a major reason why I distanced myself from it. When I stopped all the drunken parties, I then distanced myself from the whole thing. (Cited in Wahlstrom 2001, 18)

Another commented that what he really wanted was "to be part of a disciplined movement. Then you see it's not going to happen because there are so many idiots and nutters" (cited in Wahlstrom 2001, 18). Others, I was told by interviewers, "exit" in a rather respectable way: they get married and begin families. "They got a lot of positive regard for that because they were perpetuating the white race. It was simply the easiest way out," said Robert. "No one bothers you if you've got a wife and a Volvo," added Pelle.

Others drift away into other sorts of activities. Some move into more serious criminality and "had to grow their hair and fit in so they wouldn't be noticed, or they would have been ineffective in the criminal underworld," noted Pelle. A few become bikers or other marginal, hypermasculine outlaws. Not an insignificant number actually switch sides and become violent antiracists. "All these groups offer the same sort of brotherhood and community," Robert says, "so they drift into other arenas. It's almost never about making a life-long commitment to Nazi opinions."

The most common reason for leaving was, as they described it, getting "burned out." The life is demanding—drinking and fighting, constant arrests, constant violence—and requires such a steady supply of rage that eventually it begins to dissipate. "Am I going to be doing this when I'm forty?" Robert asked himself one day.

Pelle described a sort of economy of emotions. "I used anger to express every emotion. If you're disappointed, get angry. If you're sad, get angry. If you're frustrated, get angry. Eventually, I got tired of only expressing anger. I didn't run out of anger, exactly. I just got interested in other feelings." "It's a lot easier to shout at someone than it is to cry," he concluded.

Exit Through "EXIT"

The success of EXIT has been based, in large part, on its treatment of Nazism as an adolescent search for manhood rather than a commitment to ideology. "Most young neonazis eventually get bored with the ideology," states the organization's brochure. "The most common motive for leaving neonazi groups is personal development and maturity" (Exit 2000, 9).

Kent Lindahl, the group's founder, states as his axiom: "Love the neonazi, not his opinions." While this may sound like the Catholic Church's notion of loving the sinner but not the sin, it speaks, instead to the relative weights the group gives to ideology and the quest for identity. Indeed, ideology is not discussed with the potential exiter until well into the exiting process, after they have already jumped. Only outside the movement can the young man "reflect" on his ideology and see that it can be easily detached from the demonstration and proof of masculinity.

Personal development and maturity is often accompanied by a good deal of guilt. Several spoke of feeling "ashamed" or "guilty" about what they did, or what others did when they were around. "You could say I had too much of it," says one. "I couldn't bear it, I felt bad about all the stuff I did. I wanted something else, this chaos was not what I wanted." Another said he "started to feel bad about myself and realized that none of us lived the life we talked about" (Exit 2000, 4). Markus Olsson, who now works for EXIT, says that he does so, "to pay off my debt to society. But I just can't forgive myself" (Exit 2000, 10).

EXIT provides group meetings and individual therapy for these boys and young men seeking to leave the movement. They offer practical advice on rearranging social lives, returning to school, and help in a search for a job. And they offer a way to negotiate exit from groups that do not take particularly kindly to those who seek to leave its ranks. Recall, for example, the stories of David and Andrew: Andrew's mother's friend's association with Hell's Angels enabled Andrew to avoid being threatened by his group's leader; indeed, now that leader offers him rides home from school.

Others report constant threats. The one who quits is a traitor, who deserves to be assaulted or killed, they believe. In one survey, all subjects had been threatened; some actually assumed new identities in different towns or cities (Arnstberg and Hallen 2000, 37). "They were everywhere," recalls one guy. "Once, when I looked out the window in my mom's kitchen, I saw this car packed with skinheads staring straight at me." Another reports:

> It got so bad, I had to hide for five months. I couldn't even go out in the open. There was a price on my head. Everybody was chasing me and everybody was going to kill me. I hid in Stockholm for two weeks too. The more I hid, the more they wanted to get me, for they knew I was afraid of them.

EXIT can, in extreme cases, suggest potential "safe" houses and in many cases advise the young man about how to avoid retaliation.

NAZISM AS A MASCULINE RITE OF PASSAGE

According to those who have left the movement, participation in neo-Nazi groups was a rite of passage for alienated and insecure adolescent males. Their commitments were to a masculinizing project, not a National Socialist ideology. Ex-Nazis in Scandinavia appear to be far less interested in ideology than in action. Indeed, it was very difficult to extract the sorts of racist comments from them that come so casually and effortless out of the mouths of the American Aryan supremacists. In part, this reflects the fact that I interviewed ex-Nazis in Scandinavia, but it also reflects their young ages. Compared to American Aryan supremacists who enter in their late teens and early twenties, their years of participation were, on average, from thirteen to sixteen years, with some beginning as early as ten years but none of them remaining beyond age twenty. So the Scandinavian Nazis were leaving just as the Americans were entering.

Perhaps Pelle expressed this rite of passage best. Becoming a skinhead and a neo-Nazi enabled him to express his rage and, eventually, he says, to put it behind him. In leaving, he was forced to examine who he was and who he wanted to be, to delve into the lineaments of identity and discard those elements that were destructive. Now twenty-seven, and ten years out of the movement, Pelle is, like many of the long-time ex-Nazis I met, soft-spoken, thoughtful, and deliberate in speech. "I'm a better man for having been a Nazi," he says. Fortunately, for most men, in Scandinavia and elsewhere, there are other routes available to become "better men."

NOTES

1. I have changed the names of individual interviewees and changed a few details so they would not be recognizable. Names of staff at EXIT and other names have not been changed. All quotes are from interviews, except as noted.

2. This project, "Globalization and its Mal(e)contents: The Gendered Moral and Political Economy of the Extreme Right" is sponsored by the generous support of the Carnegie Corporation. The research in Scandinavia was supported by a summer research fellowship from the American Scandinavian Foundation. I am grateful to those organizations, and also to Robert Orell and the staff at EXIT in Stockholm for facilitating my work there. Amy Aronson, Klas Hyllander, and Jens Mallstrom provided moral, logistical, translation, and emotional support.

REFERENCES

Arnstberg, Karl-Olov, and Jonas Hallen. 2000. *Smaka Kanga: Intervjuer med avhoppade nynazister.* Stockholm: Fryhusset.

Back, Les. 2002. Wagner and power chords: Skinheadism, White Power music, and the Internet. In *Out of whiteness: Color, politics and culture,* edited by Vron Ware and Les Back, 94–132. Chicago: University of Chicago Press.

Bjørgo, Tore. 1997. *Racist and right-wing violence in Scandinavia: patterns, perpetrators, and responses.* Leiden: University of Leiden.

———. 1998. Entry, bridge-burning, and exit options: what happens to young people who join racist groups—and want to leave?" In *Nation and race: The developing Euro-American racist subculture,* edited by Jeffrey Kaplan and Tore Bjørgo, 231–258. Boston: Northeastern University Press.

Blee, Kathleen M. 2002. *Inside organized racism: Women in the hate movement.* Berkeley, CA: University of California Press.

EXIT. 2000. *EXIT: A way through. Facing neoNazism and racism among youth.* Sweden: EXIT.

Fangen, Katrine. 1998a. Living out our ethnic instincts: Ideological beliefs among rightist activists in Norway. In *Nation and race: The developing Euro-American racist subculture,* edited by Jeffrey Kaplan and Tore Bjørgo, 202–230. Boston: Northeastern University Press.

———. 1998b. Right-wing skinheads: Nostalgia and binary oppositions. *Young* 6(2): 33–49.

———. 1999a. A death mask of masculinity. In *Images of masculinities: Moulding masculinities,* edited by Søren Ervø and Thomas Johansson, 184–211. London: Ashgate.

———. 1999b. On the margins of life: Life stories of radical nationalists. *Acta Sociologica* 42(4): 357–373.

———. 1999c. Pride and power: a sociological interpretation of the Norwegian radical nationalist underground movement. PhD diss., Department of Sociology and Human Geography, University of Oslo.

———. 2000. Norwegian skinheads. In *White power encyclopedia,* edited by Jeffrey Kaplan. Walnut Creek, CA: Alta Mira.

Ferber, A. L. 1998. *White man falling: Race, gender and white supremacy.* Lanham, MD: Rowman and Littlefield.

Hallen, Jonas. 2000. Chronicle of a racist. *Metro,* November 30.

Kimmel, Michael. 2006. *Manhood in America: A cultural history.* 2nd ed. New York: Oxford University Press.

Kimmel, Michael, and A. Ferber. 2000. "White men are this nation": Right wing militias and the restoration of rural American masculinity. *Rural Sociology* 65(4): 582–604.

Loow, Helene. 1994. "Wir sind wieder da"—From National Socialism to militant race ideology: The Swedish racist underground in a historical context. Paper presented at the XIII World Congress of Sociology, Bielefeld, July.

———. 1998a. Racist youth culture in Sweden: Ideology, mythology, and lifestyle. In *Racism, ideology and political organization,* edited by C. Westin, 77–98. Stockholm: CEIFO Publications, University of Stockholm.

———. 1998b. White power rock 'n' roll: A growing industry. In *Nation and race: The developing Euro-American racist subculture*, edited by Jeffrey Kaplan and Tore Bjørgo, 126–147. Boston: Northeastern University Press.
Wahlstrom, Katja. 2001. *The way out of racism and nazism*. Stockholm: Save the Children Foundation.

*Michael Kimmel** is professor of sociology at SUNY–Stony Brook in the United States.

Kimmel, Michael. "Racism as Adolescent Male Rite of Passage: Ex-Nazis in Scandinavia." *Journal of Contemporary Ethnography* 36 (2007): 202–218.

Part 2: Issues

Some of the key issues related to youth and the extreme right are ethnic prejudice, (in)tolerance, and violence. While extreme-right ideology includes many ethnic prejudices (including anti-Semitism, racism, and Romaphobia), Islamophobia is undoubtedly the most important prejudice in contemporary Western democracies. Particularly in Western Europe, where Muslims constitute a large portion of the migrant communities, prejudice against Islam and Muslims is a major component of extreme-right propaganda. In "Young People's Attitudes Towards Muslims in Sweden," Pieter Bevelander and Jonas Otterbeck provide one of the first detailed studies of young people's attitudes toward Muslims.

Directly related to the topic of prejudice is the issue of tolerance. Liberal democracies are based on the values of both freedom and tolerance, but the two do not always go hand in hand. Particularly with regard to intolerant political groups, like the extreme right, the issue of whether freedom is absolute or should be restricted comes up regularly. Should governments limit the freedom of speech of the majority to protect the minority? Allison Harrell's article, "The Limits of Tolerance in Diverse Societies," looks at the complicated issue of the limits of tolerance in increasingly diverse societies and, especially, at hate speech and tolerance norms among young people in Canada.

. Violence is often seen as the most threatening aspect of extreme-right youths, but it is also one of the most alluring features of the extreme right to many young people. But violence and the extreme right are not synonymous: many extreme-right youths are not involved in political violence, while most extreme-right violence is perpetrated by people who are not involved in extreme-right organizations. In "Right-Wing Extremist Perpetrators from an International Perspective," Heléne Lööw surveys the international literature on perpetrators of extreme-right violence to see whether there is a specific profile of the violent right-wing extremist. She distinguishes between two groups, which are often collapsed into one in the media: those individuals with a background in extreme-right organizations and those without, finding that many factors play a role in attracting youth to extreme-right violence, but that no clear profile of an archetypical violent right-wing extremist exists. Meredith Watts looks at the group that probably has received most media attention in the sensationalist reporting on extreme-right violence: skinhead and neo-Nazi youth in Germany. In particular, she highlights the important role of the Internet in the growth and support of extreme-right groups.

As you read through the articles, think about the following questions:
- Should the intolerant be tolerated in a liberal democracy?
- Are extreme-right organizations the main cause of extreme-right violence?
- What is the effect of the media and the Internet on the spread of extreme-right attitudes and violence?

Young People's Attitudes Towards Muslims in Sweden

by Pieter Bevelander and Jonas Otterbeck*

Abstract

With the use of multiple regression technique, the principal objective of this study is to clarify and examine young people's attitudes towards Muslims, and the relationships between these attitudes and a large number of background factors. We use a representative sample of 9,498 non-Muslim youths between 15 and 19 years of age. The main results show that, when controlling for several background variables simultaneously, the country of birth, socio-economic background and school/programme factors all have an effect on the attitude towards Muslims. Moreover, socio-psychological factors, the relationship to friends and the perceptions of gender role patterns are found to be important. In addition, local factors like high levels of unemployment, high proportions of immigrants in a local environment also have an effect. No differences in the attitudes of boys and girls were found. Further, the study establishes a correlation between negative attitudes and right-wing populist seats in local government.

INTRODUCTION

The Swedish Muslim population increased substantially during the last quarter of the twentieth century. Although Sweden has no statistical records by religion, it is estimated that the number of individuals with a Muslim background has increased from a couple of families in the 1950s, via approximately 100,000 at the end of 1980s, to approximately 400,000 individuals in 2007.[1] The majority have come to Sweden as refugees or as [a] family of refugees, only a small minority as labour migrants. There is also an increasing Swedish-born Muslim population. Approximately one third of the Muslim population is of school age or younger (Anwar, Blaschke and Sander 2004).

To become integrated into another society, economically, socially, politically and culturally, takes time. To evaluate and translate prior educational credentials and labour-market experience can be a long process. For some, economic integration has gone better than for others. Bosnians, generally having a Muslim background, constitute one of the immigrant groups in Sweden with the highest labour-market attachment despite a relatively short stay in the country. For immigrants from Iraq, mainly Muslims, on the contrary, we find low employment rates (Bevelander and Lundh 2007). It is obvious that Muslims are not a homogeneous group in Sweden. Rather, the Muslim population have diverse backgrounds when it comes to ethnicity, citizenship, educational history, class and so on, but Muslims are often 'ethnified,' i.e. turned into an ethnic group and ascribed a homogeneous culture (Roy 2004). Strong evidence suggests that Muslims especially are perceived as a religiously distinct group by non-Muslims in Sweden. To be categorized as religiously different can create barriers and aggravations in daily life and can lead to lower chances in the housing and labour markets (Carlsson and Rooth 2006). Sometimes structures in laws, educational systems and other societal sectors cause religious minorities to get into difficult situations (Otterbeck 2004), for example in respect of religious rules on slaughter of animals or religious education. At the same time Swedish society is slowly adapting to the demographic changes in an ongoing process (Otterbeck and Bevelander 2006).

Due to this new demographic situation and to the rising discussions about racism and Islamophobia, the Living History Forum and the Crime Prevention Board in Sweden conducted a major questionnaire resulting in a report (*Intolerans* 2004). The empirical material was rich and complex and it was decided that a second wave of analyses was to be conducted. This article is one of the results of that effort.

The main aim of this article is to study the attitudes of non-Muslim youth in Sweden on Muslims. Furthermore, since few studies have been conducted in a more explorative way, this study will explore to what extend these attitudes could be explained by a number of background factors: (a) demographic factors, (b) socio-economic factors, (c) local/regional factors, (d) school factors, (e) psychosocial factors, (f) parental factors, (g) friend factors, (h) exclusion factors and (i) gender factors.

THEORY AND EARLIER RESEARCH

A number of theoretical propositions have been brought forward to explain the mechanisms behind negative or positive attitudes towards others and more extreme variations of negative attitudes like xenophobia, racism and Islamophobia. Below, some crucial theoretical concepts, stemming from the individual level, the group level or the societal level, are given, followed by an account of some studies with a focus on attitudes towards Muslims.

The Individual Level

One of the best-known studies focusing on individual prerequisites and characteristics is Adorno *et al.* (1950). This study connects the so-called authoritarian personality to anti-democratic behaviour combined with anti-Semitism, ethnocentrism, etc. A more recent variation of this theory was proposed by Tajfel (1982) who developed the so-called social identity theory. It presents the idea that ethnocentrism, negative attitudes and discrimination are based on the tendency individuals have to categorize themselves in so-called 'in' and 'out' groups. This in turn depends on a deeper need to get or uphold status, which can be achieved by comparing in- and out-groups. The more an individual identifies with his/her in-group, the stronger a negative attitude he/she will have to an out-group. However, this theory does not explain divergence in attitudes between different out-groups (for example different immigrant or ethnic groups). Nor does it explain why certain individuals systematically have a more negative attitude than others.

Studies of youth active in right-wing movements, or, at least, circles, tend to stress that these youths long to identify with a strong in-group excluding out-group members in harsh ways. These youths tend to have a long history of failure in school, have parents with lower education than average, tend to feel alienated by the middle-class ideals governing schools and tend to object to these ideals in a counter-cultural way (*Intolerans* 2004).

Other theories concentrate on the development of attitudes in adolescence and concentrate on the personal development of the individual. Robinson, Witenberg and Sanson (2001) stress the importance of socialization and especially parental practices (not only verbal tolerance) and education for the development of a 'tolerant' mind. Further, young adolescents seem to be more negative towards those holding opposing beliefs than older adolescents who tend to be more open and understanding. At the same time, according to Robinson, Witenberg and Sanson (2001), individuals do not hold either positive or negative attitudes; both attitudes coexist in all individuals. Rather, attitudes are situational.

Group and Societal Level

A more sociological explanatory concept is the so-called realistic conflict theory which stresses real conflicts of interests between groups and competition for scarce resources like education, employment and housing (Sherif 1966). A development of this theory is the so-called power-threat hypothesis. According to this, a negative attitude towards certain groups is due to the fact that these groups are seen as economic competitors and challenge the social and political power of another (Blalock 1967). A more socio-ecological variation emphasizes the environment individuals live in and is more or less a variation of the power-threat hypothesis. A feeling of threat increases with immigration of new groups. These groups become more visible, which diminishes the social distance from the majority. When symbolic dominance is felt to be threatened, racism and negative attitudes flourish. For example, visibly religious otherness might be perceived as a threat (McLaren 2003).

A variant of the above is called defended neighbourhoods theory, and it states that a fear of losing one's identity increases with a faster pace of change in neighbourhood composition (Dustmann, Fabbri and Preston 2004). Finally, and in contrast to the rather negative focus of Dustmann, Fabbri and Preston, according to Allport's (1958) contact hypothesis attitudes towards other groups are more positive when contacts between groups increase, especially when individuals have the same socio-economic background and try to obtain the same goals. This theory has generated much discussion and suggestions about the kind and the quality of the contact needed if a positive result is to be gained. Researchers tend to agree that in particular having friends among those who are constructed as the other tends to be strongly associated with positive attitudes (McLaren 2003).

Structural Level

Another set of theories is based on a more structural understanding of prejudices and racism. The theories attempt to uncover how economic, political and social power over states and institutions (re)produce discursive orders, benefits and resources along ethnic, racial, cultural, religious or other lines, securing the power position of a presumed elite (see, for example, *Integrationens svarta bok* 2006). These theories often focus on how cultures (and religions) are essentialized, seen as separate from each other and, finally, are ordered in hierarchies (Fredrickson 2002). A common trait is that theories on racism today often stress culture, rather than race, and how culture is made the functional equivalent of race in the sense that it becomes inherent in the individual classified as belonging to a specific culture (Balibar 2002; Solomos and Back 1999). These orders, at times invisible but always present, saturate public discourse and are manifested in stereotypes, jokes, popular culture but also in laws, politics and discrimination in the labour and housing markets. The orders often have long histories and are in the West European and North American case more often than not connected with the colonial period. Thus, while the studies above focus on personal characteristics or interpersonal relations, these theories focus on well-spread discourses and power relations with a long history.

ATTITUDES TO ISLAM AND MUSLIMS

Earlier quantitative research on attitudes towards Islam and Muslims in Sweden was carried out primarily on the adult population. The first study was done in 1990 by Hvitfelt (1991). He found that almost 65 per cent of the population was fairly to very negative towards Islam, 88 per cent was of the opinion that the Islamic religion was incompatible with the democratic system and 62 per cent had the view that the religion led to female repression. Finally, 53 per cent were of the opinion that the immigration of Muslims should be reduced. Hvitfelt's study makes use of bivariate analysis but refrains from theoretical explanations apart from vague references to negative stereotypes in media and studies on prejudice. The conclusion is that higher education, female sex and younger age generally lead to a higher degree of positive attitudes towards Islam, but that even the more positive were rather negative. However, this study was performed in connection with a period, the late 1980s, in which non-European immigration had increased dramatically which affected the discussion about Muslims. For example, certain members of the new right-wing populist political party, New Democrats (Ny Demokrati), claimed the increased numbers of Muslims were a threat to Swedish culture and prosperity.

Later studies have mainly been commissioned by the Swedish Integration Board (*Integrationsverket*). The *Integrationsbarometer* (2005, 2006) studied the attitudes of the general public with the use of a couple of indicators. These studies show that those who have a more positive attitude towards Muslims and Islam are women more than men, individuals living in large cities more than those living in smaller towns or the countryside and the higher educated more than the lower educated. This study also measured an age effect: the younger the respondents, the more positive towards Muslims and Islam. One question is similar to one in Hvitfelt's study. In the *Integration Barometer* 39 per cent (2005) and 37 per cent (2006) of the respondents think that Muslim immigration should be restricted, compared to 53 per cent in Hvitfelt's. Otherwise, most questions in the *Integration Barometer* are about Muslims rather than about Islam as in Hvitfelt's. This seems to have the effect that the attitudes are not as harsh. It is also possible that the population grew more accustomed to Muslims during the fifteen years that passed between the questionnaires and that this might have had an effect.

The results of the Swedish studies on attitudes are largely in line with those found in Germany and Switzerland. The theoretical base of the *Integration Barometer* stems primarily from Wilhelm Heitmeyer's research (2002, 2003, 2005; Heitmeyer and Zick 2004). These studies operate with ideas on social dominance similar to the meso-level theories mentioned above and also with theories on authoritarian personalities. Heitmeyer found that men had a less positive attitude towards Muslims than women. Furthermore, a more negative attitude was measured with increased age and a more positive with increased education. Political affiliation showed that individuals more to the right had less positive attitudes than those more to the left, who were more positive. Higher levels of unemployment and a larger share of immigrants living in the state were correlated with a less positive attitude towards Muslims. In the latest study a difference between 'east' and 'west' Germany is observed, with a more negative attitude towards Muslims by people living in 'west.' In addition, it shows that individuals more affected by social dominance, e.g. the feeling that one's existence is becoming less secure by the settlement of others, are less positive to Muslims. Finally, individuals with authoritarian perceptions also held slightly more negative attitudes to Muslims than others. For Switzerland, Cattacin *et al.* (2006) found that approximately 30 per cent of the population had Islamophobic attitudes, which is slightly higher than for Germany (20–25 per cent). Moreover, Cattacin's study found little correlation between Islamophobia and racism, xenophobia and anti-Semitism.

To our knowledge only one study has been conducted for the Netherlands focusing on youth and attitudes towards Muslims and Islam (Dekker, van der Noll and Capelos 2007). In this study, 581 students aged 14–16 were asked about their opinions on Islam and Muslims, but also on individuals of Turkish and Moroccan descent, with 54 per cent proving negative towards Muslims. Lack of positive, direct contacts with Muslims was seen as the most important factor in this result. Other factors explaining the result were if the individuals held negative stereotypical ideas about Muslims, got negative messages from family and friends about Muslims or had the conviction that Muslims and Islam were a threat to security.

The only study for Sweden that has focused on attitudes on Muslims by young people is the previously mentioned report *Intolerance* (2004). Using the same questionnaire as the present article, the *Intolerance* report tried to measure the attitudes of young people in Sweden towards Muslims, Jews, homosexuals and immigrants. Contrary to earlier studies and certainly compared to the study performed in 1990 by Hvitfelt (1991), this study showed that young people generally had rather positive attitudes. Only 5 per cent had negative attitudes, out of which 1.7 per cent were extremely negative. When it comes to attitudes specifically towards Muslims, 8 per cent had negative attitudes. Moreover, this study also tried to link a number of background factors with a so-called intolerance measure. Cross-tabulations showed that individuals with more negative attitudes towards Muslims were, for example, boys, youth having parents with a lower socio-economic background, youngsters who are enrolled in lower-level educational programmes, young people living in the countryside and those born in Sweden. Like earlier studies this study did not make use of more sophisticated statistical methods. The design of the questionnaire is, however, thoroughly based in micro- and meso-level theories on attitudes with clear references to Heitmeyer's study and to Scandinavian studies on racist and prejudiced attitudes of youth.

Other studies have discussed the representation of Islam. According to a number of research reports, youth in Sweden live in a media climate that is not particularly sympathetic towards Islam. For example, the news, popular culture and textbooks are often accused of superficial portrayals of Islam (Berg 1998; Hvitfelt 1998; Otterbeck 2005; Kamali 2006). In brief, when Islam is seen as something negative (which is not always the case) it is presented as a threat, uniform, undemocratic, patriarchal and different.

The above-discussed societal factors, an increasing population with a Muslim background and the relatively slow economic integration process of some Muslim groups, a relatively negative media climate on Muslims and Islam, as well as the fact that relatively few studies have been undertaken on this subject, make studies on the attitudes of the majority on the Muslim minority of great importance.

DATA, MODEL AND METHOD

The data used are based on a classroom questionnaire carried out during the month of December 2003 among pupils in the two highest levels of primary school and the three following levels at upper secondary schools.[2] The individuals who answered the questionnaire are pupils between the ages of 15 and 19. Cluster sampling on the total population in these ages was used to have an equal number of primary and secondary schools as well as having schools from different parts of the country. The total sample consists of 230 schools, 762 classes and 13,898 individuals. Classes that would not be in the study as well as internal drop out left us with basic material that comprises a representative sample of 10,599 individuals. This is approximately 2 per cent of the total population in these age categories in Sweden. Of these, 565 individuals have indicated that they are Muslims and are therefore excluded from the analyses. An internal reduction of 536 individuals who have not answered all questions used in this analysis means that the material for our analysis comprises 9,498 individuals, 4,680 girls and 4,818 boys.[3]

The dependent variable is a constructed attitudinal scale or index based on eight separate statements indicating a more positive or negative attitude towards Muslims. In Appendix A these separate statements are given as well as the means, percentages for the five alternative answers and standard deviations for girls and boys. The alternative answers on these statements were: yes, this is correct; this is relatively correct; unsure/doesn't know; this is rather incorrect; no, this is incorrect. Since a large correlation in the answers between the statements could be measured, an attitude index is created.[4] The index is constructed so that an increasing level indicates a more positive attitude towards Muslims.

The independent variables[5] are based on the questions asked in the questionnaire and to a large extent formulated in line with the earlier discussed theoretical propositions at the individual, group and societal level. Some of these questions are dealing with *demographic characteristics* like age, gender and country of birth, whereas others are connected to the *socio-economic background* of the respondents. In this case the socio-economic status of the parents, split into eight categories, was used; whether the individual lived in a single-parent family or not and if one or both parents were unemployed were also used as indicators for socio-economic background. According to earlier studies and the above-mentioned theories, we expect that increased age, being a girl, being born outside Sweden and having a higher socio-economic background is correlated with a more positive attitude towards Muslims. If one or both parents are unemployed and if the adolescent lives in a single-parent household that should lead to economic stress in the family and is expected to have a negative effect on the attitude towards Muslims. *Local and regional factors* are primarily based on which municipality an individual lives in. Moreover, this variable is categorized in various ways to 'catch' different aspects assumed to be connected to attitudes towards Muslims. This variable is categorized according to type of municipality,[6] level of unemployment in municipality, proportion of foreign-born population in the municipality, the relative proportion of the manufacturing sector in the municipality and, finally, a dummy variable constructed on the basis of whether a municipality had right-wing populist mandates in the local parliament or not.[7] The local and regional indicators are assumed to measure differences in regional and local context of the individual. Economic stress factors at this level and a more negative regional/local attitude towards immigrants in general are expected to be measured by these included variables. In other words, we expect a correlation between increased negative attitudes towards Muslims and the higher the unemployment rate, the higher relative proportion of the manufacturing sector in the municipality, as well as the higher the percentage of immigrants living in the municipality. Individuals living in municipalities with a right-wing mandate in the local parliament are expected to be more negative towards Muslims. *School factors* like how comfortable the pupil is at school and the respondent's grade level are included as index variables. The kind of programme the respondent is following, categorized into four levels, is also integrated in the model. This variable is assumed to catch the effect of socio-economic background on the level of attitudes towards Muslims. According to earlier studies, these variables certainly have a strong connection to the socio-economic background of the parents (Lange and Westin 1981). Moreover, *social psychosocial indicators* are all index questions and constitute the following: aggressiveness, restlessness, risk preference and nervousness. These factors are assumed to measure the individual psychosocial behaviour of the adolescents. The expectation is that the more aggressive, restless, risk preferable and nervous the individual is, the more negative an attitude towards Muslims should be measured. Other indices in the model include one dealing with *parental factors* which is assumed to measure contact between parents and adolescents. Here it is expected that a 'better' parent contact with the adolescent is connected to a more positive attitude towards Muslims. *Friend factors* are assumed to measure the influence of friends on behaviour. We measure general friend relations with an index and this factor is assumed to measure the effect of friends on the attitude towards Muslims. Better friend relations in general are expected to be connected to a more positive attitude towards Muslims. Moreover, we also measure whether the individuals know a Muslim (or Muslims) personally. This variable is assumed to measure a better knowledge about individuals having Islam as religion and we expect those who know a Muslim to be more positive towards Muslims than those who do not know a Muslim. To know (in Swedish 'att känna') is a broader category than to have as a friend. Still it is a neutral to positive expression when you state that you know someone, though less likely to be said of someone you dislike. Societal belonging at a general level is measured by inclusion of the question as to whether the respondent has *feelings of exclusion from society*. It is expected that a higher belonging is correlated with a more positive attitude towards Muslims. Finally, *gender role patterns* are included and assumed to measure whether attitudes towards gender role patterns are congruent with attitudes towards Muslims. It is expected that more traditional gender role patterns are connected to more negative attitudes towards Muslims if the attitude is based on a general xenophobia. But if it is rather based on specific stereotypes about Muslims and Islam generally including the idea of Muslim men and Islam as utterly misogynistic and Muslim women as oppressed one ought to find a correlation between progressive attitudes to gender roles and a negative attitude to Muslims.[8]

Many questions in the questionnaire that are included in the model are on an ordinal level and recoded to scales with the use of factor analysis. With the use of multiple regression technique, OLS, we estimate the effect of the various variables on the constructed index of attitudes towards Muslims. Variables based on constructed indices are standardized. The model presented in the analysis includes all variables presented earlier as well as a separate analysis for girls and boys.

RESULTS OF MULTIVARIATE ANALYSIS

In the Table 1 the results of three regressions are presented, including all background variables. The first regression shows the results for both girls and boys. Given that earlier studies showed a difference in attitudes towards Muslims by sex the second and third regression is for girls and boys separately. The results indicate that some variables have no statistically significant effect on the attitude towards Muslims by young people, whereas other variables show either positive or negative effects. In the following we discuss the results by variable group.

Demographic Factors

When it comes to age/grade the results of the regression for both girls and boys show few differences in effect of age/grade on the attitude towards Muslims. With the exception of those who attend the highest grade of secondary schooling (consequently also age) no significant effect could be measured on the attitude towards Muslims, which is in line with the means shown in the earlier section. However, the regressions for girls and boys separately show that, for boys attending the second year of secondary schooling, a significant positive effect is measured. Girls attending the highest level of primary schooling also have a significant positive attitude towards Muslims.

Boys born outside Sweden have a more positive attitude towards Muslims relative to boys born in Sweden. We also found that girls born outside Europe have a more positive attitude towards Muslims than those born in Europe. Moreover, a young person who knows a Muslim has a significantly more positive attitude towards Muslims relative to somebody who does not know a Muslim. Also, individuals born outside Sweden and especially those born in southern Europe and outside Europe know a Muslim far more often than individuals born in Sweden. A possible explanation for these results could be that young people from outside Europe to a larger extent are living in areas and attend schools with relatively more Muslims.

Table 1. Adolescent attitudes towards Muslims: multivariate regression

	All	Girls	Boys
Boys	0.034	–	–
Grade 9	−0.007	0.058	−0.067
1st grade secondary	−0.052	−0.086*	−0.020
2nd grade secondary	0.026	0.013	0.059
3rd grade secondary	0.084**	0.102**	0.107**
North/West/Eastern Europe	0.100***	0.052	0.135***
Southern Europe	0.159**	0.147	0.173*
Outside Europe	0.178***	0.167***	0.206***
Skilled worker	0.009	−0.004	0.031
Lower civil servant	0.040	0.044	0.034
Intermediate civil servant	0.133***	0.123***	0.136***
Higher civil servant	0.162***	0.143***	0.173***
Occupations with academic education	0.143***	0.191***	0.098
Entrepreneur	0.040	0.028	0.064
Agricultural worker	0.093	0.133	0.071
Single-parent family	−0.016	0.012	−0.056*
Mother unemployed	0.032	−0.006	0.053
Father unemployed	−0.029	−0.098	0.058
Gothenburg	−0.052	−0.181**	0.172
Malmoe	0.245**	0.384**	0.091
Other larger cities	0.054	0.067	0.057
Medium-sized cities	−0.016	0.024	0.031
Large municipalities	0.049	0.084	0.049
Smaller municipalities	−0.038	−0.083	0.036
Country site	0.073	0.103	0.080
Share unemployed	−0.012*	−0.007	−0.019**
Share immigrants	−0.005***	−0.003*	−0.007***
Size manufacturing sector	−0.004***	−0.001	−0.007***
Right-wing populist mandate	−0.178***	−0.136***	−0.204***
Mean grade level	0.142***	0.191***	0.090***
Well-being at school	0.084***	0.065***	0.102***
University and occup. prep. programme	−0.033	0.104	−0.103*
Occupational prep. programme	−0.186***	−0.016	−0.346***
Individual programme	−0.332***	−0.338***	−0.385***
Restlessness (index)	−0.040***	−0.049***	−0.031*
Aggressiveness (index)	−0.062***	−0.042***	−0.080***
Risk preference (index)	0.013	0.010	0.016
Nervousness (index)	0.057***	0.046***	0.068***
Parent communication (index)	−0.048***	−0.042***	−0.051***
Parent knowledge recreational activities (index)	−0.016	−0.025*	−0.008
Parent reaction problematic behavior (index)	0.054***	0.046***	0.057***
Friend relations (index)	0.009	0.024*	−0.001
Knows Muslim	0.095***	0.129***	0.073***
Does not know Muslim	−0.165***	−0.123***	−0.203***

Feelings of exclusion from society (index)	–0.128***	–0.128***	–0.128***
Gender role patterns (index)	–0.316***	–0.321***	–0.308***
Constant	2.874***	2.674***	3.072***
Adjusted R²	0.369	0.352	0.352
Number	9498	4680	4818

Notes:
***p<0.001, **p<0.005, *p<0.01
Reference categories for dummy variables in regression are girls, grade 8, Swedish born, unskilled worker and Stockholm

Interestingly, the results indicate no difference in attitude towards Muslims between boys and girls. This is different from what was measured in the earlier discussed descriptive section. This result is mainly due to the inclusion of the variable stereotypical gender role ideas in the model.

Socio-Economic Factors

While we assume a more stepwise, 'the higher, the more positive,' connection between attitudes and socio-economic background, the regressions presented in the table show that only pupils with parents having academic occupations have a more positive attitude towards Muslims. For all other occupations we find no statistically significant effect. Boys living in single-parent families have a more negative attitude towards Muslims than those who live with both parents. For girls no significant effect of this variable could be measured.

Local and Regional Factors

In earlier reports it was indicated that the more urban the environment a person is living in, the more positive he or she is towards Muslims. As described in an earlier section, this study uses a different geographical division for region of living and finds for boys no statistically significant difference in attitude towards Muslims by region. For girls, however, we find an interesting difference, with the cities Gothenburg and Malmoe on one side and all other regions (including Stockholm) on the other. Girls in Gothenburg have a somewhat less positive attitude towards Muslims, while girls in Malmoe clearly have a more positive attitude. For the other regions, no statistical significant difference could be measured relative to the reference category, Stockholm.

However, economic factors at the local level have a certain importance for young people's attitudes towards Muslims. Boys who live in municipalities with a relatively large manufacturing sector, a higher level of unemployment and a

higher proportion of immigrants living in the municipality have a more negative attitude towards Muslims than boys who live in municipalities with the
opposite conditions. One possible explanation for this result could be that a
relative large manufacturing sector exposed to competition is related to larger
business cycle variation and fluctuations in unemployment. One interpretation
could be that some boys in these municipalities blame this situation on immigration in general and Muslims in particular. For girls we do not find significant
results for these variables.

Finally, our categorization of municipalities into a binary variable wherein
either a municipality has right-wing populist political seats in local government
or not, shows that young people who live in municipalities where these parties
have seats have more negative attitudes towards Muslims than young people
living in municipalities without such seats. A possible explanation could be that
the attitude towards Muslims by young people is also affected by other negative
attitudes on immigrants and Muslims in the local community.

School Factors

School and programme factors are important explanatory factors for the attitude towards Muslims by pupils. An increased individual grade is correlated
with a more positive attitude towards Muslims. Pupils who attend the individual
programme (lowest) have a more negative attitude towards Muslims relative to
those in the other secondary programmes. In line with earlier studies we also
find a strong correlation between the occupational distribution of the parents
and school performance of pupils.

Social Psychological Factors

Social psychological factors like restlessness and aggressiveness also affect
the attitude towards Muslims of both girls and boys. This is in line with earlier
research that has indicated that so-called intolerant youth are more restless.
It is most likely that these young people also have negative attitudes towards
Muslims. A hypothetical explanation for the result that was found for 'increasing nervousness' and increasing positive attitude could be that this is a proxy
for emotional sensitiveness and a more nuanced concept of reality, which in
turn could lead to more positive attitudes towards those who are perceived as
different.

Family Factors

In the model questions were also included that measured the effect of degree of confidential communication with parents, parent knowledge about the recreational activities of their child and the reaction of parents to problematic behaviour of their children on the attitude towards Muslims. According to the analysis, pupils with parents who reacted strongly to their problematic behaviour have a more positive attitude towards Muslims. Surprisingly we found the opposite signs for the other measurements.

Friend Factors

If girls have good relationships they have a more positive attitude towards Muslims relative to if they have less good relationships. This relation was not found for boys. One explanation for this could be that among boys 'good relationships' can be related to having the company of 'intolerant groups of friends' (*Intolerans* 2004) which is statistically less likely for girls.

Feelings of Exclusion from Society

The question on feelings of exclusion from society is based on the idea that attitudes to immigrants and minorities vary with the degree of trust in other human beings and is asked with the aim of measuring to what extent pupils feel in or excluded from society on a general level. The analysis shows that this variable has a significant effect on the attitude towards Muslims for both boys and girls. The higher the feeling of exclusion, the more the negative attitude is measured.

Gender Role Patterns

Finally an index measuring gender-role patterns among pupils is included in the model. The idea behind this inclusion is that the attitude towards Muslims could be influenced by 'gender-role ideals' by both girls and boys. The results show that both boys and girls with more stereotypical, inflexible gender-role perceptions have a more negative attitude towards Muslims relative to those who have other perceptions about gender roles.

SUMMARY AND DISCUSSION

Earlier Swedish and international statistical studies on attitudes towards

Muslims have included relatively few explanatory variables and used only basic statistical tools to measure variation in attitudes towards Muslims. The present study shows, with the use of multiple regression technique, that many variables have a significant, either positive or negative, effect on young people's attitude towards Muslims. Returning to the earlier studies and the theoretical considerations described initially, various propositions in these are supported by the results of the study. We have divided this discussion into three levels, while well aware of them overlapping each other.

Starting at the individual level, we find that individual characteristics have an important influence on the attitude towards others, in this case Muslims. Socio-psychological factors like aggressiveness and restlessness clearly influence held attitudes. This was an expected result in line with the analysis in the 2004 *Intolerance* report, with theories on attitudes of right-wing youth but also socio-psychological theories like Tajfel's (1982). Moreover, our analysis shows that individuals holding stereotypical understandings of gender and a negative perception of society have more negative attitudes to Muslims. Interestingly, and in contrast to bivariate analyses, no difference between girls and boys was measured.

Robinson *et al.* (2001) suggested that attitudes were interconnected with socialization and parental practices, but also with successive maturity. In the present study, the socio-economic background of parents affected the attitude of youths. If the result from earlier studies of the adult population is taken into account—parents with less education and lower socio-economic statues are more likely to hold negative attitudes towards Muslims—it is to be expected that these youths' attitudes are in line with their parents' and that the prejudices are likely to be part of their socialization. The opposite situation also holds. The children of those with a higher socio-economic status and higher education generally have more positive attitudes. The age hypothesis is more difficult to confirm. We cannot observe a successive increase in positive attitudes; rather, no significant difference can be measured between in the eighth grade (about 14 years old) and those in the second grade of the gymnasium (17 years). But in fact, the oldest respondents, those in the third grade, have the most positive attitudes.

An interesting, significant result is that both girls and boys born outside Sweden, and especially outside Europe, have more positive attitudes to Muslims. The likeliness of knowing a Muslim increases if you live in immigrant-dense areas. It is also possible that the joint experience of feeling excluded from the category 'Swedish' and being labelled 'immigrant' can lead to solidarity and positive, inclusive attitudes. These interpretations are in line with the contact hypothesis stressing both general contact and common goals and experiences.

When analysing the results solely on an individual level, attitudes primarily depend on the social situation of the individual, his or her psychic well-being and possibly on age. The results of our analysis further indicate clear support for the contact hypothesis which is based on the idea that increased contact with the other induces more positive attitudes towards others. Taken all together, negative attitudes would then be caused by the life situation of the individual rather than by a specific Islamophobia. However, we argue for a need to take other possibilities into account for a more complex understanding.

At the group and societal level, measuring the general friend factors, we find a more ambiguous result. For girls, friend factors have a significant positive effect on the attitude towards Muslims. For boys we do not find an effect of this factor. This difference between the sexes could be due to boys being more involved in so-called intolerant groups of friends. Besides, we found that economic, political demographic factors are important factors in explaining attitude towards Muslims, especially for boys. Increased number of immigrants and higher unemployment level correlate with a more negative attitude by boys towards Muslims, who can be seen as threats to the status quo and increased competition for scarce economic resources in the locality. This result supports the theoretical propositions of the power-threat hypothesis. We also find support for the idea that factors at the regional level, in this case right-wing political ideas that have been translated into actual political parties and seats in the local government, correlate with young individuals' attitudes towards Muslims. Also this is in line with the power-threat hypothesis but more on a political level.

While the immediate reaction might be that these analyses are sufficient when explaining the attitudes, those who propose a structural analysis prefer to make additions to be able to answer questions like why specifically Muslims are targeted. There is a claim that negative discourses on Islam and Muslims are especially strong and that there is a widespread Islamophobia in Sweden reproduced in, for example, different kinds of media and popular culture. Why is this not visible in our study? Or is it? The previous study on the same statistical material shows that the attitudes to Jews, homosexuals, immigrants and Muslims are similar, albeit marginally harsher against Muslims (*Intolerans* 2004). In our analysis it is clear that it is the well-adjusted children of the well-educated and employed who are the most positive to Muslims. Could it be that they also hold a competence for expressing positive attitudes in questionnaires, thus concealing other forms of othering? According to Olivier Roy (2004), one of the principal misconceptions of Muslims is to perceive them as a group not a mere population with diverse interests. Étienne Balibar (2002) further claims that a dominating form of new racism is when cultural identity is ascribed to individuals and when group categories are closed, not allowing hybridity and transformation. Thus the mere fact that the questionnaire groups Muslims together as 'Muslims' helps the middle class to avoid exposing the foundation of their cultural assumptions, i.e. that Muslims are primarily different. Positive attitudes towards the other are a norm, but it helps to conceal the fact that at the bottom of that norm lies a political act of othering. This line of reasoning cannot be tested with the help of our material but it would be interesting to design questionnaires taking these theoretical ideas into account.

Concluding, our analysis sheds some light on what factors seem to be relevant to explaining the attitude towards Muslims by young people. Since these results are highly contextual and difficult to generalize we are careful about stating that the measured effects will last in different environments. Our recommendation is therefore increased future research, both comparative and longitudinal, that could confirm or refute our results.

Notes

1. The number of 400,000 Muslims in 2007 is an assumption based on earlier figures given by Anwar, Blaschke and Sander (2004, p. 224) updated with net migration to Sweden from Muslim countries up to 2007.

2. The Swedish school system has nine obligatory grades followed by a three-year upper secondary school where students can choose between different programmes.

3. The reduction of responses is higher with increased age and a possible explanation for this is that in higher grades students have fewer classroom lectures and more apprenticeship hours. Since increased age induced higher positive attitudes towards Muslims we probably slightly underestimate the positive attitude towards Muslims by the population. See also *Intolerans* (2004) for more on the initial questionnaire, method of selection, reduction of responses, etc.

4. The internal correlation is 0.90 measured as the Cronbach alpha coefficient, which is on a satisfactory level. Since some of the statements were stated in the opposite direction, we reversed the coding for all statements in the same direction.

5. See Appendix B for an overview. Construction of all indices and the questions asked are available from the author upon request.

6. Available from author upon request.

7. The population and labour-market indicators are based on data from Statistics Sweden. The political indicator is based on statistics of the local elections of 2002.

8. Test for multicollinearity of both the variables *feelings of social exclusion from society* and *gender role patterns* gave a correlation of 0.23 and 0.44 respectively.

REFERENCES

ADORNO, THEODOR W., et al. 1950 *The Authoritarian Personality*, New York: Norton

ALLPORT, GORDON W. 1958 *The Nature of Prejudice*, Reading, MA: Addison-Wesley

ANWAR, MUHAMMAD, BLASHKE, JOCHEN and SANDER, ÅKE 2004 *State Policies towards Muslim Minorities: Sweden, Great Britain and Germany*, Berlin: Edition Parabolis

BALIBAR, ÉTIENNE 2002 'Finns det en "nyrasism"?', in É. Balibar and I. Wallerstein (eds), *Ras, nation, klass: Mångtydiga identiteter*, Göteborg: Daidalos

BERG, MAGNUS 1998 *Hudud: Ett resonemang om populärorientalismens bruksvärde och världsbild*, Stockholm: Carlson

BEVELANDER, PIETER and LUNDH, CHRISTER 2007 'Employment integration of refugees: the influence of local factors on refugee job opportunities in Sweden', *IZA-Discussion Paper*, no. 2551

BLALOCK, HUBERT M. 1967 *Toward a Theory of Minority-Group Relations*, New York: Wiley

CARLSSON, MAGNUS and ROOTH, DAN-OLOF 2006 'Evidence of ethnic discrimination in the Swedish labour market using experimental data,' *IZA-Discussion Paper*, no. 2281

CATTACIN, S. et al. 2006 'Monitoring misanthropy and rightwing extremist attitudes in Switzerland, an explorative study,' *Research Report PNR 40*, Geneva: University of Geneva

DEKKER, HENK, VAN DER NOLL, JOLANDA and CAPELOS, TEREZA 2007 'Islamofobie onder jongeren en de achtergronden daarvan,' mimeo, Universiteit Leiden, Departement Politieke Wetenschap

DUSTMANN, C., FABBRI, F. and PRESTON, I. 2004 'Ethnic concentration, prejudice and racial harassment towards minorities in the UK, manuscript, University College, London

FREDRICKSON, GEORGE M. 2002 *Racism: A Short History*, Princeton, NJ: Princeton University Press

HEITMEYER, WILHELM (ed.) 2002 *Deutsche Zustände, Folge 1*, Frankfurt am Main: Suhrkamp

——— 2003 *Deutsche Zustände, Folge 2*, Frankfurt am Main: Suhrkamp

——— 2005 *Deutsche Zustände, Folge 3*, Frankfurt am Main: Suhrkamp

HEITMEYER, WILHELM and ZICK, ANDREAS 2004 'Anti-Semitism, Islamophobia and group-focused enmity in Germany,' research note at Institute for Interdisciplinary Research on Conflict and Violence, University of Bielefeld

HVITFELT, HÅKAN 1991 'Svenska attityder till islam,' in S. Holmberg and L. Weibull (eds), *Politiska opinioner, SOM-undersökningen 1990*, SOM-rapport 6, Gothenburg University

——— 1998 'Den muslimska faran—om mediabilden av islam,' in Y. Brune (ed.), *Mörk magi i vita medier: svensk nyhetsjournalistik om invandrare, flyktingar och rasism*, Stockholm: Carlssons

INTEGRATIONENS SVARTA BOK: agenda för jämlikhet och social sammanhållning 2006 SOU 40, Stockholm: Fritzes

INTEGRATIONSBAROMETER 2004 2005 *En rapport om allmänhetens inställning till integration, mångfald och diskriminering 2003 och 2004*, Integrationsverkets skriftserie V, Norrköping: Integrationsverket

INTEGRATIONSBAROMETER 2005 2006 *En rapport om allmänhetens attityder, erfarenheter och kunskaper inom områdena integration, mångfald och diskriminering*, Integrationsverkets rapportserie 5. Norrköping: Integrationsverket

INTOLERANS 2004 Antisemitiska, homofobiska, islamofobiska och invandrarfientliga tendenser bland unga, Stockholm: Forum för Levande Historia and Brottsförebyggande Rådet

KAMALI, MASOUD 2006 'Skolböcker och kognitiv andrafiering,' in L. Sawyer and M. Kamali (eds), *Utbildningens dilemma: Demokratiska ideal och andrefierande praxis*, SOU 40, Stockholm: Fritzes

LANGE, ANDERS and WESTIN, CHARLES 1981 *Etnisk diskriminering och social identitet: Forskningsöversikt och teoretisk analys*, Stockholm: Liber/Publica

MCLAREN, LAUREN 2003 'Anti-immigrant prejudice in Europe: contact, threat perception, and preferences for the exclusion of migrants,' *Social Forces*, vol. 81, no. 3

OTTERBECK, JONAS 2004 'The legal status of Islamic minorities in Sweden,' in R. Aluffi B.-P and G. Zincone (eds), *The Legal Treatment of Islamic Minorities in Europe*, Leuven: Peeters

——— 2005 'What is reasonable to demand? Islam in Swedish textbooks,' *Journal of Ethnic and Migration Studies*, vol. 31, no. 4

OTTERBECK, JONAS and BEVELANDER, PIETER 2006 *Islamofobi: en studie av begreppet, ungdomars attityder och unga muslimer utsatthet*, Stockholm: Forum för Levande Historia

ROBINSON, JULIE, WITENBERG, RITVKA and SANSON, ANN 2001 'The socialisation of tolerance,' in M. Augoustinos (ed.), *Understanding Prejudice, Racism, and Social Conflict*, London: Sage

ROY, OLIVIER 2004 *Globalised Islam: The Search for a New Ummah*, London: Hurst

SHERIF, MUZAFER 1966 *Group Conflict and Co-operation: Their Social Psychology*, London: Routledge & Kegan Paul

SOLOMOS, JOHN and BACK, LES 1999 *Theories of Race & Racism: Reader*, Florence, KY: Routledge

TAJFEL, HENRI 1982 'Social identity of inter-group relations,' *Annual Review of Psychology*, no. 1

Appendix A. Adolescent attitudes towards young Muslims, mean of index, standard deviation and the percentage by category of answer

Girls Statement	Mean	SD	4	3	2	1	0
Most Muslims are decent people ...	3.00	0.980	36.8	35.4	21.2	4.1	2.4
It would be entirely OK to have a steady Muslim as a neighbour ...	3.57	0.841	72.8	17.0	6.6	1.7	1.9
Muslims in Sweden should have the right to build mosques ...	2.56	1.352	33.6	21.2	25.2	7.4	12.7
There are far too many Muslims in Sweden ...	2.54	1.286	32.9	16.5	31.5	10.0	9.1
You cannot trust a Muslim ...	3.02	1.090	46.9	18.4	27.0	4.6	2.9
It should be forbidden for Muslims to vote in elections ...	3.37	1.031	66.9	11.5	16.3	2.3	3.1
Most immigrated Muslims are very likely law-abiding ...	2.67	1.074	29.2	34.2	25.3	7.1	4.2
Most Muslims only want to live on social security ...	2.41	1.158	23.2	20.6	36.4	13.9	6.0
Boys Statement	**Mean**	**SD**	**4**	**3**	**2**	**1**	**0**
Most Muslims are decent people ...	2.68	1.110	25.8	35.3	25.4	7.9	5.7
It would be entirely OK to have a steady Muslim as a neighbour	3.28	1.087	58.9	22.5	10.9	2.7	5.0
Muslims in Sweden should have the right to build mosques ...	2.24	1.469	27.9	18.5	24.2	8.7	20.7
There are far too many Muslims in Sweden ...	2.12	1.354	22.4	14.9	31.1	15.4	16.2
You cannot trust a Muslim ...	2.69	1.206	35.0	20.0	30.3	8.5	6.2
It should be forbidden for Muslims to vote in elections ...	3.08	1.257	57.3	12.5	18.8	4.0	7.4
Most immigrated Muslims are very likely law-abiding ...	2.38	1.260	22.3	28.1	26.0	12.7	10.8
Most Muslims only want to live on social security ...	2.03	1.294	17.7	16.8	31.5	18.7	15.3

Notes: The alternative answers on these statements were: yes, this is correct; this is relatively correct; unsure/doesn't know; this is rather incorrect; no, this is incorrect. For some statements we change the order of answering. For all statements, a higher mean, close to 4, implies a more positive attitude towards Muslims.

Appendix B. Independent variables

Variables	Categories	Variables	Categories
Demography		*School/programme factors*	
Gender	Girls/boys	Mean grade level	Index
Grade	Grade 8 (15 years old)	Well-being at school	Index
	Grade 9 (16 years old)	Programme	University preparation
	Secondary 1st grade		University and professional preparation
	Secondary 2nd grade		Professional preparation
	Secondary 3th grade	*Individual*	
Region of birth	Sweden	*Social psychological factors*	
	North/West/ Eastern Europe	Restlessness	Index
	Southern Europe	Aggressiveness	Index
	Outside Europe	Risk preference	Index
Socio-economic background		Nervousness	Index
Parents' socio-economic background	Non-skilled worker	*Family factors*	
	Skilled worker	Parent communication	Index
	Lower civil servant	Parent knowledge recreational activities	Index
	Intermediate civil servant	Parent reaction problematic behaviour	Index
	Higher civil servant	*Friend factors*	
	Occupations with academic education	Friend relations	Index
	Entrepreneur Agricultural worker	Knows Muslim *Exclusion*	No/yes
Single-parent family	No/yes	Feelings of exclusion from society	Index
Mother unemployed	No/yes	*Gender role factors*	
Father unemployed	No/yes	Gender role patterns	Index

Local/regional factors	
Municipality type	Stockholm
	Gothenburg
	Malmoe
	Other larger cities
	Medium-sized cities
	Large municipalities
	Smaller municipalities
	Country site
Unemployment level (municipality)	Continuous
Share foreign born (municipality)	Continuous
Size manufacturing sector (municipality)	Continuous
Right-wing populist mandate in municipality	No/yes

*Pieter Bevelander is associate professor in the Department of International Migration and Ethnic Relations at Malmö University.

Jonas Otterbeck is assistant professor in the Department of International Migration and Ethnic Relations at Malmö University.

Bevelander, Pieter, and Jonas Otterbeck. "Young People's Attitudes Towards Muslims in Sweden." *Ethnic and Racial Studies* 33, no. 3 (2010): 404–425.

Reprinted by permission of the publisher (Taylor & Francis Ltd., http://www.tanf.co.uk/journals).

The Limits of Tolerance in Diverse Societies: Hate Speech and Political Tolerance Norms Among Youth

by Allison Harell*

Abstract. Conventional measures of political tolerance have tended to assume that people see all forms of speech as equally legitimate (or equally illegitimate). This article develops an alternative view, and measure, of political tolerance to account for individual distinctions across types of speech. Political tolerance is conceptualized using three individual-level dispositions. The intolerant reject speech rights for all objectionable groups; absolute tolerators endorse speech rights for all groups viewed as objectionable; and multicultural tolerators support free speech except when such freedoms are used to target racial and ethnic minorities. Survey data from close to 10,000 youth in Canada and Belgium show that multicultural tolerance reflects civil liberties attitudes among many young citizens. These youth do see exclusionary speech as a special category of "intolerable" speech, consistent with legal restrictions on hate speech in many industrialized democracies. Such target group distinctions are an under-studied and underspecified component of contemporary political tolerance judgments.

Freedom of speech is a fundamental value in democratic politics. Citizens are expected to respect the rights of others to express themselves publicly, regardless of whether they endorse the ideas espoused by others. The capacity to do this is captured by the concept of political tolerance, which is usually defined as "a willingness to 'put up with' those things one rejects or opposes. Politically, it implies a willingness to permit the expression of ideas or interests one opposes" (Sullivan et al., 1982: 2). Traditional liberal definitions of tolerance require that all groups—even groups that fundamentally challenge a minority group's right to exist—be tolerated. Although there has been recognition that political tolerance is often at odds with other democratic values (Marcuse, 1969; Nelson et al., 1997; Peffley et al., 2001; Sniderman et al., 1996), its current conceptualization does not fully account for the ways in which individuals distinguish various types of speech.

This is clearly the case when free expression collides with concerns about preventing discrimination in contemporary, multicultural democracies. There have been successive legislative and legal attempts, especially since the 1980s, to criminalize prejudicial behaviour in industrialized countries. This can be seen in employment equity legislation, antidiscrimination provisions and legal cases that challenge discriminatory behaviour on the part of governments and organizations. It can also be seen in the trend toward regulating racist speech, with hate speech legislation being present in most European countries and in Canada (Coliver et al., 1992).

Such legislative restrictions are completely at odds with current conceptualizations of political tolerance as a citizen value. While attitudes toward free speech have been examined empirically since the 1950s (Stouffer, 1963), there have been few attempts to examine specific target groups or the relationship between them. In this article, I argue that exclusionary speech—such as incitement of racial hatred, Holocaust denial and other forms of hate speech—poses a fundamental challenge to how we think about, and in turn measure, political tolerance. Target group distinctions are an under-specified source of variation in political tolerance judgments.

To examine these contentions, I rely on a unique comparative dataset of young people in Canada and Belgium. Young people in these two countries have grown up during a period of unprecedented racial and ethnic diversity and under legislative regimes that, at least officially, place severe sanctions on the expression of hatred. Given this, youth in these two countries are considered critical cases (Eckstein, 1975) for testing the presence of inter-target group distinctions in political tolerance judgments.

The findings, in general, support the idea that the youngest generation is balancing the need for social inclusion with individual rights to speech, rather than siding consistently with individual rights (absolute tolerance) or consistently censoring speech across the board (intolerance). A substantial proportion of youth see hate speech as outside the realm of legitimate democratic debate, while still permitting the expression of other objectionable ideas. This distinction is at the heart of the concept of multicultural political tolerance developed in this article.

DEFINING POLITICAL TOLERANCE

Tolerance is traditionally understood to imply restraint when confronted with a group or practice found objectionable (Cohen, 2004; Heyd, 1996; Horton and Nicholson, 1992; Mendus, 1988, 1989; Sullivan et al., 1979). Political tolerance typically refers to individual-level attitudes that permit groups to express opinions or maintain practices that a majority finds objectionable. It thus refers to the willingness to refrain from preventing people (or groups of people) from expressing their disliked opinions, lifestyles, preferences or world views (McKinnon, 2003: 55–61; see also Walzer, 1997; Weissberg, 1998). In practice, a citizen's degree of tolerance is assessed based on whether people agree that controversial groups should be allowed to participate in expressive activities, such as giving public speeches, holding rallies, or having books in local libraries. When respondents agree to extend civil liberties, they are providing tolerant answers. When they disagree, it is considered intolerant.

Two key features of this definition of political tolerance are the presence of prior disagreement and content neutrality. First, political tolerance is essentially about overcoming objection, and thus is only relevant for situations of disapproval (Sullivan et al., 1979). If a person agrees with, or is indifferent toward, a viewpoint, tolerance is not applicable because there is nothing to which the person objects. The other feature of conventional political tolerance measures is their unified nature. While the targets of tolerance must provide an opportunity for objection on the part of the respondent, there has been little attempt to distinguish between types of objectionable speech. Although there has been recognition that the targets of intolerance vary by country (Sullivan et al., 1985), only a few studies have focused on specific types of target groups, such as extreme religious sects, racists or pornographers (Chong, 2006; Davis, 1995; Gross and Kinder, 1998; Lambe, 2004; O'Donnell, 1993).Much like American First Amendment jurisprudence, the concept of political tolerance has been constructed as essentially content neutral.[1]

Prior objection and content neutrality are important concepts in the current measurement of political tolerance. These standards isolate the concept of tolerance from acceptance and ensure that both right-leaning and left-leaning citizens have an opportunity to express intolerance. Yet, from a comparative perspective, the emphases on prior disagreement and content neutrality create a situation in which citizens are considered intolerant *even when* the laws of their country permit certain types of censorship.

This is evident for what is commonly referred to as hate speech, usually defined as speech intended to incite hatred or promote genocide of minority groups. Legislation and legal interpretations that place restrictions on the expression of hate have been widely adopted in contemporary democracies, with the United States being the most notable exception (Cohen-Almagor, 2000; Coliver et al., 1992; Douglas-Scott, 1999). Defenders of such restrictions usually focus on the impact of hate speech on minorities. For example, Matsuda has argued, "The negative effects of hate messages are real and immediate to victims. Victims of vicious hate propaganda experience physiological symptoms and emotional distress ... Victims are restricted in their personal freedom ... As much as one may try to resist a piece of hate propaganda, the effect on one's self-esteem and sense of personal security is devastating" (1993: 24–25).Such a perspective is supported by recent work dealing with the effects of hate crimes and hate speech on victims (Boeckman and Turpin-Petrosino, 2002).

Hate speech also arguably plays a role in perpetuating hate organizations and hate crimes. Sumner (2004: 162–63), for example, sees hate speech as serving primarily as a means of recruitment for and identification with hate organizations that have been linked to racial violence.[2] In studies of genocides and large-scale discrimination, hate speech serves to stigmatize a group and normalize discriminatory treatment of them (Bosmajian, 1974; Cortese, 2006; Mullen, 2001; Tsesis, 2002).At the individual level, there is evidence that witnessing ethnic slurs or other derogatory comments directed at a minority can make majority group members feel more negatively toward them (Greenberg and Pyszczynski, 1985; Kirkland et al., 1987; Simon and Greenberg, 1996).

In other words, hate speech is viewed as a distinct type of expression. Unlike other potentially objectionable speech, hate speech serves to negatively impact the psychological and physical well-being of racialized minorities, effectively impacting the equal ability of people to enjoy the rights accorded to them as citizens. This distinction is fundamental, and is well captured by Harel's distinction (1996: 122) between inclusionary intolerance and exclusionary intolerance. Inclusionary intolerance arises in circumstances where minority groups are trying to fully participate in society by restricting the expression of prejudice directed at them. In other words, inclusionary intolerance involves restricting the rights of the intolerant. Preferential hiring regulations would be an example of inclusionary intolerance; such regulations limit the rights of employers to hire (or rather not hire) whom they want. Indeed, most anti-discrimination legislation could be considered as inclusionary intolerance as it limits the right of people to act on their biases in areas like employment and housing. Restrictions on hate speech, similar to other anti-discrimination measures, are a form of inclusionary intolerance. They limit individuals' right to express themselves in a manner that arguably hinders the full participation of others. Harel argues that inclusionary intolerance (restricting the rights of the intolerant) is more easily justified based on liberal democratic norms than other restrictions on rights.

The success of hate speech laws in effectively countering the societal problems they are said to address is, of course, a contentious issue (Braun, 2004; Coliver et al., 1992). Suppressing the expression of ideas, as Locke informed us long ago, does not necessarily change the ideas people hold, yet the extent of support for hate speech legislation and its relationship to other forms of intolerance is an empirical question. Current conceptualizations of political tolerance fail to recognize the possibility that restrictions on certain forms of speech are democratically defensible and are in fact restricted in most advanced industrialized democracies.

This shortcoming is particularly evident in attempts at assessing citizens' attitudes toward free speech, where there has been little effort to incorporate distinctions between inclusionary and exclusionary censorship practices. Typically, political tolerance is assessed either through the summing of responses to civil liberties questions about various target groups, similar to the early scales developed by Stouffer (1963) or by asking citizens which groups they dislike and then measuring their willingness to extend civil liberties to this group, referred to as the least-liked method of Sullivan and colleagues (1979). Both measures reflect the objective of content-neutrality, and indeed the least-liked method is designed specifically to be "content controlled" (Sullivan et al., 1981). Neither method for assessing political tolerance allows for the consideration of distinctions between various types of target groups, yet these two measurement techniques have been widely used to study citizens' political tolerance levels (see, for example, Chong, 2006; Gibson, 1998, 2006a; Marcus et al., 1995; Marquart-Pryatt and Paxton, 2006; Mondak and Hurwitz, 1998; Mutz, 2002).

Using citizens' support for the protection of racist speech as a test of political tolerance, then, may underestimate a citizen's commitment to the ideals of free speech. A willingness to curb racist speech may reflect the adoption of a more general approach to political expression that views some ideas as outside the realm of democratic discourse, as indeed many democratic governments and courts have maintained. One of the consequences of content neutrality in the measurement and operationalization of political tolerance is that we know little about the extent to which citizens view hate speech as distinct from other types of objectionable speech. The basic puzzle motivating this research is whether a willingness to restrict hate speech is simply a manifestation of political intolerance like any other or if individuals can be politically tolerant while still placing limits on specific types of speech. Unlike past research on political tolerance, this study rests fundamentally on the idea that speech associated with the promotion of hatred is viewed as particularly detrimental to democratic politics.

Redefining Tolerance

Rather than a view of political tolerance that prioritizes content neutrality, Harel's distinction (1996), as well as the comparative juridical prominence of hate speech restrictions, suggests that political tolerance should not be conceptualized as a binary concept where one is either intolerant or tolerant. Rather, conceptual room must be made for those who distinguish between the speech of the intolerant and other objectionable ideas. Censoring speech is usually problematic because it serves to (or at least has the potential to) restrict free and open debate that is considered fundamental to the democratic process. Yet some speech arguably serves exclusionary purposes and aims to delegitimize the voices and experiences of marginalized communities in the democratic process. A redefinition of political tolerance judgments that takes this into consideration results in three possible types of responses[3]:

(1) *Intolerance.* These individuals do not support speech rights for any objectionable group. Most research on political tolerance is actually concerned with this group of individuals.

(2) *Multicultural tolerance.* Individuals who support speech rights for objectionable groups, but do not extend them to groups that promote hatred.

(3) *Absolute tolerance.* Individuals who extend speech rights, irrespective of the target group.

While intolerance and absolute tolerance are well captured by current conceptualizations of political tolerance, the idea of multicultural political tolerance relies on the ability of citizens to distinguish hate speech from other speech that they find objectionable. Those who make such distinctions cannot possibly be captured using current techniques. They would be either categorized as intolerant if they chose a racist group as their least-liked using Sullivan and colleagues' content-neutral strategy (1979), or as somewhat intolerant based on a Stouffer-like scale. Yet, given the presence of such distinctions in the legal regimes of most industrialized countries, it seems essential to ask whether citizens are capable of (and in fact do) make such distinctions. I refer to this as multicultural political tolerance because it reflects contemporary discourses about the inclusion of various ethnic, racial and religious communities in the democratic process (Kymlicka, 1995, 2001; Young, 1990).[4]

This typology, in part, addresses a recent concern expressed by Mondak and Sanders (2003: 496–97), who argue that absolute tolerance (that is, tolerance for all groups) is fundamentally different from variations in intolerance. They argue that when individual tolerance judgments are simply summed together across target groups, those who are tolerant of some are fundamentally different than those who respond tolerantly to all groups. They recommend only considering the extreme of the scale as tolerant, in line with the concept of absolute tolerance noted above.

The problem with their approach is that there is no consideration of how variations across target groups are conceptualized, leaving everything but the extreme of the scale as representing simple variation in intolerance. The definition developed here, in contrast, includes a theoretically driven explanation of this variation by focusing on the types of groups in the scale. Furthermore, this framework specifies the types of target groups driving the variation. The measure controls for disagreement and is not limited by the number of groups in total that the respondent finds objectionable. While Mondak and Sanders may consider this distinction between groups simply a specification of levels of intolerance, the distinction—if found to reflect significant patterns in line with the legislative norms of democratic politics today—is more fundamental than that.

CASE SELECTION, DATA AND METHODS

In order to test whether there is evidence that citizens do in fact make distinctions between hate speech and other types of objectionable speech, this study relies on a critical case studies approach (Eckstein, 1975). As the concept of multicultural political tolerance represents a significant departure from conventional conceptions of political tolerance, this study provides a first test relying on samples in which I most expect to find inter-target group distinctions. The case countries for consideration are Canada and Belgium. A key criterion for their inclusion in this study is that both have civil and criminal laws prohibiting hate speech. The presence of such legislation should make it more likely that citizens adopt similar limits on speech rights. Along with the presence of such legislation, both these countries also share structural characteristics, including two major linguistic communities that are regionally concentrated and a federal system of government. These similarities reduce the possibility that inter-country differences in political tolerance can be attributed to variation in structural characteristics.

The critical difference between the countries, and comparative advantage of this study, is that Canada has a longer history of multicultural policies and much higher levels of racial and ethnic diversity than Belgium. While the primary goal of this article is to assess if citizens are capable of distinguishing between hate speech and other types of objectionable speech, the study also provides an important opportunity to explore the circumstances in which it is most likely to emerge. Canada was the first country to adopt an official policy of multiculturalism. In part due to open immigration policies, its actual levels of racial, ethnic and religious diversity are higher than most advanced industrialized democracies, including Belgium. Belgian politics have been marked by more open hostility to racial and ethnic diversity, notably in the popularity of the *Vlaams Blok*, a right-wing anti-immigrant party which has garnered substantial portions of the vote there (Billiet and De Witte, 1995). While both countries provide crucial case studies for the presence of inter-target group distinctions, their differences also provide some leverage in explicating the institutional and social bases of multicultural tolerance.

This initial test also focuses on a specific age cohort. Given the importance of early experiences to the socialization of political values and behaviours (Gerber et al., 2003; Hooghe, 2004; Plutzer, 2002), the youngest generation is considered the most likely to espouse new norms around the limits of free speech in multicultural democracies. Evidence suggests that attitudes toward diversity in these countries have become increasingly open over time, and this appears to be particularly true among the younger generations (Inglehart, 1997; Nevitte, 1996; Wilkes et al., 2008). Furthermore, there is some evidence that more supportive attitudes toward diversity and multicultural policies have been accompanied by increased hostility toward hate speech among younger people (Chong, 2006; Harell, 2008). If some citizens do distinguish between hate speech and other types of objectionable speech, they would most likely be found among youth in countries with strong legal frameworks restricting hate speech.

The Comparative Youth Survey (CYS) provided the data used in this analysis (Stolle and Hooghe, 2006). Surveys were conducted with students in grades 10 and 11 in Canada and Belgium during the 2005–2006 school year. In Canada, students were sampled in schools from seven cities in Ontario and Quebec.[5] Six cities were selected to vary in terms of size and were "matched" across provinces. The largest city was selected in each province (Toronto and Montreal), along with two medium-sized cities of approximately 150,000 inhabitants and two small towns with approximately 15,000 inhabitants. A second small town was also surveyed in Ontario that included a substantial French-speaking minority to facilitate inter-language and inter-province comparisons. Schools were intentionally selected to vary in terms of the socio-economic status of students and the homogeneity of the student population.[6] In the medium and small towns, all school boards were contacted and an effort was made to survey as many schools as possible in each setting. In total, 3334 respondents completed the self-administered questionnaire. Within each city, the socio-economic and linguistic backgrounds of the students are similar to the city in which they were sampled, and the distribution of schools approximates the language and public/ private distribution of schools in the cities.[7]

The Belgian sample was a stratified sample of secondary schools in ten provinces in the French and Flemish communities, with an over-sampling of five additional Dutch-speaking schools in Brussels. The schools were randomly selected and match the distribution of school types present. In total, 6265 students completed the survey. The average age of respondents in both surveys was 16 years old.

The main variables of interest derive from a tolerance battery. Modified from commonly used tolerance batteries, the goal was to include a number of potentially objectionable groups that differ in the exclusionary nature of their speech, their ideological association and their salience in the two contexts. The final battery includes five different potentially objectionable groups: racists, skinheads, radical Muslims, gay rights activists and Quebec/Flemish separatists. Racists and skinheads were included to represent groups associated with hate speech.[8] For each group, the respondent is asked to indicate whether they should be allowed to 1) hold a peaceful march in the respondent's neighbourhood and 2) talk on public television about their views. The answer categories are dichotomous (yes or no).

Importantly, the respondent was also asked to indicate their level of agreement or disagreement with each group on an 11-point Likert scale. The inclusion of this last item allows replication of a modified version of the least-liked methodology created by Sullivan and colleagues (1979) where respondents preselect their most objectionable group. Unlike the method developed by Sullivan and colleagues, where respondents are required to rank groups by level of dislike, this question format allows the respondent to find multiple groups equally objectionable and therefore allows for a controlled comparison across different objectionable groups. Its advantage over traditional Stouffer-like batteries where responses are summed across groups is that disagreement can be controlled.[9]

Based on these questions, a tolerance score is calculated for each target group and activity pair by limiting the analysis to individuals who expressed prior disagreement with the group.[10] Unlike studies that simply sum the number of tolerant responses, this methodological approach allows for a comparison of the nature of tolerance decisions and, importantly, whether young citizens make distinctions between the two hate groups in the survey and the other three groups, while controlling for the varying levels of disagreement across target groups. A composite measure based on these items is then developed to represent the three typologies presented earlier and a brief exploration of the significant demographic and political correlates of multicultural tolerance is provided. These include the level of political activism (0 to 5 or more), political knowledge (scale from 0 to 1 based on 3 questions), organization involvement (0 to 4 or more organizations), gender (1 = female), racialized minority status (1 = non-white respondent), urban/rural (1 = urban), parental education level (1 = one or both parents university educated), religious affiliation (non-religious is reference category) and religious attendance (0 = never to 4 = more than once a week).

TARGET GROUP DISTINCTIONS AND TOLERANCE NORMS

If individuals do make distinctions between exclusionary speech and other types of objectionable speech, one would expect that the aggregate level of tolerance for exclusionary groups would be lower than for other objectionable groups. Figure 1 presents the levels of tolerance for each of the two civil liberties activities in each country. The results are presented only for respondents who disagreed (and highly disagreed) with each group in order to more accurately capture the concept of tolerance. Note that the levels of tolerance for talking on television are expected to be higher than for peaceful marches because the proximity of the latter activity makes it more threatening—an "in your face" activity that has more potential to affect the respondent and would be harder to ignore if it occurred (Gibson and Bingham, 1985; Marcus et al., 1995). Figure 1 bears this expectation out. Indeed, in almost every single case, the tolerance level in each country is higher in the television scenario than it is for the peaceful march scenario.

What is more noteworthy is the variation across target groups within each scenario. First, the percentage of respondents in Canada and Belgium who were willing to tolerate each group talking on television about their views follows the hypothesized pattern: racists and skinheads, who represent exclusionary groups, are less likely to be tolerated than radical Muslims, gay rights activists or separatists.[11] In the Canadian sample, racists and skinheads receive the lowest levels of tolerance, with only about one in five young people permitting them to talk on public television about their views. This is in contrast to the other three target groups that receive between 35 and 63 per cent tolerance. In the Belgian data, racists and skinheads again receive the lowest levels of tolerance (17 and 15 per cent respectively) whereas over twice as many respondents were willing to allow gay rights activists and Flemish separatists to talk on television about their views. Radical Muslims, on the other hand, only receive slightly higher levels (19 per cent).[12] The gap between the most and least tolerated groups is more than 40 points in the Canadian sample, and over 20 points among Belgian youth.

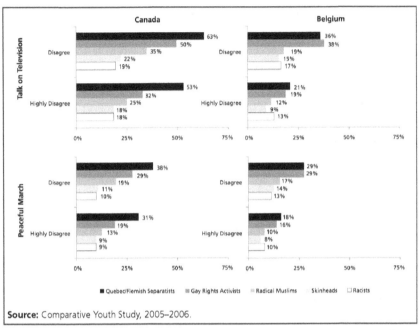

Source: Comparative Youth Study, 2005–2006.

Figure 1. Percent Tolerant by Activity, Country, and Disagreement Level

A similar pattern emerges when respondents were asked if each group should be allowed to hold a peaceful march in their neighbourhood. As expected, levels of tolerance for each group are lower for this more threatening activity, but the distribution across groups is consistent with the talking on television scenario. Almost 30 points separate the tolerance levels of racists and skinheads from gay rights activists and separatists in the Canadian sample, and over 16 points separate these groups in the Belgian sample.

Some might argue that this variation is driven solely by the fact that young people in both countries find hate groups more objectionable. Respondents did disagree most heavily with racists and skinheads in the full sample.[13] This is hardly a surprising finding, and in fact reflects the primary contention of this research: exclusionary speech is more objectionable to many young people precisely because it conflicts with other values, like social inclusion. As one might expect when limiting the sub-sample to only those who highly disagree with a target group (that is, where the respondent reported a 0 on the 0–10 disagree/agree scale), tolerance levels for those groups that were less objectionable on average decrease more substantially than for groups that were already found, on average, to be more objectionable.[14] For example, willingness to allow gay rights activists to talk on television drops from 50 per cent to 32 per cent among Canadian youth. The parallel drop for racists and skinheads is only a couple of percentage points. Thus, one of the reasons for the variation across target groups is the difference in the levels of aggregate disagreement.

That being said, this reduction in variation does not radically change the observed pattern, suggesting that level of disagreement is an important control but does not fully explain the aggregate level variations. Individuals continue to be less willing to extend civil liberties to exclusionary groups than to other groups, even under the most stringent conditions (high disagreement X high threat). Clearly, more young people find it harder to tolerate exclusionary speech than other forms of speech. As expected, these gaps are largest in Canada. While the samples across countries are not identical, and thus prevent a rigorous test of differences between the countries, the greater divergence between exclusionary and other objectionable groups in Canada is suggestive. Canada's longer history of multicultural policies and substantially higher levels of racial and ethnic diversity, especially in Central Canada from which the sample is drawn, should promote the free speech balancing act consistent with multicultural tolerance. Yet, in both Canada and Belgium, target group variation is clearly present, albeit at different levels.

The evidence provided so far only demonstrates this distinction at the aggregate level. One of the strengths of the question format developed here is it allows an examination of how individuals who disagree with multiple groups make distinctions between them. On average, respondents indicated some level of disagreement with just over three groups, of which two on average were rated highly objectionable. Racists and skinheads were among the group many respondents' objected to, but the vast majority of those finding at least one exclusionary group objectionable *also* disagreed with one of the remaining three groups. In fact, 80 per cent of respondents disagreed with at least one of each type of group, allowing for a comparison of tolerance judgments at the individual level.

Table 1 (Canadian data) and Table 2 (Belgian data) capture these distinctions by presenting the differences in the percentage tolerant of one target group compared to another target group limiting each dyad to only those individuals who found *both* groups objectionable.[15] Percentages close to zero imply that when respondents tolerated (or not) the group listed in the column, they responded similarly to the group listed in the row. A higher percentage indicates the difference in tolerance levels between the column and row groups for each activity. If exclusionary speech is less tolerated than other types of speech, one would expect a higher positive percentage among dyads that include both an objectionable group in the column and an exclusionary group in the row. This implies that individuals were more likely to tolerate objectionable speech than

Table 1.
Difference in Tolerance Levels within Group Dyads in Canada

	Gay Rights Activists	Quebec Separatists	Radical Muslims	Skinheads
Tolerance of Talking on Public Television				
Quebec Separatists				
% Point Difference	-8%			
n	713			
Radical Muslims				
% Point Difference	20%	29%		
n	735	1204		
Skinheads				
% Point Difference	27%	42%	14%	
n	811	1376	1772	
Racists				
% Point Difference	29%	45%	17%	4%
n	864	1471	1935	2182
Holding a Peaceful March in Respondent's Neighborhood				
	Gay Rights Activists	Quebec Separatists	Radical Muslims	Skinheads
Quebec Separatists				
% Point Difference	-3%			
n	727			
Radical Muslims				
% Point Difference	10%	19%		
n	743	1218		
Skinheads				
% Point Difference	14%	27%	8%	
n	823	1401	1782	
Racists				
% Point Difference	15%	29%	9%	2%
n	873	1492	1944	2202

Note: The percentage is the percentage point difference in the aggregate level of tolerance for the row group compared to the column group. Positive numbers indicate greater tolerance for the column group, and negative numbers indicate higher levels of tolerance for the row group. Within each pair, only respondents who disagreed with both groups were included. The number is represented by the n for each pair of groups.
Source: Comparative Youth Study, 2005–2006.

they were to tolerate exclusionary speech. Likewise, tolerance values between pairs of objectionable groups or between pairs of exclusionary groups are expected to be closer to zero.

Table 2.
Difference in Tolerance Levels within Group Dyads in Belgium

Tolerance of Talking on Public Television				
	Gay Rights Activists	Quebec Separatists	Radical Muslims	Skinheads
Flemish Separatists				
% Point Difference	4%			
n	*932*			
Radical Muslims				
% Point Difference	21%	18%		
n	*1178*	*2125*		
Skinheads				
% Point Difference	23%	21%	3%	
n	*1115*	*2036*	*2630*	
Racists				
% Point Difference	20%	21%	4%	0%
n	*1044*	*2164*	*2874*	*2714*
Holding a Peaceful March in Respondent's Neighborhood				
	Gay Rights Activists	Quebec Separatists	Radical Muslims	Skinheads
Flemish Separatists				
% Point Difference	0%			
n	*1048*			
Radical Muslims				
% Point Difference	15%	14%		
n	*1307*	*2245*		
Skinheads				
% Point Difference	16%	16%	2%	

Note: The percentage is the percentage point difference in the aggregate level of tolerance for the row group compared to the column group. Positive numbers indicate greater tolerance for the column group, and negative numbers indicate higher levels of tolerance for the row group. Within each pair, only respondents who disagreed with both groups were included. The number is represented by the n for each pair of groups.

Source: Comparative Youth Study, 2005–2006.

Both Table 1 and Table 2 present patterns consistent with these expectations. Turning first to tolerance of talking on television in the Canadian sample, consider the dyads that contrast tolerance levels of gay rights activists and separatists with skinheads and racists in the television scenario. These are found in the lower left-hand corner of Table 1. For individuals who disagree with both groups in the dyads, tolerance levels are still between 27 and 45 percentage points higher for gay rights activists and separatists than for the two exclusionary groups. In contrast, the difference that emerges between tolerance levels of gay rights activists and separatists is only 8 percentage points in favour of Quebec separatists. Similarly, the difference between tolerance of racists and skinheads is only 4 percentage points. Dyads that include radical Muslims are less consistent. While they do receive higher levels of tolerance than skinheads and racists (14 and 17 percentage points respectively), they receive substantially lower tolerance levels than gay rights activists and separatists.

The results for holding a peaceful march indicate an almost identical pattern, although the differences are less dramatic as might be expected in the higher threat scenario. The largest differences (between 14 and 29 points) emerge between exclusionary groups and gay rights activists and separatists, even after limiting the comparisons to only those who find both groups objectionable.

A similar pattern emerges in the Belgian data. Considering young people's tolerance of a target group talking on television, a difference of over 20 percentage points exists between those tolerating either gay rights activists or Flemish separatists and each of the exclusionary groups. It is noteworthy that similar gaps in tolerance also exist in this sample between gay rights activists or Flemish separatists and radical Muslims. This suggests that there is an added distinction being made with respect to radical Muslims. The results for holding a peaceful march mimic this pattern. Importantly, the results in Tables 1 and 2 control for prior disagreement with groups (hence the different sample size in each dyad) and provide strong support for the contention that young people distinguish exclusionary speech from other objectionable speech.

What does this mean for our understanding of political tolerance judgments? Clearly, some young people do make distinctions across target groups when deciding whether or not to extend certain civil liberties. This is particularly evident for civil liberties activities that are more distant and less "in your face." These differences are not simply an artifact of varying levels of objection. Rather, it seems that some groups are viewed as more legitimate participants in democratic debate, in spite of any objection to the point of view being expressed.

Multicultural Political Tolerance among Youth

Clearly, there is evidence that at least some young people are distinguishing between hate speech and other objectionable speech. This is consistent with the concept of multicultural political tolerance, yet to fully highlight the extent of target group distinctions, it is necessary to identify the extent to which youth are making these distinctions. For this, a categorical variable has been developed that captures three types of individuals in the CYS study that correspond to the three types of tolerance dispositions developed here: intolerance, multicultural tolerance and absolute tolerance. A respondent who is unwilling to allow at least one exclusionary group and at least one other objectionable group to hold a march and talk on television is coded as intolerant. Conversely, a respondent who is willing to allow both an exclusionary group and another objectionable group to hold a march and talk on television is coded as an absolute tolerator. Finally, those who allow at least one objectionable group to do both civil liberty activities but deny them to at least one exclusionary group are coded as multicultural tolerators.

A choice was clearly made to force respondents to allow at least one objectionable group to participate in *both* of the civil liberties activities asked about in the survey, rather than at least one of the two activities. This was intentional in order to ensure respondents applied rights judgments in a principled manner, rather than simply responding to the threatening stimulus of the march scenario. This is also an attempt to make this a stricter test of the hypothesis that tolerance distinctions emerge based on target group distinctions (and not distinctions between situations where tolerance is asked to be applied).[16]

Table 3 provides the breakdown by each category. It demonstrates that multicultural tolerance is, in fact, characteristic of a substantial portion of young people's thinking. In the Canadian sample, 55 per cent of respondents are categorized as multicultural tolerators when any level of prior disagreement is used as the basis for determining tolerance judgments. Another 33 per cent responded in an intolerant manner, and only 11 per cent were willing to extend civil liberties judgments across groups.[17] Similarly, about 11 per cent of the Belgian sample qualifies as absolute tolerators. The difference is that in Belgium, the intolerant account for 49 percent of the sample compared with 40 percent who were coded as multicultural tolerators.[18]

The difference in levels of multicultural tolerance between Canada and Belgium are significant (p<.01) and in the hypothesized direction. While sampling differences cannot be fully ruled out as a source of these differences, the evidence is at least suggestive that countries with greater openness toward racial and ethnic diversity should be more likely to view hate speech as intolerable. Given the importance that ethnocultural diversity plays in Canadian discourses around identity, it should not be surprising that young people in that context are more likely to fall into the multicultural tolerance category.

Table 3.
Breakdown by Type of Tolerance

	Canadian Sample	Belgian Sample	Significance
Intolerance			
%	33%	49%	***
N	811	2033	
Multicultural Tolerance			
%	55%	40%	***
N	1352	1672	
Absolute Tolerance			
%	11%	11%	
N	278	438	
Total	2441	4143	

Note: The disagreement breakdown excludes 1598 respondents who did not find at least one of each type of target group objectionable, as well as 1482 respondents who failed to complete the tolerance battery. Significance calculated using a two-group mean comparison t-test (one-sided) where *** means $p < .01$.
Source: Comparative Youth Study, 2005–2006.

The prominence of multicultural tolerance, especially in the Canadian context, raises the question of who is most likely to make such distinctions. Clearly, the extensive literature on political tolerance points to a number of key correlates of political intolerance (for reviews, see Gibson, 2006b; Sullivan and Transue, 1999). Here, I focus primarily on demographic and political correlates of intolerance. In terms of demographic characteristics, gender, urban/rural status, education and religiosity are examined. Previous research has shown that men, those living in urban areas, those with more education and less religiously involved express greater political tolerance (Marcus et al., 1995; Nie et al., 1996; Stouffer, 1963). There is also an expectation that involvement in the political system is supposed to foster knowledge of the rules of democratic politics as well as facilitate the ability of individuals to apply general democratic principles to specific situations (Finkel and Ernst, 2005; Fletcher, 1990; Peffley and Rohrschneider, 2003).[19] These findings have largely been reproduced among youth samples, with the exception of gender (Sotelo, 1999, 2000).

If multicultural tolerance is, in fact, a unique tolerance disposition, then the expectation is that the traditional correlates of tolerance should help to distinguish multicultural tolerance from intolerance. Furthermore, I have argued that multicultural tolerance does not simply represent a midpoint on a scale from intolerance to tolerance, either. If multicultural tolerance reflects contemporary norms of political tolerance, then one might expect that traditional correlates of intolerance should do little to differentiate multicultural from absolute tolerance.

To test these contentions, Table 4 presents separate multinomial logistic regressions. The reference category for the analysis is multicultural tolerance, which means that the results should be read essentially as tests of the impact each independent variable has on the likelihood of intolerance or absolute tolerance compared to the reference category. The coefficient should be interpreted as providing the direction of effects.

The first contention is that traditional correlates of intolerance should distinguish multicultural tolerance from intolerance, and this appears to largely be reflected in the models presented in Table 4. As expected, the intolerant in both countries appear to be less politically knowledgeable and engaged compared to those in the multicultural tolerance category (p<.01). They are also likely to attend religious services more often compared to multicultural tolerators. Like Sotelo (1999), I find that young women have a greater probability of being tolerant of the civil liberties of some groups compared to men. There are some inter-country differences that emerge, although in each case the significant effect goes in the expected direction. In short, traditional correlates of intolerance seem to distinguish the intolerant from multicultural tolerators, despite the fact that these individuals would likely be considered intolerant based on a least-liked approach.

Perhaps more enlightening are the effects of these variables on the likelihood of absolute tolerance compared to multicultural tolerance. As mentioned previously, the alternative to a least-liked methodology is to sum the number of tolerant responses across target groups. Such an approach would make multicultural tolerance a midpoint on the scale, as respondents have provided some tolerant responses and some intolerant responses. The implication would be that multicultural tolerators should be found "between" the intolerant and absolute tolerators on many of the important correlates of intolerance. However, the results in Table 4 shed doubt on such a linear interpretation. In both the Canadian and Belgian data, fewer coefficients are significant, but more importantly, the direction of these effects are *opposite* of what would be expected from a linear view of political tolerance. At least in the Canadian case, the likelihood of absolute tolerance decreases as youth are more politically active and knowledgeable about politics. Conversely, those who display greater religiosity are more likely to fall into the absolute tolerance category. At the same time, those from Catholic and Jewish background were less likely to be in this category, compared to multicultural tolerance. Racialized minorities, as might be expected given the role of hate speech in the categorization of multicultural tolerance, were also less likely to be absolutely tolerant.

Table 4.
Political and Demographic Correlates of Tolerance

	Canada					
	Intolerance vs. Multicultural Tolerance			Absolute Tolerance vs. Multicultural Tolerance		
	Coef.	(s.e.)		Coef.	(s.e.)	
Political Knowledge Scale	-1.12	(.18)	***	-0.38	(.24)	a
Political Activism Scale	-0.22	(.03)	***	-0.12	(.05)	***
Number of Organizations	0.03	(.05)		0.15	(.07)	**
Female	-0.74	(.12)	***	0.13	(.16)	
Urban	0.03	(.23)		-0.21	(.24)	
Parent(s) University Educated?	-0.35	(.12)	***	-0.13	(.15)	
Racialized Minority	0.50	(.13)	***	-0.39	(.22)	*
Catholic	0.16	(.16)		-0.51	(.16)	***
Other Christian	0.53	(.16)	***	-0.26	(.25)	
Jewish	-0.10	(.50)		-0.54	(.31)	*
Religious Attendance	0.27	(.05)	***	0.19	(.08)	**
Constant	0.51	(.28)	*	-0.91	(.36)	**
McFadden's Pseudo R-Squared	0.066		N		2120	
Nagelkerke Pseudo R-Squared	0.160		Prob > Chi-Squ.		0.00	

	Belgium					
	Intolerance vs. Multicultural Tolerance			Absolute Tolerance vs. Multicultural Tolerance		
	Coef.	(s.e.)		Coef.	(s.e.)	
Political Knowledge Scale	-0.42	(.14)	***	-0.26	(.20)	
Political Activism Scale	-0.16	(.03)	***	0.00	(.04)	
Number of Organizations	-0.10	(.04)	***	-0.01	(.06)	
Female	-0.35	(.09)	***	-0.03	(.10)	
Urban	-0.20	(.11)	*	-0.25	(.15)	a
Parent (s) University Educated?	-0.15	(.10)		-0.05	(.13)	
Racialized Minority	0.14	(.13)		-0.42	(.22)	*
Catholic	0.00	(.09)		-0.06	(.14)	
Other Christian	0.16	(.22)		-0.06	(.37)	
Jewish	n/a			n/a		
Religious Attendance	0.17	(.05)	***	0.08	(.08)	
Constant	0.83	(.12)	***	-1.09	(.15)	***
McFadden's Pseudo R-Squared	0.022		N		3489	
Nagelkerke Pseudo R-Squared	0.049		Prob > Chi-Squ.		0.00	

Note: Multinomial logistic regressions are presented, where multicultural tolerance is the reference category, and standard errors are adjusted for clustering. The variable for Jewish has been dropped in the Belgian regression due to small subsample size. ***p<.01; **p<.05; *p<.10; ap<.15.

Source: Comparative Youth Study, 2005–2006.

In some ways, then, multicultural tolerators seem to share the democratic qualities of absolute tolerators—they are as, if not more, knowledgeable and engaged in politics—while their social backgrounds distinguish them equally well from the intolerant. Multicultural tolerators are distinct from the intolerant, despite the fact that the least-liked methodology would often categorize them as intolerant. A targeted intolerance of racist speech, then, appears fundamentally different than intolerance of other speech. This casts doubt on a linear conception of political tolerance and points instead to the benefits of examining the role that inter-target group distinctions play in understanding contemporary civil liberties judgments. Developing a measure that can capture such distinctions opens up new avenues of research into what type of people are most likely to set limits on exclusionary speech. The preliminary examination of the correlates of multicultural tolerance provides support for the view of multicultural tolerance as a unique disposition more akin to tolerance than intolerance. It also casts further doubt on the ability of conventional measures to fully capture how the next generation is making civil liberties decisions.

Balancing Rights in Multicultural Democracies

Democratic politics is a balancing act. In multicultural democracies, this balancing act sometimes brings the rights of individuals into conflict with the rights of groups. The public expression of exclusionary ideas is such an instance: individual rights to free expression must be balanced against the rights of minorities to live free from harassment and prejudice. In many advanced, industrialized democracies, there is room for the courts to decide in favour of the rights of minorities in such instances, despite the overwhelmingly absolute nature of free speech in much of the political science literature. As Horton notes, "What we need to recognize is that any inculcation of the virtue of toleration (and any coherent form of multiculturalism) must attend to questions about what it is reasonable to object to, as well as about which of those things that are objectionable should be tolerated and which should not" (1996: 37).

In contemporary democracies, one thing that most would agree is unreasonable to object to is skin colour or ethnic origin. On the other hand, it seems perfectly reasonable, and indeed desirable, to object to racial and ethnic prejudice. The normative question, for academics as well as citizens, then becomes whether to tolerate the latter, given the unreasonableness of the former. The answer to this question is contested because both responses at their core have a desire to ensure freedom and facilitate the healthy functioning of democratic politics.

While the normative implications of a more multicultural form of tolerance are beyond the scope of this article, the empirical evidence presented suggests that the study of political tolerance needs to move beyond questions of the degree of tolerance and intolerance to the ways in which people distinguish across target groups. It is clear that a substantial portion of young people do indeed favour some limits on speech in line with the legislative norms in their countries. Hate speech has a legal status as a prohibited form of speech in many countries, and the evidence presented here suggests that many young people in Canada and Belgium recognize it as such. They are in turn far less willing to permit its public expression, despite the fact that they are generally tolerant of other objectionable ideas. This distinction is at the heart of the concept of multicultural political tolerance.

While a rich research tradition exists into the correlates of political *intolerance*, an understanding of politically tolerant attitudes in multicultural democracies requires researchers to examine the nature of the limits people place on speech rights. While this article has developed a typology of tolerance dispositions based on theoretically driven distinctions between types of speech and has presented an initial test of the demographic and political correlates, future research will need to unpack the causes of such distinctions. Threat is a key variable in understanding tolerance decisions (Duch and Gibson, 1992; Gibson and Gouws, 2001; Huddy et al., 2005; Marcus et al., 1995; Stouffer, 1963; Sullivan et al., 1981). It may well be that exclusionary groups are seen as more threatening, and this is the reason for the distinctions documented across groups here. Unfortunately, there is no direct measure of threat available to test this contention in the CYS. This is an empirical question for future research and a potentially fruitful way of understanding what it is about exclusionary groups that make them particularly likely to be censored by the next generation.

In conclusion, young people can and do make distinctions across different types of speech they find offensive. Documenting such distinctions provides a better understanding of the way people balance the sometimes competing demands of individual rights and the inclusion of ethnic, racial and religious minorities in public life. As immigration continues to change the demographic realities in liberal democracies, this article has pointed to one way in which public opinion reflects support for such competing rights. In doing so, it has challenged current conceptualizations of political tolerance as an absolute democratic value and provided substantial evidence of inter-target group distinctions. The concept of multicultural tolerance developed here reflects the ways in which many young citizens set predictable limits on speech which reflect both the legal realities in Canada and Belgium and the increasing acceptance of proactive measures to combat discrimination.

Acknowledgments: The author is grateful to the principal investigators of the Comparative Youth Study, Dietlind Stolle and Marc Hooghe, for their collaboration in collecting the data used in this article. The Social Science and Humanities Research Council (SSHRC), the Fonds Québécois de la Recherche sur la Société et la Culture (FQRSC), the Fonds Wetenschappelijk Onderzoek Vlaanderen and the Bijzonder Onderzoeksfonds, K.U. Leuven provided financial support for the data collection. I would also like to thank to Elisabeth Gidengil, Stuart Soroka and two anonymous *CJPS* reviewers for useful comments provided on earlier drafts and the American Association of University Women whose financial support made this research possible.

NOTES

1. The content-neutral component of speech regulation was solidified in US Supreme Court case *R.A.V v. St. Paul* (1992), where the court overturned the conviction of individuals for setting a cross on fire on a black family's lawn because the ordinance specified specific types of speech.

2. While white supremacy groups in the US are the most common example, the presence, and some argue increase, of such groups in Canada and Europe is well documented (Fraser, 2001; Kinsella, 2001).

3. A fourth possibility, of course, is that citizens permit hate groups to express themselves but deny them to other groups. The contention here is that in contemporary, multicultural democracies, it should be far more likely that a citizen will deny civil liberties to a racist group than to another group that is not characterized by exclusionary goals. It is expected that when people do make distinctions across target groups, they are likely to make predictable distinctions in line with multicultural tolerance.

4. While I am not aware of any previous attempt to define multicultural political tolerance as developed here, a large body of theoretical work exists that problematizes the absolute nature of the concept of political tolerance and its usefulness as a guide to resolving liberal dilemmas of accommodating diversity. See, for example, Heyd (1996), Murphy (1997), Galeotti (2002), and Jones (2007).

5. Ideally, the Canadian sample would include youth from across Canada. The focus on Central Canada, however, allows for a controlled comparison between the two provinces and across cities.

6. Provincial educational statistics, when available, were combined with census tract information, statistics gathered from individual school websites and rankings from the Frasier Institute to ensure variation in terms of the ethnic and socio-economic composition of schools.

7. For detailed information about the sampling technique, see Harell et al. (2008).

8. The five groups were selected by the author to ensure the inclusion of two hate groups, and were pretested to ensure comprehension among a youth sample. "Racist" is a commonly included item in tolerance batteries, and "skinhead" was included to provide a second measure of a racist group that during pre-testing proved to be comprehensible to this age group. The other three items were included to represent similar and salient cleavages in Canada and Belgium. Muslims and homosexual groups are commonly included in tolerance batteries, and the separatist item was included to represent a politically relevant and comparable cleavage in both countries.

9. For a comparison of these two methods, see Gibson (1992).

10. Disagreement with the group means the respondent rated the group between 0 and 4 on the 0–10 disagree/agree scale.

11. While the French-speaking populations in each country report slightly lower levels of tolerance across groups, the overall pattern between target groups remains the same (results not shown).

12. Unlike lower levels of tolerance for hate groups, the lower levels of tolerance for radical Muslims in Belgium appears to reflect greater levels of xenophobia in the Belgium sample (analysis not shown).

13. The one deviation from this pattern is the skinhead group in the Belgian sample that received a slightly higher score than radical Muslims, although the difference is not statistically significant.

14. Obviously, this method is not identical to the least-liked methodology, where respondents must choose the group they dislike the most. In the CYS, respondents were allowed to give a score of 0 to as many groups as they wanted. Two, on average, were coded as such.

15. The advantage to the dyadic approach is that a true test of inter-target group distinctions requires that we limit the comparisons to individuals who express prior disagreement with each group, and the size of this group varies considerably across dyads. Factor analysis using tetrachoric correlations to account for the dichotomous nature of the five civil liberties items reveals that they do fall onto two dimensions, with racists and skinheads on one and the other three objectionable groups on the other (results not shown). However, this does not allow a control for prior disagreement, making the dyadic approach conceptually more appropriate.

16. It is also possible that citizens allow exclusionary groups speech rights but deny them to other groups. The framework developed here suggests this is highly improbable: it should be far more likely that a citizen will deny civil liberties to a racist group than to another group that is not characterized by exclusionary goals. This assertion holds empirically: once disagreement is controlled, less than 2 per cent of respondents permitted racist speech but denied them to other potentially objectionable groups. These respondents have been coded as intolerant, because they fail to extend civil liberties to objectionable groups.

17. Francophones (60 per cent) are slightly more likely to be in the multicultural tolerance category compared to Anglophones (51 per cent) in Canada.

18. Francophones show slightly higher levels of intolerance (55 per cent) and slightly lower levels of absolute tolerance (6 per cent) compared to Dutch-speakers in Belgium (49 per cent and 13 per cent respectively).

19. Psychological variables have also played an important role in explaining tolerance judgments (Sullivan and Transue, 1999). Limited measures are available for these variables in the CYS, and thus beyond the scope of the present inquiry.

REFERENCES

Billiet, Jaak and Hans De Witte. 1995. "Attitudinal Dispositions to Vote for a 'New' Extreme Right-Wing Party: The Case of 'Vlaams Blok.'" *European Journal of Political Research* 27: 181–202.

Boeckman, Robert J. and Carolyn Turpin-Petrosino. 2002. "Understanding the Harm of Hate Crime." *Journal of Social Issues* 58 (2):207–225.

Bosmajian, Haig. 1974. *The Language of Oppression*. Washington DC: Public Affairs Press.

Braun, Stefan. 2004. *Democracy Off Balance: Freedom of Expression and Hate Propaganda Law in Canada*. Toronto: University of Toronto Press.

Chong, Dennis. 2006. "Free Speech and Multiculturalism In and Out of the Academy." *Political Psychology* 27 (6): 29–54.

Cohen, Andrew Jason. 2004. "What Tolerance Is." *Ethics* 115: 68–95.

Cohen-Almagor, Raphael, ed. 2000. *Liberal Democracy and the Limits of Tolerance: Essays in Honor and Memory of Yitzhak Rabin*. Ann Arbor: University of Michigan Press.

Coliver, Sandra, Kevin Boyle and Frances D'Souza. 1992. *Striking A Balance: Hate Speech, Freedom of Expression and Non-Discrimination*. London: Article 19.

Cortese, Anthony Joseph Paul. 2006. *Opposing Hate Speech*. Westport CT: Praeger Publishers.

Davis, Darren W. 1995. "Exploring Black Political Intolerance." *Political Behavior* 17 (1): 1–22.

Douglas-Scott, Sionaidh. 1999. "The Hatefulness of Protected Speech: A Comparison of American and European Approaches." *William and Mary Bill of Rights Journal* 7: 305–46.

Duch, Raymond M. and James L. Gibson. 1992. "'Putting Up With'" Fascists in Western Europe: A Comparative, Cross-Level Analysis of Political Tolerance." *The Western Political Quarterly* 45 (1): 237–73.

Eckstein, Harry. 1975. "Case Study and Theory in Political Science." In *Handbook of Political Science*, ed. Fred I. Greenstein and Nelson W. Polsby. Reading MA: Addison-Wesley.

Finkel, Steven E. and Howard R. Ernst. 2005. "Civic Education in Post-Apartheid South Africa: Alternative Paths to the Development of Political Knowledge and Democratic Values." *Political Psychology* 26 (3): 333–64.

Fletcher, Joseph F. 1990. "Participation and Attitudes toward Civil Liberties: Is There an "Educative" Effect?" *International Political Science Review/Revue internationale de science politique* 11 (4): 439–59.

Fraser, Nicholas. 2001. *The Voice of Modern Hatred: Tracing the Rise of Neo-Fascism in Europe*. Woodstock NY: Overlook Press.

Galeotti, Anna E. 2002. *Toleration as Recognition*. New York: Cambridge University Press.

Gerber, Alan S., Donald Green and Ron Shachar. 2003. "Voting May Be Habit-Forming: Evidence from a Randomized Field Experiment." *American Journal of Political Science* 47 (3): 540–50.

Gibson, James L. 1992. "Alternative Measures of Political Tolerance: Must Tolerance be 'Least-Liked'" *American Journal of Political Science* 36 (2): 560–577.

Gibson, James L. 1998. "A Sober Second Thought: An Experiment in Persuading Russians to Tolerate." *American Journal of Political Science* 42 (3): 819–50.

Gibson, James L. 2006a. "Do Strong Group Identities Fuel Intolerance? Evidence from the South African Case." *Political Psychology* 27 (5): 665–706.

Gibson, James L. 2006b. "Enigmas of Intolerance: Fifty Years after Stouffer's *Communism, Conformity, and Civil Liberties*." *Perspectives on Politics* 4: 21–34.

Gibson, James L. and Richard D. Bingham. 1985. *Civil Liberties and Nazis: The Skokie Free-Speech Controversy*: Westport CT: Praeger.

Gibson, James L. and Amanda Gouws. 2001. "Making Tolerance Judgments: The Effects of Context, Local and National." *Journal of Politics* 63 (4): 1067–90.

Greenberg, Jeff and Tom Pyszczynski. 1985. "The Effect of an Overheard Slur on Evaluations of the Target: How to Spread a Social Disease." *Journal of Experimental Social Psychology* 21: 61–72.

Gross, Kimberly A. and Donald R. Kinder. 1998. "A Collision of Principles? Free Expression, Racial Equality and the Prohibition of Racist Speech." *British Journal of Political Science* 28 (3): 445–71.

Harel, Alon. 1996. "The Boundaries of Justifiable Tolerance: A Liberal Perspective." In *Toleration: An Elusive Virtue*, ed. David Heyd. Princeton: Princeton University Press.

Harell, Allison. 2008. "The Micro-Story of Multiculturalism: Diverse Social Networks and the Socialization of Tolerance." Doctoral dissertation. McGill University, Montreal, Quebec.

Harell, Allison, Valerie-Anne Mahéo and Dietlind Stolle. 2008. "Canadian Youth Study (CANYS), Wave 1: Technical Report and Codebook." Montreal, QC: McGill University.

Heyd, David. 1996. *Toleration: An Elusive Virtue*. Princeton: Princeton University Press.

Hooghe, Marc. 2004. "Political Socialization and the Future of Politics." *Acta Politica* 39 (4): 331–41.

Horton, John. 1996. "Toleration as a Virtue." In *Toleration: An Elusive Virtue*, ed. David Heyd. Princeton: Princeton University Press.

Horton, John and Peter Nicholson, eds. 1992. *Toleration: Philosophy and Practice*. London: Ashgate Publishing.

Huddy, Leonie, Stanley Feldman, Charles Taber and Gallya Lahav. 2005. "Threat, Anxiety and Support of Antiterrorist Policies." *American Journal of Political Science* 49 (3): 595–608.

Inglehart, Ronald. 1997. *Modernization and Postmodernization: Cultural, Economic and Political Change in 43 Countries*. Princeton: Princeton University Press.

Jones, Peter. 2007. "Making Sense of Political Toleration." *British Journal of Political Science* 37: 383–402.

Kinsella, Warren. 2001. *Web of Hate: Inside Canada's Far Right Network*. Toronto: HarperCollins.

Kirkland, Shari L., Jeff Greenberg and Tom Pyszczynski. 1987. "Further Evidence of the Deleterious Effects of Overheard Ethnic Slurs: Derogation beyond the Target." *Personality and Social Psychology Bulletin* 13: 216–227.

Kymlicka, Will. 1995. *Multicultural Citizenship: A Liberal Theory of Minority Rights*. Oxford: Clarendon Press.

Kymlicka, Will. 2001. *Politics in the Vernacular: Nationalism, Multiculturalism, and Citizenship*. Oxford: Oxford University Press.

Lambe, Jennifer. 2004. "Who Wants to Censor Pornography and Hate Speech." *Mass Communication and Society* 7 (3): 279–99.

Marcus, George E., John L. Sullivan, Elizabeth Theiss-Morse and Sandra L. Wood. 1995. *With Malice Toward Some: How People Make Civil Liberties Judgments*. Cambridge: Cambridge University Press.

Marcuse, Herbert. 1969. "Repressive Tolerance." In *A Critique of Pure Tolerance*, ed. Robert Paul Wolff, Barrington Moore and Herbert Marcuse. Boston: Beacon Press.

Marquart-Pryatt, Sandra and Pamela Paxton. 2006. "In Principle and In Practice: Learning Political Tolerance in Eastern and Western Europe." *Political Behavior* 29 (1): 89–113.

Matsuda, Mari J. 1993. "Public Response to Racist Speech: Considering the Victim's Story." In *Words That Wound: Critical Race Theory, Assaultive Speech, and the First Amendment*, ed. Mari J. Matsuda, Charles R. Lawrence III, Richard Delgado and Kimberlè Williams Crenshaw. Boulder CO: Westview Press.

McKinnon, Catriona. 2003. "Toleration and the Character of Pluralism." In *The Culture of Toleration in Diverse Societies*, ed. Catriona McKinnon and Dario Castiglione. New York: Manchester University Press.

Mendus, Susan, ed. 1988. *Justifying Toleration: Conceptual and Historical Perspectives*. Cambridge: Cambridge University Press.

Mendus, Susan. 1989. *Toleration and the Limits of Liberalism*. Atlantic Highlands NJ: Humanities Press International.

Mondak, Jeffery J. and Jon Hurwitz. 1998. "Values, Acts, and Actors: Distinguishing Generic and Discriminatory Intolerance." *Political Behavior* 20 (4): 313–39.

Mondak, Jeffery J. and Mitchell S. Sanders. 2003. "Tolerance and Intolerance, 1976–1998." *American Journal of Political Science* 47 (3): 492–502.

Mullen, Brian. 2001. "Ethnophaulisms for Ethnic Immigrant Groups." *Journal of Social Issues* 57 (3): 457–75.

Murphy, Andrew R. 1997. "Tolerance, Toleration, and the Liberal Tradition." *Polity* 29: 593–623.

Mutz, Diana. 2002. "Cross-Cutting Social Networks: Testing Democratic Theory in Practice." *American Political Science Review* 96 (1): 111–26.

Nelson, Thomas, Rosalee Clawson and Zoe Oxley. 1997. "Media Framing of Civil Liberties Conflict and Its Effect on Tolerance." *American Political Science Review* 91 (3): 567–83.

Nevitte, Neil. 1996. *The Decline of Deference: Canadian Value Change in Cross-National Perspective*. Peterborough: Broadview Press.

Nie, Norman H., Jane Junn and Kenneth Stehlik-Barry. 1996. *Education and Democratic Citizenship in America*. Chicago: University of Chicago Press.

O'Donnell, John P. 1993. "Predicting Tolerance of New Religious Movements: A Multivariate Analysis." *Journal for the Scientific Study of Religion* 32 (4): 356–65.

Peffley, Mark, Pia Knigge and Jon Hurwitz. 2001. "A Multiple Values Model of Political Tolerance." *Political Research Quarterly* 54 (2): 379–406.

Peffley, Mark and Robert Rohrschneider. 2003. "Democratization and Political Tolerance in Seventeen Countries: A Multi-Level Model of Democratic Learning." *Political Research Quarterly* 56 (3): 243–57.

Plutzer, E. 2002. "Becoming a Habitual Voter: Inertia, Resources, and Growth in Young Adulthood." *American Political Science Review* 96 (1): 41–56.

Simon, L. and Jeff Greenberg. 1996. "Further Progress in Understanding the Effects of Derogatory Ethnic Labels: The Role of Preexisting Attitudes Toward the Targeted Group." *Personality and Social Psychology Bulletin* 22 (12): 1195–1204.

Sniderman, Paul M., Joseph F. Fletcher, Peter H. Russell and Philip Tetlock. 1996. *The Clash of Rights: Liberty, Equality, and Legitimacy in Pluralist Democracy.* New Haven CT: Yale University Press.

Sotelo, Maria Jose. 1999. "Gender Differences in Political Tolerance among Adolescents." *Journal of Gender Studies* 8 (2): 211–17.

Sotelo, Maria Jose. 2000. "Individual Differences in Political Tolerance Among Adolescents." *Social Behavior and Personality* 28 (2): 185–92.

Stolle, Dietlind and Marc Hooghe. 2006. "Comparative Youth Survey: First Wave." McGill/Leuven.

Stouffer, Samuel Andrew. 1963. *Communism, Conformity, and Civil Liberties: A Cross-Section of the Nation Speaks Its Mind.* Gloucester MA: P. Smith.

Sullivan, John L., George E. Marcus, Stanley Feldman and James E. Piereson. 1981. "The Sources of Political Tolerance: A Multivariate Analysis." *The American Political Science Review* 75 (1): 92–106.

Sullivan, John L., James E. Piereson and George E. Marcus. 1979. "An Alternative Conceptualization of Political Tolerance." *American Political Science Review* 73 (3): 781–94.

Sullivan, John L., James E. Piereson and George E. Marcus. 1982. *Political Tolerance and American Democracy.* Chicago: University of Chicago Press.

Sullivan, John L., Michal Shamir, Pat Walsh and N.S. Roberts. 1985. *Political Tolerance in Context.* Boulder CO: Westview.

Sullivan, John L. and John E. Transue. 1999. "The Psychological Underpinnings of Democracy: A Selective Review of Research on Political Tolerance, Interpersonal Trust, and Social Capital." *Annual Review of Psychology* 50: 625–50.

Sumner, L.W. 2004. *The Hateful and the Obscene: Studies in the Limits of Free Expression.* Toronto: University of Toronto Press.

Tsesis, Alexander. 2002. *Destructive Messages: How Hate Speech Paves the Way for Harmful Social Movements.* New York: New York University Press.

Walzer, Michael. 1997. *On Toleration* .New Haven: Yale University Press.

Weissberg, Robert. 1998. *Political Tolerance: Balancing Community and Diversity.* Thousand Oaks CA: Sage Publications.

Wilkes, Rima, Neil Guppy and Lily Farris. 2008. "'No Thanks, We're Full': Individual Characteristics, National Context, and Changing Attitudes toward Immigration." *International Migration Review* 42 (2): 203–329.

Young, Iris Marion. 1990. *Justice and the Politics of Difference.* Princeton: Princeton University Press.

***Allison Harrell** is regular professor in the Department of Political Science at the University of Quebec in Montreal, Canada.

Harrell, Allison. "The Limits of Tolerance in Diverse Societies: Hate Speech and Political Tolerance Norms Among Youth." *Canadian Journal of Political Science* 43, no. 2 (2010): 407–432.

Right-Wing Extremist Perpetrators from an International Perspective

by Heléne Lööw*

Waves of violence directed against foreigners have repeatedly swept across Europe in the post-war era. In the late 1950s and early 1960s, they included anti-Semitic graffiti and the desecration of Jewish cemeteries, starting with the defacement of a Cologne synagogue in December of 1959. The violence spread to the U.S., Latin America, Australia and Africa, and when this wave ended in February and March of 1960, over 2,500 anti-Semitic incidents had been reported from more than 400 places around the world (Bachner 1999, 137). France experienced waves of anti-foreign violence in 1961, 1973 and 1982, and again in the late 1980s, as did the Netherlands in the 1970s and early 1980s (Merkl 1995). Another wave of violence, now directed against immigrants, refugees, and refugee camps, swept over parts of Europe (including Germany and Sweden) during the late 1980s and early 1990s.

The issue of violence that is motivated by various forms of intolerance has received increasing attention from politicians, government officials, the media, and the scientific community, or in other words from society as a whole. Research has tended to focus on the perpetrators, public responses (the legal, social, political and preventative strategies used), and support for racist, xenophobic, anti-Semitic, islamophobic, homophobic and other intolerant ideas among the general population. However, in recent years more and more attention has been paid to the victims of various forms of hate crimes, to the process involved in leaving a right-wing extremist or racist milieu, and to a lesser extent, the issue of how various forms of intolerant ideas and attitudes are transmitted from one generation to the next, and transformed in the process.

The main focus here is on the perpetrators of hate crimes. They fall into two categories: perpetrators with a background in various racist organizations (or who sympathize with such organizations), and perpetrators who lack such background (at least with respect to the role ideology plays in their willingness to commit hate crimes). It will also address how ideas are transmitted from one generation to the next.

Hate Crime Violence . . .

The victims of hate crimes range from asylum seekers and foreigners to political opponents, members of ethnic and religious minorities, and homosexuals (Schmid and Storni 2007)—multiple targets of hostility and violence exist. While interest during the 1990s mainly focused on violence and hostility directed against asylum seekers and refugees, what victims have in common is that perpetrators define them as "enemies," whether of the "nation" or the "race," as enemies of "native ethnic and cultural homogeneity," or, as in the case of homosexuals, as "foes of morality."

When it comes to perpetrators with backgrounds in organized groups or from loose networks of the kind found in the racist underground—which itself harbors groups ranging from national socialist parties to Christian Identity groups, and even occult groups that promote racist ideologies—the violence needs to be divided into two major categories. One is violence directed against groups, or individuals, who belong to those who are defined as "enemies." The other is violence directed against representatives of the "system," which may include government officials, politicians, anti-racists, or journalists. These alleged "representatives" are targeted because they are seen as part of a "system" that, according to activists, is "run by the Jews" or is part what they call "the Zionist Occupation Government" (ZOG).

The notion that ZOG exists is shared by most European and American White Power groups. The Israeli researcher Ehud Sprinzak writes: "For European right-wingers just as for their American colleagues, it was an appealing post-communist answer to their quest for demons. The communist 'evil empire,' which had long haunted the extreme right and served as its great satanic enemy, may be gone, but the real demonic people, the Jews, were still around" (Sprinzak 1995). An example of crimes directed against individuals regarded as ZOG representatives was provided by the wave of violence that swept through Sweden in 1999, including a car bombing (injuring an investigative reporter and his son in Nacka, near Stockholm[1]), the murder of two police officers by a group of activists during a bank robbery outside the small town of Malexander, and the murder of the syndicalist trade union activist Björn Söderberg.

In a statement issued after the murder of the two police officers, the more radical parts of the racist underground stated that:

> "Those who died were not fathers, they were no one's children, and they were not innocent. They had made their choice, just as the ones who walked into the bank in Kisa. They took on the uniform of the state, in order to uphold that same state's criminal laws. They took orders from a

Jew [referring to the then-head of the Swedish police] and arrest Swedish youngsters who are of an independent mind. People who do this shall receive no mercy. There were no innocents that died; it was police officers, officers who had chosen to fight against their own people" (Lööw 2000, 479).

The individuals who engaged in this series of violent acts did so largely for ideological reasons. A number of them had no previous criminal records; most of those involved in killing Björn Söderberg, for example, had no known background in raceideological organizations. Once arrested, they refused to talk to the police. They had maintained a low profile before the murder in order to not draw attention to themselves (Lööw 2000, 479 ff.).

The same is true of a splinter group of the Swedish National Socialist Front Party that began their "war against a society run by ZOG" in 2004 by planning a series of sabotage acts they believed would lead to a "racial holy war." These activists were the first in Sweden to be prosecuted under anti-terrorist laws passed after 9/11, and the leading members of the group saw themselves as "prisoners of war," and as a result gave only their names and social security numbers to the police.

Members of this group were not convicted for acts of terrorism but for acts of vandalism instead. Their sentences did not change their attitudes. One said he hoped a full-scale war would break out in 10–20 years, and hoped he would be able to fight that war, if he was not already dead by then. Another of the leading members, a 31-year-old father of two children, said his prison sentence had strengthened him in his belief that society must be destroyed by force. His time in prison had only strengthened him: "Now I have the patience and will not let things happen as fast as they did two years ago. We lost the first battle, but it only made us stronger, and the most important thing, after all, is to win the war" (Sandelin 2007, part I).

The Order, an American white supremacist group active in 1983 and 1984, provided the model, ideology, and heroes for racist activists in Sweden and elsewhere and still has a tremendous influence on the tactics used. In 2007, an international campaign for imprisoned members of the Order was launched by racist activists around the world.[2]

The Order was founded in 1983 by Robert Jay Mathews, and soon thereafter started its "War against ZOG." In the autumn of 1984, more than 75 individuals with connections to The Order were arrested. Thirty of them were charged with murder, arson, armed robbery and conspiracy. Mathews managed to break free of his captors by opening fire, and escaped, along with other members of his group, to a farm on Whidbey Island outside of Seattle. On the morning of December 7, 1984, the FBI surrounded the farm; the battle ended 36 hours later when the farm was firebombed, killing Mathews (Flynn and Gerhardt 1989). Remaining members of The Order, in particular David Lane, carried on the legacy. Until his death in 2007, Lane was one of the most influential ideologists of the racist underground.

HATE CRIMES AMONG ADOLESCENTS

The recent study conducted by Martin Schmid and Marco Storni of adolescents living in and around Basel, Switzerland, found that 10.8% had experienced either right-wing extremist violence or had been threatened by right-wing extremist youths on at least one occasion between 2000 and 2005. Almost a third of them were victimized owing to supposed or real differences in political attitude, nationality or ethnic background. Other violent conflicts that study identified were embedded within juvenile subcultures, and here victims did not belong, as a rule, to any group especially targeted by the extreme right (Schmid and Storni 2007).

The findings from this study correspond with the results of a Swedish study conducted by the National Council for Crime Prevention and the Living History Forum. The main questions in the Swedish survey focused on anti-Semitic, homophobic, Islamophobic and anti-immigrant tendencies among youths, including their exposure to abuse or participation in abuse, and the social and psychosocial characteristics of tolerant and intolerant youth.

The survey was national, with 10,600 students completing the questionnaire. It found that verbal insults were the most common form of victimization, with 40% of foreign-born students teased at some point as a result of their origins, 6.6% of students of immigrant background reported they had been physically abused during the previous year as a result of their nationality origins, and 15% reported being threatened. Students who experienced victimization reported they had recently experienced negative feelings, or felt depressed, angry, anxious, or had difficulties sleeping; these symptoms were reported more often than among those who did not report any victimization (Ring and Morgentau 2005).

This Swedish study did not, as in the Swiss study, address the issue of what strategies victims used to deal with the verbal or physical abuse or its long term consequences. These questions have been addressed in several studies by the Swedish criminologist Eva Tiby, however, with respect to the victims of homophobic hate crimes. In one study, she found that most victims reported psychological problems that were related to abuse, and had suffered serious fear. Because individuals were attacked for their identity, the abuse they suffered led to more damaging psychological effects than was the case for the victims of other categories of violent abuse (Tiby 1999).

This is the case among all victims of hate crimes. It is an individual's religion, ethnic or nationality background, or other characteristic that defines them as "the enemy" in the eyes of the perpetrator(s). Racist ideology is based on a belief that certain people do not 'belong' in the community, and are by definition outsiders who should treated accordingly. Therefore, terrorizing groups or individuals thought to belong to a particular group considered to be inferior is a means for exerting control.

That may be a reason why most perpetrators never try to apologize for their brutal acts, or why so few explanatory ideologies exist in this cultural milieu. Acts deem reasonable and natural do not, in the eyes of the perpetrators, require justification (Sprinzak 1995). Instead, explanatory ideology is reserved for "the war against ZOG" rather to justify acts of violence directed against groups or individuals considered inferior. As the raceideological Swedish magazine *Storm* put it in 1993, "To eliminate an enemy of our people or of the nation is moral, humane and responsible, and is something based in our natural instincts. We hate everyone who wishes to harm, and hate leads to action and revenge. All according to the laws of nature."[3]

The activist interpretation of reality makes the idea of ZOG into something more than just ideology. The activist can no longer distinguish between the state and "the other," which includes Jews, Africans, homosexuals, or other despised groups. It's all mixed together in a world of secret conspiracies, and activists tend to withdraw from society both mentally and physically—a society they literally see as demonic. To strike against ZOG's different faces, in the eyes of activists, is to fight "the devil himself" (Lööw 2000, 306).

THE PERPETRATORS

But who are the perpetrators? In a study of the first generation of perpetrators of anti-foreigner violence in Germany in early 1990s, the German researcher Helmut Willems divided them into four categories: right-wing extremist activists, ethnocentric youth, criminal youth, and fellow travelers.

Perpetrators who belong to the first category have a strong right-wing ideology and identity, and a politically motivated and legitimate—in their eyes—

willingness to resort to violence (e.g., instrumental violence). They have prior police records for political crimes, which are often multiple, and typically come from the lower and middle class. Even so, they typically have no family, private problems or problems on the job, and while their educational level may only be low or middling, they have often been successfully trained for jobs and have low unemployment.

In the case of ethnocentric youths, perpetrators are typically strongly hostile toward foreigners and agree in part with right-wing ideology and slogans. They have a propensity to use violence as an expression of sub-cultural values and as means to provoke (e.g., expressive and hedonistic violence). They, too, have prior police records for juvenile crimes, and typically come from the lower middle class. However, they also tend to come from problem families, and may have had some private or job-related problems. Their educational level is often low, and they may be somewhat unsuccessful in employment, both in terms of unsuccessful job training and in having higher rates of unemployment.

Perpetrators who belong to the category of criminal youth partly agree with right-wing ideology and slogans and partly hold racist or ethnocentric attitudes and beliefs. For them, violence is seen as a normal, everyday means to deal with conflicts (e.g., it does not need legitimizing). They have long police records and show criminal career patterns. They are typically lower class, and have numerous family, private, and job problems, as well as deficits in socialization. They are unsuccessful in school—often dropouts or without diplomas—and frequently have had no job training, leaving them with high and recurring unemployment rates.

Finally, among the 'fellow travelers'—a term associated in the past with those who sympathized with the left, and with Communism in particular—one finds no right-wing ideology, or firm racist or ethnocentristic attitudes. On the other hand, they may engage in violent behavior as a result of group dynamics or peer pressure (e.g., there is no general propensity for violence). Those in this category have no prior police record, and typically do not come from problem families or have private or job problems. Often from the lower and middle class, they have low and middling levels of education, and tend to be successful in the labor market, meaning they have low levels of unemployment and have successfully completed job training (Willems 1995). Similar patterns could be found among the first generation of perpetrators of anti-foreigner violence in Sweden in the early 1990s. A survey of the motives behind attacks on refugee camps in Sweden in 1988–1992, based on court verdicts and police interrogations, points to three main motives behind the crimes.

First, there are the "private" motives. That is, the offender claims that he or persons close to him have been robbed by refugees from the local refugee hostel, or that "the refugees behave badly," or that they "insult us Swedes" or "laugh at us."

The second are "frustration and protest" motives. Here, a perpetrator claims he was to "put the refugee question on the political agenda" or "make people wake up." Sometimes perpetrators claim that attacking a refugee hostel is the only remaining way to protest, because "the politicians" are not listening to them. In other cases offenders see themselves as local heroes, claiming "everyone in the village thinks like us, but no one except us dares to do anything about the refugees." In some cases, perpetrators may indeed have received passive support and understanding from some parts of the local population. The third are "hate and dislike" motives. The perpetrators in this category simply say they "hate the bastards" (Lööw 1995).

The Swedish hate crime statistics from 2005 indicate the following about suspects:

Table I. Age and motive of Suspects in anti-immigrant, anti-semitic, homophobic and racially-motivated crimes, 2005[4]

Motive	Age							
	Under 14	15–17	18–24	25–39	40+	totals	of these racist	perpetrator average age
Anti-immigrant	35	132	162	154	272	755	49	34
Anti-Semitic	4	–	4	3	3	14	3	27
Homophobic	25	53	58	42	27	205	25	25
Raceidological	23	62	52	21	10	168	168	21
Totals	87	247	276	220	312	1142		

82% of the suspects were male and 18% female.[5] The statistics reveal that anti-immigrant, anti-Semitic, homophobic and hate crimes related to racist motives are by no means limited to youngsters: perpetrators come from all age groups, with an average of 34 among those who commit crimes with an anti-immigrant motive.

A similar pattern was found in a 2004 study of the 367 perpetrators of homophobic hate crimes in Sweden. Of the 333 cases (90% of 367) in which the suspect's age was known, the breakdown was as follows:

Table 2. Age of suspects

Under 15	23%
15–20	29%
21–30	17%
31–40	12%
41–50	11%
51–60	7%
Over 60	1%

In 306 (83% of 367) cases, there is information about the relationship between perpetrator and victim, and in approximately half of these, the perpetrator is unknown to the victim. This result is quite similar to Schmid and Storni's (2007) Swiss findings that 57.8% of the victims did not know their aggressors. Among the other half, however, the relationship consisted of school friends (16%), acquaintances (14%), neighbors (8%), client or company (7%), ex-partners (4%), teacher or pupil (3%), and colleagues at work (1%). Over half of the perpetrators are under 20, and 80% of the perpetrators and the victims are male (Tiby and Sörberg 2006, 17).

Thus, both the more general statistics for 2005 and the homophobic hate crime statistics from 2004 indicate that these types of crimes are by no means limited to youngsters. Still, are perpetrators really any different from common criminals? They are in terms of the motives for the crimes—but maybe not in other aspects. Swedish crime statistics for 2006 show that 21% of the criminals convicted were aged between 15 and 20, yet adolescents form only 10% of the total population. In the general crime statistics, 18% are committed by women. So in terms of age and gender, those who commit hate crimes fit well into the general pattern of perpetrators: the differences lie in the motives behind the crimes, the selection of the victims and occasionally, as has been true for a number of murders of male homosexuals, in the extreme violence used.

The study of Swedish youth noted above also addressed the issue of young perpetrators, of whom 1.5% reported having hit someone because of their foreign background. These youths were also asked whether they had committed any of a number of acts against someone as "a result of their foreign origins, religion or skin colour," frozen someone out, spread lies about or bad-mouthed, started a fight with or shoved someone, or destroyed something. A total of 13% reported having committed one of these acts during the previous twelve months. The study also showed a clear correlation between intolerance and participation in anti-social behavior. The higher the level of intolerance, the more common it was to have teased, threatened or hit someone (Ring and Morgentau 2005).

VICTIM ONE DAY—PERPETRATOR THE NEXT?

On the one hand, as Schmid and Storni point out, measures to help the victim should be strengthened. On the other hand, extreme nationalists, and members or sympathizers of the raceideological subculture, are themselves subjected to abuse and violence, which society as a whole tends to ignore. Dead members of the militant raceideological underground do not—or at least not in Sweden and probably not in most countries—create public outcry or lead to public demonstrations. This neglect and readiness look the other way generates further radicalization, in the end leading to still more violence. It can function as a recruiting factor for various right-wing groups (Lööw 2000). Ignorance and trivialization of both categories of victims will encourage a further polarization of youth subcultures and result in still more violence. The conflicts—often violent—between a militant racist underground and an equally militant anti-racist underground, [are] a phenomenon that can be observed in a number of European countries.

The absence of genuine borders in Europe anymore also means racist and anti-racist activists alike travel freely to take part in confrontations that almost routinely occur during larger demonstrations or commemorations extreme nationalists or the militant raceideological underground organize. These kinds of clashes between militants of both political extremes have been going on since the mid-1980s, and by the early 1990s took the form of clashes between underground racist right-wing groups and anti-fascist, left-wing, activists. These conflicts tend to follow a cyclical pattern, with periods of relative calm followed by periods in intense conflict.

The violence started to escalate again in 2000 in Sweden. That August, a member of the Blood & Honor group was shot in Klippan but survived. A Molotov cocktail was thrown at an apartment where another activist lived, but missed, hitting a flat that belonged to an immigrant family (Lööw 2000). The violence has continued to escalate since, with serious incidents in 2007 as well. Both racist groups and the militant anti-fascists fill their homepages on the Web with ongoing reports "from the battlefield."[6] Neither subculture wants to involve the police, and in many cases such conflict festers in local communities without the wider public being aware of it—not just in Sweden but in a number of other European countries as well.

EXITING THE SCENE

When it comes to prevention, a key question what motivates individuals to enter or exit the right-wing extremist scene. Kassis et al. (in this volume)

have pointed to six factors that contribute to the motivation to leave:
- The right-wing extremist scene as a dysfunctional system
- Positive contact experiences with "outsiders" or "foreigners" under certain conditions
- A lack of effectiveness regarding political/ideological ambitions
- Over-saturation because needs are lived out
- Burnout
- Criminal procedure that are perceived to be a strain

They also point to two other influences on the motivation to exit: personal influences (developmental tasks that are achieved, identity-creating capital such as hobbies, talents, and success experiences) and the social influences (such as clique type, position in the clique, peer networks, family, and so forth) that strengthen or weaken the effectiveness of the factors listed above.

Their findings correspond with similar studies conducted in other countries (Björgo 1997), but such studies do raise some questions. In leaving the right-wing extremist scene, do activists also abandon its values and ideas in the process? Or do they maintain their beliefs even if they no longer act them out? Some undoubtedly do so, while others don't, or they might even return at a later stage, in some form, to the extremist scene. There is very little research that has been done over longer time periods, say 10 or 15 years, both about those who leave the scene and those who re-enter it. Perhaps they slip back into society, or enter a different extremist scene, or become members of a criminal subculture. In my own research, I have noticed individuals who float in and out of the scene. There are those who re-enter the scene, sometimes decades after they left, and perhaps not at the violent street level but in other capacities, and there are those who appear to have left but in reality never do. Questions as to why or why at a particular point in time remain to be answered.

XENOPHOBIA AND THE QUESTION OF INHERITANCE AND FAMILY STRUCTURE

As Mäder et al. have pointed out (in this volume), xenophobia has been generally seen as a youth phenomenon, at least in Western Europe. But xenophobia and other forms of intolerance are by no means limited to the young, which raises some important questions about the interaction between youths and adults and how extremist ideas are transmitted from generation to generation. A number of studies indicate that various forms of intolerance are found to varying degrees in the population as a whole.

The statistics also show that hate crimes are by no means a youth phenomena. A recent study of anti-Semitism in Sweden (Bachner and Ring 2006) pointed out that the correlation between anti-Semitism and age is relatively weak, but also that attitudes vary by age. There are fewer in the oldest age category who reject prejudice against Jews, and the share that are ambivalent or systematically anti-Semitic is also somewhat higher in this age group than in younger age groups.

Xenophobia and other forms of intolerance are a concern for the population as a whole. True, violent behavior is often found among the young, but they in turn interact with their adult surroundings. As Husbands puts it, "There are some older and more middle-class racists who do not attack black people on the streets or in their homes, even if they might have done so had they been younger and not middle-class. However, they may not be above making malicious and anonymous reports to child protection agencies or environmental health services about purported child abuse infractions of health regulations either by individual black households or perhaps by ethnically-owned restaurants" (Husbands 1993). This type of harassment is harder to investigate than actual physical attacks, but points to the possibility that different age groups or social groups choose different methods to express similar distastes. The young perpetrator who attacks someone in the street because he dislikes the victims' religious or ethnic background, or sexual orientation, is not necessarily any more hostile than the older man or woman who sends anonymous notes to various authorities commenting about their immigrant or homosexual neighbor.

It is of equal importance on another level to—as noted in the study by Gabriel (in this volume)—to ask why some young people are susceptible to xenophobic ideologies and engage in violence, while others who live under similar conditions do not. Gabriel's study points out that intolerant values are found among the parents, grandparents, and other individuals close to the respective adolescents, and they are also found in the immediate cultural environment.

This pattern corresponds with research findings for Sweden and Norway. In the Swedish raceideological subculture, the older generation of activists has very high status among the young, and since the 1990s, more and more of them have become active again. One of these members of the old generation, a former Waffen SS volunteer, explained why he had chosen to associate himself with the new generation of racists: "We are not ordinary people. When you have done what I have done and seen what I have seen, you never become ordinary again, and that is why I'm here, because the boys are like we were. They are us and we are them, we are the same kind of people." Some activists are even literally the children or grandchildren of the older generation of activists. To belong to a family with a long history of activism gives an individual a high status within a group, but also raises the expectations placed on them. Members of the old national socialist parties have played an important role for at least some modern activists in how, when, and why they became politically active (Lööw 1995). Gabriel's study also pointed to the violence factor, the disregard for others and the search for recognition, as well as the search for experience, visibility and difference.

The aforementioned Swedish youth study also noted that high levels of intolerance tend to be associated with

- Low levels of educational achievement and social class among parents
- Certain individual level and emotional factors such as restlessness, aggressiveness, and a lack of empathy (but not nervous problems)
- Poor school performance and adjustment to school
- Certain types of problematic family situations such as low levels of parental knowledge as to the youth's socialization patterns
- Stereotypical gender norms (male chauvinist attitudes)
- Feelings of social alienation
- Higher than average association with a few older friends

These findings does not exclude the possibility that the xenophobic and racist underground culture may for various reasons exercise such a strong attraction for others, who do not suffer from problems of this kind, that they are drawn towards it.

The results of the findings from the Swiss projects correspond with findings from other countries and contribute to the understanding both of the victims and of the perpetrators of hate crimes. There may be national differences, but the issue of intolerance, of violence, and of growing conflicts between various militant subcultures is a European problem much as the historical inheritance of intolerant ideas such as anti-Semitism or racism is a part of the history of Western civilization.

Notes

1. The case is still unsolved.

2. http://www.freetheorder.org/.

3. En annan syn på saken, Storm 9-10/1993, 2.

4. The term racist or white power motives is used in the statistics for crimes with a clearer and more systematic ideological background.

5. Brå 2006.

6. RF ledare konfronterad och förnedras, 2006-09-10, www.info14.com/inrikes. för andra konfrontationer se RF-ledare neutraliserad vid angrepp, 2007-01-11, www.info14.com/inrikes.

REFERENCES

Bachner, H. 1999 Återkomsten, antisemitism i Sverige efter 1945, Uddevalla: Natur och kultur.

Bachner, H, and Ring, J. 2006 Antisemitiska attityder och föreställningar I Sverige, The National Council for Crime Prevention and the Living History Forum.

Björgo, T. 1997 Patterns, Perpetrators and Response, Oslo: Tano.

Brå. (National council for crime prevention) 2006 Hatbrott 2005 'en sammanställning av polisanmälningar med främlingsfientliga, antisemitiska, homofobiska och vit makt ideologiska motiv,' Webbrapport 3, www.bra.se.

Flynn, K. and Gerhardt, G. 1989 The Silent Brotherhood; Inside America's racist underground, New York: McMillan.

Husbands, C.T. 1993 'Racism and Racist violence: Some Theories and Political Perspectives,' in T. Björgo and R. Witte (eds.) Racist Violence in Europe, Basingstoke: Macmillan.

Lööw, H. 1995 'Racist Violence and Criminal Behaviour in Sweden: Myths and Reality,' in T. Björgo (ed.) Terror from the Extreme Right, London: Frank Cass, pp. 119–161.

Lööw, H. 2000 Nazismen i Sverige 1980—1997, 2nd Edition, Stockholm: Ordfront [first published in 1998].

Merkl, P.H. 1995 'Radical Right Parties in Europe and Anti-Foreign Violence: A Comparative Essay,' in T. Bjorgo (ed.) Terror from the Extreme Right, London: Frank Cass, pp. 96–118.

Ring, J. and Morgentau, S. 2005 Anti-Semitic, Homophobic, Islamophobic and Xenophobic tendencies among the young, Stockholm: The National Council for Crime Prevention and the Living History Forum.

Sandelin, M. 2007 Extremister; en berättelse om politiska våldsverkare i Sverige, Stockholm: bokförlaget DN.

Sprinzak, E. 1995 'Right-wing Terrorism in Comparative Perspective: The Case of Split Delegitimation,' in T. Björgo (ed.) Terror from the Extreme Right, London: Frank Cass, pp. 17–43

Schmid, M. and Storni, M. [Year] Youth victims of right-wing extremist violence. A survey of victims in the northwestern part of Swi tzerland.

Tiby, E. and Sörberg, A.-M. 2006 En studie av homofobiska hatbrott i Sverige, Stockholm: The Living History Forum.

Tiby, E. 1999 Hatbrott? Homosexuella kvinnors och mäns utsatthet för brott, Thesis, University of Stockholm.

Willems, H. 1995 'Development, Patterns and Causes of violence against Foreigners in Germany. Social and Biographical Characteristics of Perpetrators and the Process of Escalation,' in T. Björgo (ed.) Terror from the Extreme Right, London: Frank Cass, pp, 162–181.

*Heléne Lööw is researcher in the Department of History at Uppsala University in Sweden.

Lööw, Heléne. "Right-Wing Extremist Perpetrators from an International Perspective." In Right-Wing Extremism in Switzerland: National and International Perspectives, edited by Marcel Alexander Niggli, 170–180. Baden-Baden: Nomos, 2009.

Aggressive Youth Cultures and Hate Crime: Skinheads and Xenophobic Youth in Germany

by Meredith W. Watts*

Contemporary bias crime in Germany increased dramatically after unification and remained at a relatively high, though fluctuating, level for the decade. Right-wing skinheads and neo-Nazis played a significant role in the violence, but at least one third of the violent incidents came from informal groups of young males who were not affiliated. This represents a shift in anti-Semitic and antiforeigner violence from the 1980s and earlier, when the perpetrators were likely to be older and affiliated with identifiable ideological groups. Contemporary xenophobia is not only linked to aggressive elements of youth culture but appears to be increasingly connected to local and international ideological networks. Electronic media such as the Internet have given both the political and commercial entities of skinhead and right-wing culture a means of support and growth.

Xenophobic aggression in postunification Germany is not identical with what is called hate crime or hate violence in the United States, nor are the official data kept by the Federal Office for the Protection of the Constitution to monitor bias-inspired crimes directly comparable with U.S. definitions. The law in the Federal Republic of Germany reflects a reaction against the Nazi past and aims to forbid "Nazi" speech and propaganda. The law also provided for the monitoring of acts motivated by right-wing extremism, anti-Semitism, and antiforeigner bias. This produces several special categories of crime that may seem unusual to citizens of the United States, such as (a) disturbing or defaming the dead (the charges invoked to sanction desecration of Jewish grave sites and memorials), (b) "public incitement" and "instigation of racial hatred" (charges used to suppress racist public speech), and (c) distribution of Nazi propaganda or "literature liable to corrupt the young."

Other aspects of German law forbid the promotion of a Nazi-like political party, denial of the Holocaust, and use of the symbols associated with officially banned groups. The latter provision criminalizes the display of Nazi-era symbols (e.g., the swastika, the "Hitler greeting") but has been steadily expanded to forbid a wide variety of flags, emblems, and other symbols that were employed by groups banned by the Federal Constitutional Court.

What these laws do not do (compared to bias crime legislation in the United States) is define hate crime or hate violence as such, nor do they include any special recognition of gender, disability, or sexual orientation. On the other hand, they go much further than laws in many other contemporary democracies in limiting certain types of biased or racist speech, particularly when it is directed at groups victimized in the Holocaust.

Although the German law obviously reflects a special set of historical and legal circumstances, it results in an exemplary national data effort in certain categories of bias crime. The law requires national reporting of incidents by all police agencies. This ensures data gathering that is more intensive and more complete than is currently the case in most other nations (particularly in comparison with the United States where hate crime reporting is still voluntary and highly variable). As a result, German data provide a better basis than that of most nations for examining trends and developments in certain categories of hate-motivated violence. This feature of the law makes it possible to analyze trends in right-wing and xenophobic[1] violence in Germany, developments that reflect a particular national situation but that also show international characteristics that may help us understand hate violence in other societies as well.

THE COURSE OF RIGHT-WING VIOLENCE

Perhaps the first question concerns the basic historical development of right-wing violence in Germany. Table 1 and Figure 1 place the era of "modern" xenophobia in Germany in perspective. In 1989 and 1990, immediately prior to unification, there were fewer than 200 violent incidents per year. That figure more than quadrupled by 1992 and reached its contemporary peak in the following year. Shock of the German public (expressed dramatically by candlelight processions in sympathy with the victims), consolidation of the criminal justice agencies in the new federal states in the east, and stepped-up enforcement activities by security agencies all played a part in the decline. Since then, there have been oscillations between 600 and 800 violent incidents per year—a decline from the peak but still high compared to the preunification period (for a more extended discussion, see Watts, 1997, chap. 2).

A second question concerns the targets of violence. Unlike federal (and some state) hate crime statutes in the United States, German law does not provide for special reporting of violence based on sexual orientation, gender, or disability. However, it is quite specific about crimes that can be attributed to anti-Semitic, antiforeigner, or right-wing motivation. Since unification (beginning officially in 1990), the targets of attack have remained relatively constant. As Table 2 shows, about 60% of the violent incidents have been directed against foreigners. Anti-Semitic attacks, including desecration of graves and memorial sites, have accounted for about 2% of all violent incidents. Foreigners are a significant presence in Germany (with a population of more than 7 million) and account for the vast majority (60%) of attacks against persons. By contrast, the number of Jews in Germany is probably not much more than one hundredth that of foreigners, even allowing for a doubling of the Jewish population over the decade (due primarily to immigration from the former Soviet Union). Thus, whereas only 2% of the total offenses involve Jewish persons or institutions, the per capita rate is high.

Table 1. The Course of Right-Wing Violence in Germany, 1989–1998

Year	Number of Violent Acts[a]
1989	173
1990	178
1991	849
1992	1,485
1993	1,322
1994	784
1995	612
1996	624
1997	790
1998	708

Source: Bundesamt für Verfassungsschutz [Federal Office for Protection of the Constitution] (1997, 1998d). See also Watts (1997, chap. 2).
[a] The official term refers to violent acts "with demonstrated or assumed right-wing motivation."

Political opponents such as "autonomous" leftist groups and rival youth cultures accounted for another 14% of the total. The last category ("other") contained 24% of the incidents; it refers to offenses where the perpetrators were identifiably right wing but the victims were not foreigners, Jews, or political enemies (examples might be damage to property during a demonstration or assaults against police or bystanders).

Who are the Perpetrators?

But who are these "rightists?" Increasingly, the perpetrators of hate violence of the past decade have tended overwhelmingly to be young males, usually acting in groups. But how young? And in what kind of groups—skinheads, neo-Nazis, or informal groups of young men looking for excitement?[2] As Table 3 shows, modern xenophobia indeed has a youthful face. Data from 1996 show that 30% of the perpetrators were ages 16 to 17 and that more than two thirds of all perpetrators were 20 years of age or younger.

This aggressive activism on the part of teenaged and young adult males represents a historical "modernization" of xenophobic violence. Prior to 1980, those younger than 20 years of age accounted for only 40% of the incidents (see Watts, 1997, p. 269). The earlier form of rightist activism involved somewhat older perpetrators who were more likely to be associated with neo-Nazi groups (and, presumably, had more developed right-wing ideological positions than today's younger activists). In comparison with this earlier period, today's typical activist is much younger[3] and less likely to be a member of a neo-Nazi organization.

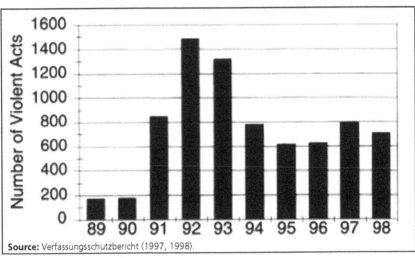

Source: Verfassungsschutzbericht (1997, 1998).

Figure 1. Right-Wing Violence

Table 2. Targets of Right-Wing Violence in Germany, 1995–1998

Type	Number of Offenses[a]	Percentage of Total
Antiforeigner	1,269	60
Anti-Semitic	38	2
Against political opponents	303	14
Other[b]	512	24
Total	2,122	100

Source: Bundesarnt für Verfassungsschutz [Federal Office for Protection of the Constitution] (1997, 1998d).
a. The official term refers to violent acts "with demonstrated or assumed right-wing motivation."
b. "Other" includes acts of violence where the perpetrators are identified as "rightists" but where the incident or target does not involve the previous three categories. Examples might be a march in which store windows are broken or a confrontation with citizens or bystanders.

Accompanying this shift toward youthful activism has been a trend away from classic, membership-based organizational forms. The young perpetrators are less likely than their predecessors to be ideologically sophisticated and organizationally connected. This does not mean they are isolated; on the contrary, they are part of a xenophobic culture that includes both the older organizational forms and a heterogeneous (and often highly spontaneous) youth culture. This last point is not an obvious one, but we can make sense of it looking at recent skinhead history and at the data on the organization connections of actual perpetrators. Here, we have two questions: How have developments in the skinhead scene contributed to the subculture of racism? and How much have skinheads contributed to the rise in violence?

Table 3. Age of Perpetrators (1996)

Age	Percentage	Cumulative Percentage
16–17	30	30
18–20	37	67
21–30	27	94
31–40	3	97
Older than 40	3	100

Source: Bundesamt für Verfassungsschutz [Federal Office for Protection of the Constitution] (1996). (For earlier years, see Watts, 1997, p. 269.)

Trends in Extremism and Aggressive Subcultures

Historically, only a portion of the skinhead style has been explicitly racist or neo-Nazi. Most histories of the movement point to its British working-class origins and to its multiracialism in membership and music tastes. But, those accounts also point to the split of the skinheads into "left" and "right" factions in the 1980s. Somewhere in between these politicized factions are the apolitical skins (who probably make up the majority). The actual numbers in each group are difficult to identify because the boundaries are fluid, and stylistic variations are not always recognizable to the outsider. To make things more difficult, it is not unusual for German skins to refer to themselves as "more or less left" when they actually mean that they are not right. For young Germans in the east, to be truly left was largely discredited with the fall of the East German regime. This was particularly the case for skinheads, who were likely to see being right as the logical place for rebellion to take place in a socialist society.

The right-wing scene has been notorious for its fluidity and unpredictable actionism, a frustration both for the more orthodox rightists who would like to organize them and for the security agencies who would like to monitor them.

However, there is a countervailing tendency that seems to have been accelerating throughout the decade—there are signs that such international groups as the Blood and Honour (British) and the Hammerskins (United States) have added discipline, ideology, and an international network to the right-wing skinhead culture. Not only do both movements have global pretensions, but the latter group refers to itself, ominously, as the Hammerskin Nation.

All this points to a rightist milieu that contains a diverse mix of elements— informal groups of xenophobic youth; "subcultures" with a recognizable, aggressive style (such as skinheads); and ideological groups that are disciplined and organized. Those who identify themselves as rightist skinheads are a dramatic presence among perpetrators (Anti-Defamation League, 1995; Hamm, 1993), but available data suggest that they are only one part of a much broader class of aggressive xenophobes.

In his study of perpetrators in the early 1990s, Willems found that 38% of those arrested for antiforeigner violence in the early 1990s were identified as skinheads (Willems, 1995). Heitmeyer and Muller (1995) found that 46% of their interviewees who were involved in antiforeigner violence thought of themselves as skinheads. Prior to 1990, however, the term *skinhead* hardly surfaced with respect to anti-Semitic or antiforeigner violence—not only was there a smaller amount of violence, but some 90% of the perpetrators in that earlier period were identified with neo-Nazi or other classic right-wing extremist groups (Kalinowsky, 1990). In other words, the 1990s were characterized by a surge in xenophobic violence that was carried by aggressive subcultures that were different from the traditional ideological groups on the right.

In comparison to Germany, information on the role of skinheads in the United States is somewhat less systematic and therefore less conclusive. Levin and McDevitt (1993) estimated that the most ideological perpetrators of hate crimes are probably no more than 1% of the total perpetrators. The authors suggested that skinheads are part of this group of violent perpetrators who attack out of an ideological "mission" to drive out the target group. However, data from Germany and elsewhere suggest that skinheads and other aggressive subcultures may not act primarily from racial or ideological motivations but are motivated by "thrill-seeking" and other opportunistic or criminal motives. Thus, it is difficult to estimate the contributions of skinheads in the perpetration of hate crimes or bias-motivated attacks and just as difficult, at the moment, to compare accurately the various types of perpetrators from one nation to another.

Direct comparison across nations is also made difficult because of the nature of the data (compared to Germany, police reports in the United States are less systematic in establishing the political motivation or membership of the perpetrators). As a result, figures from the United States are not comparable (either in relative accuracy or in estimated magnitude) with that of Germany; however, it is clear that racist skinheads are involved in a number of dramatically violent incidents nationally and internationally (Anti-Defamation League, 1995; Southern Poverty Law Center, 1998).

Thus, to reiterate an obvious point: Only some skinheads are racists, and most racists are not skinheads. Yet, skinheads have played a growing role in xenophobic violence. But, what do we know of the "skinhead" contribution to the broader culture of aggressive xenophobia? To put the numbers in perspective, Willems (1995) found that in addition to the 38% who were identifiable with skinhead culture in some way, about 25% of the perpetrators were associated with right-wing extremist groups. Another 19% were members of informal groups or cliques with no specific ideological identification (most of the remaining perpetrators not accounted for in the above categories had prior records and were classified as "criminal," though this category no doubt overlaps the others). Heitmeyer and Muller (1995) found that roughly 27% of the rightist youth they interviewed were associated with neo-Nazi (rather than skinhead) groups. Taken together, these studies indicate that skinheads make up the largest single category of perpetrators in Germany, with members of neo-Nazi organizations a distant second. By either account, at least one third of the attacks are committed by youth who are not associated with these easily identifiable groups.

Skinheads have represented a major portion of the problem, but they were still only one part of a much broader pattern of violence. According to the German Federal Office for the Protection of the Constitution, the total estimate of "right-wing extremist potential" in Germany grew steadily in the last half of the 1990s. A closer look at the various groups (see Table 4) shows that the largest single numerical change has occurred in the estimated strength of right-extremist political parties (these are parties that are "on watch" by the agency but are not classified/banned as "neo-Nazi"). The number of hard-core ideologues represented by the neo-Nazis has remained relatively constant; other growth areas have been among those classified as "violence-prone rightists" and "other groups" (see Figure 2). The latter category contains a diverse cluster of Kameradschaften, discussion groups, and informal cliques that seem to have proliferated (but whose numbers are notoriously hard to estimate due to their informal organizational forms).

Also hard to estimate is the exact number of persons in the violence-prone category; yet, it is on this diffuse group that the federal office has focused much of its concern over the decade. This category contains the heart of the perpe-trator category—potentially violent young people (mostly males); its numbers are largely a matter of estimate (because there are no "organizations" to infil-trate or membership records to confiscate). It is this category that contains the skinheads, the group with the most identifiable style and appearance among the violence-prone. Obviously, the German government views this category as a growing source of danger. The rise in the number estimated to be violence-prone thus reflects an increase in aggressive youth. It is also likely that the in-crease in their estimated numbers results from a heightened perception on the part of monitoring agencies that the danger from unorganized, aggressive youth is growing. If the numbers are truly on the rise, then it is an increase in the potential—rather than the actual—rate of perpetration. In recent years, the number of violent offenses has declined somewhat (see Table 1).

Table 4. Estimated Right-Wing Extremist Potential, 1995–1998

	Year			
Extremist Group	1995	1996	1997	1998
Violence-prone rightists	6,200	6,400	7,600	8,200
Neo-Nazis	1,980	2,420	2,400	2,400
Political parties	35,900	33,500	34,800	39,000
Other groups	2,660	3,700	4,300	4,500
Total	46,740	46,020	49,100	54,100
Total minus multiple memberships	44,610	45,300	48,400	53,600

Source: Bundesamt für Verfassungsschutz [Federal Office for Protection of the Constitution] (1997, 1998d).

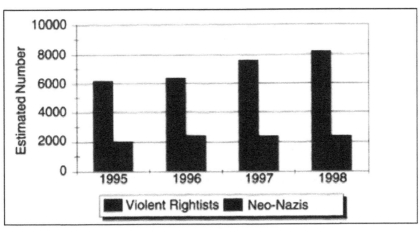

Figure 2. Trends in Right-Wing Potential

Evolution and Change in Skinhead Culture

The skinhead scene actually consists of many scenes with elements borrowed from other subcultures. For this reason, it is impossible to speak of skinheads as if they all shared an identical culture, ideology, or organizational structure; there are also evolution and change in the scene. Three types of development are worth noting: The first is adaptation of the skinhead style to fit the local political culture. The second is in the increased networking of skinhead groups; this includes organization diffusion above the local level and reflects the internationalization of skinhead style. The third is in the commercialization and commodification of skinhead culture.

In the first development, the international skinhead style (much like other subcultural styles) can be "downloaded" from international media and adapted to fit local conditions. This produces variation not only in the groups themselves but in their local "partners." As local variations include cultural elements that respond to the particular culture and community, the network of potential supporters varies from one place to another. For example, in the United States, racist skinhead groups may be allied locally with neo-Nazi groups, with traditional organizations such as the Ku Klux Klan, or with such groups as Aryan Nations or the World Church of the Creator. In Germany, rightist skinheads may find political partners with neo-Nazi groups or with Kameradschaften and political "discussion groups." White supremacist groups (often imported from the United States) also have some appeal because they offer a racist model that is not associated with the Nazi era (thereby avoiding both the stigma of association with the Nazi period and reducing the likelihood of being banned or prosecuted).

This ideological and associational variation has counterparts in the United States, as in the example of the Nazi Low Riders of Antelope Valley, California. Although the name conjures up images of Los Angeles Latino subculture, this group combined elements of skinhead culture, Nazi ideology, racism, and a business sideline in the methamphetamine trade (Finnegan, 1997). Local variations such as these show that such subcultures are dynamic and difficult to capture in a simple ideological or political definition. Local scenes show a kind of cultural entrepreneurship that combines national and international models with the political culture of the local community.

There also appears to be a growing network of rightist culture on both the local and international levels. Though their impact is difficult to estimate, there is evidence from a number of sources that the right-wing elements of the skinhead scene have become more structured and that they have increased their capacity to cooperate with other groups. Those partner groups often provide the organizational structure, capacity for logistics, and tactical planning (e.g., for demonstrations) that skinheads have traditionally lacked. Most of all, those groups may provide ideological structure and tutelage.

The hard street-fighting style of many skins has long been used by other rightist groups for its intimidation value. According to former neo-Nazi Ingo Hasselbach (1996), "The skins were our storm troopers—the idiots who cleared the streets for us and intimidated our enemies—and enjoyed a bit of violence anytime" (p. 171). However, there is evidence that by the end of the decade skins had expanded beyond this role of "useful idiots" (Hasselbach's term) and that they had done it beyond national boundaries. In early 1999, skinheads from Croatia, Slovenia, and Germany joined neo-Nazis from Hungary and elsewhere for a demonstration in Budapest. Rightist skins were a common sight at Aryan Nation meetings in the United States, the White Aryan Resistance actively recruited violent skinheads in the early 1990s, and a well-known watchdog organization argues that the skinhead scene is moving "from chaos to conspiracy" (Southern Poverty Law Center, 1998, p. 23). In Germany, connections have developed between the skins and various neo-Nazi groups and, more recently, to rightist political parties; in particular, the National Democratic Party and its youth organization, the Young National Democrats, have actively sought contact and cooperation with right-wing skins (Bundesamt für Verfassungsschutz, 1998a, 1998b, 1998c).

If the actual extent of political networking is a bit difficult to estimate, the evidence for the international commercialization of skinhead culture seems more easily quantifiable. In Germany, data on this trend come from the fact that police and government agencies monitor both "hate speech" and material that is considered "harmful to youth." For example, music and public speech can be targeted for official repression if they are placed by authorities under either of these categories. Thus, in a 1993 operation that would seem unusual to citizens in the United States, German national and provincial agencies prosecuted rightist and "White power" skinhead bands and took legal action against commercial distributors of their music.

In a similar action in 1997, police and security agencies in 10 federal states searched the homes and places of business of 24 individual and corporate distributors of music judged to be racist. Confiscated in the action were several thousand CDs and various Nazi memorabilia and propaganda material. Also captured were computers, business files, and, in one case, an automatic weapon with ammunition (Landesamt für Verfassungsschutz, 1998).

Despite these periodic waves of concerted suppression and interdiction by authorities, the number of concerts and distributors of skinhead materials (and literature) increased steadily through the late 1990s (see Figure 3). The number of bands also increased, showing a 20% surge in 1 year alone (from fewer than 80 in 1997 to roughly 100 in 1998). Repression efforts run up against two major obstacles. The first is the increase in commercialization and commodification, in which skinhead and racist culture is turned into products (e.g., music, clothes) and marketed for economic gain. This produces an economic incentive for the continuation and exploitation of skinhead and racist culture.

The second, interrelated, trend is the internationalization of that commercial culture that allows concerts and distributors to operate effectively from other countries. To escape German sanctions, bands, literature, and concerts are likely to appear in Denmark or Sweden (in fact, it was from Denmark that American neo-Nazi Gary Lauck was extradited to Germany in 1995). Of course, the United States is the prime international center for the distribution of skinhead, White power, and extremist material. The development of electronic networks such as the World Wide Web has promoted this globalization, increased the commercial availability of rightist materials, and undermined German attempts to suppress skinhead culture. Ideological/commercial Web sites (usually based in the United States but reachable from virtually anywhere) have expanded; Web sites suppressed in Canada, Germany, and elsewhere reappear in the freer cyberspace of the United States where they exist alongside entrepreneurial American extremists.

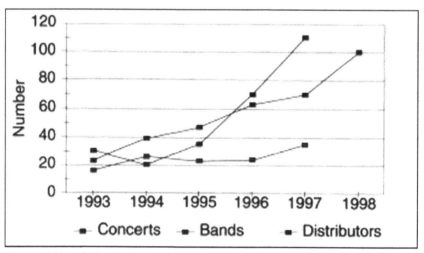

Figure 3. Trends in Skinhead Culture

Discussion

Germans are not alone in the surge of xenophobia and hate crime. There are signs that similar developments are occurring throughout industrial societies undergoing modernization and structural change, stress in employment markets, and a significant influx of people perceived as foreign. Though these structural and social problems all affect Germany, they are common throughout contemporary democracies. So, too, is xenophobic violence and bias crime.

The preceding analysis dealt with rightist potential (and the role of skinheads within it) in one country. The German data are more complete than information available in other nations, but they are not identical with what would be categorized as hate- or bias-crime in the United States. Notably, offenses based on gender and sexual orientation are not included (as indeed they are not in a number of American states). These differences in emphasis make it difficult to compare trends across nations with accuracy. Even so, the data are helpful in pointing out some of the major trends in xenophobic culture in Germany and elsewhere.

Some of our concerns go beyond what the data can clearly tell us. However, we can make some reasonably well-grounded speculations about the role of aggressive youth cultures in contemporary bias crime. I would like to suggest some propositions that seem sensible based in part on the analysis presented here. Each is supported to a greater or lesser extent by current information, but to have more certainty, more comparable data from other nations will be needed. Indeed, we will need far more systematic data for the many jurisdictions of the United States because, unlike Germany, reporting under U.S. hate crime legislation is voluntary and still far from being complete.

- First of all, youth cultures are often not just passing fads. The decline of the skinheads has long been predicted, but it has changed, expanded, and internationalized in the two or more decades since it first appeared. As a style, it has some ephemeral characteristics that will undoubtedly change further and even disappear. But, like rock and roll music (whose death has been predicted for four decades), there is no reason to doubt that this or a similar youth culture will continue to express some form of aggressive xenophobia.
- The early skinhead style originally emerged from British working-class culture as an expression of a strong, working-class masculinity. Segments of it later split into politicized left and right, with the racist segment emerging as an amalgam of aggressive masculinity and explicit xenophobia. This racist tendency was augmented by a sporadic, but growing,

connection with ideological elements of the extreme and racist right. What resulted was a three-part poison of aggression, xenophobia, and ideology that has been much more self-sustaining than any of the individual components alone. Where younger persons, particularly males, are confronted with economic modernization and dislocation for which they are ill prepared, and where scapegoats in the form of various cultural "outsiders" are perceived as threats, this three-part poison will continue to produce aggressive sub-cultures (of which skinheads are only one contemporary variant).

• The skin/fascho scene has developed elements of a subculture that includes music, fanzines (fan magazines), concerts, and other more or less organized symbolic and cultural events. This helps provide an integration of the scene as well as a sense of identity—of being part of something much larger, more powerful, and even somewhat "dangerous." This provides the basis for a self-sustaining scene—it falls short of being a "movement," but it provides a network through which movement-like connections can develop.

• The skinhead scene has broken out of its parochial/provincial boundaries to establish important links to ideological groups—groups that provide the "intellectual" part of the fascho program, offer a "standing organization," and maintain a durable political opportunity structure. The skins might not be interested in organizing, say, a Rudolf Hess Memorial day (a German neo-Nazi tribute day, substituted for Hitler's birthday, which cannot be celebrated publicly); the neo-Nazis do that. But, the skins can show up, act badly, and lend a show of force and aggressive power. They typically horrify the orthodox rightists, but both groups gain from the odd alliance. Moreover, skinheads have graduated from being what Hasselbach (1996) called "useful idiots"; some have crossed the ideological line and become part of the organizational neo-Nazi right. They maintain links to the skin scene and provide a bridge from the rowdy skinhead style to the more disciplined structures on the right.

• The scene of youthful xenophobic aggression has broken out of its provincialism to establish links to international groups. There are many reports of contacts to a variegated international network, particularly in the United States, United Kingdom, Scandinavia, the Netherlands, and to a lesser degree Spain (relations with the Czechs, Poles, Hungarians, and other central Europeans are somewhat more strained, but they exist). Explicitly racist groups such as Blood and Honour and the Hammerskin

Nation provide an international style that is easily downloaded and adapted from the World Wide Web, music, and literature. In Germany, the government estimates that there are more than 200 skinhead or racist Web sites (in the United States, there are far more, of course); many of them are in English to broaden their impact (or because they use North American Internet providers to avoid German censorship).

• Concerts of White power bands are typically discouraged, even prosecuted, in Germany. Bands are raided, CDs confiscated, concerts broken up or forbidden, and leaders prosecuted under German hate speech laws that forbid glorification of Nazis, racist speech, or defamation of victims of the Holocaust. It is even illegal to deny that the Holocaust existed or to slander Jews in public speech. This suppression is undermined by global electronic networks and by support for the scene from abroad.

• The example of skinheads provides some insight into the dynamics of international commercialization—a phenomenon that appears to help stabilize the scene, allow it to expand, and give it a longer life than might have been expected. The same is true, but more so, for right-wing extremist groups and sentiment. This commercial dimension includes cultural artifacts, memorabilia, music, and literature that provide an economic incentive for widening and deepening the scene.

• The structural conditions that produced skinhead groups all over the world are still present. Where they are not solved, skinheads or some other subcultural phenomenon is likely to persist. Status anxiety, identity problems in declining working-class culture, and the compensatory needs of underemployed or threatened young people, particularly males, are continuing problems. These problems, and the youth cultures they produced, extend well beyond the boundaries of the less advantaged. Although the expression of such xenophobia may have significant origins in threatened segments of the housing and labor markets, that xenophobia has been transported politically and culturally to a much broader segment of the population (e.g., middle-class youth, young women, and a variety of nations that have developed "copy-cat" scenes).[4]

• The psychological need for an identity and sense of meaning remains. Not all youth can answer that need with conventional achievement in work, education, and family, but some find it easier or more exciting to use physical and symbolic aggression against out-groups. This form of identity can be extremely unrealistic and dysfunctional (especially when based on a mythopoetic White race, or the like, which either does not exist or, if it does, hardly appoints these youth as its "sword and shield").

This is not a productive identity search, but it will continue to have power where other sources of positive identity are not available.

• Last, although racist skinheads and other aggressive cliques may seem atavistic, they may actually be on the cutting edge of modern xenophobia. Their spontaneous and unpredictable style was traditionally seen as a disadvantage, but a trend in the far right throughout the decade comes to favor this seemingly primitive form of action. Increased repression of extremist groups by various national governments has led to organizational innovations. In the United States, the concept of leaderless resistance sprang up on the far right to promote action that is not controlled by a specific organizational center. The concept was developed among American extremists to replace the standard organizational model that proved vulnerable to government infiltration and prosecution. But, small groups of aggressive youth had long been the source of spontaneous, "unorganized" violence. Skinheads and other aggressive subcultures are part of a fluid milieu that is held together by symbols, idea fragments, cultural events, and electronic media—but often without any classic organizational structure. This relatively unorganized base then provides a place from which the more ideological of them are likely to find their way into parties, movements, and discussion circles. Thus, the language and symbols may often sound like the "same old thing," but underlying the familiar slogans is a significant change—the right has modernized and adapted, and it has taken on a more youthful face than was the case a generation ago.

NOTES

1. The term *xenophobia* can refer to a generalized antipathy toward out-groups in general or toward a specific target group such as foreigners, Jews, homosexuals, and others. In German usage, the term *Fremdenfeindlichkeit* refers to antipathy against foreigners, although *Xenophobie* is increasingly used. I have tried elsewhere to make these distinctions somewhat more carefully. In this discussion, I try (without complete success) to use *xenophobia* when referring to the more inclusive concept. The terms *antiforeigner* and *anti-Semitic* not only denote the more specific antipathies, they also correspond to the primary categories in the official Germany agency reports.

2. This is not the place for an analysis of the causes and appeals of youthful xenophobia; but some useful starting points are Bergmann (1998); Boehnke, Hagan, and Hefler (1998); Hagan, Merkens, and Boehnke (1995); Oesterreich (1998); Watts (1997, 1999); Watts and Zinnecker (1998); and Willems (1995). For a closer look at the role of young females on the right, see Mushaben (1996).

3. Other discussions of aggressive German youth cultures in the early 1990s can be found in Watts, 1997 (particularly in chaps. 1, 6, 7. and 9). For a more detailed analysis of the shift in public opinion and violence during the 1980s and 1990s, see Watts, 1997 (particularly chap. 2).

A detailed chronology of postunification xenophobia is provided by Rainer Erb (cited in Kurthen, Bergmann, & Erb, 1997, pp. 263–285).

4. This conclusion obviously refers to the spread of aggressive youth culture, the primary topic of this discussion. I do not mean it to be a global proposition about the origins of xenophobia or to imply that youth are the source of xenophobia. What I have argued from the German data, though, is that xenophobic youth have been the primary source of rightist violence in the past decade.

REFERENCES

NOTE: Sources are provided in English wherever possible, though in many cases the data reported are available only in German. In those cases, I have provided a translation of the original title and institutional name (when a governmental agency is the data source). Readers interested in the extensive German literature on the subject might start with the bibliographies in Watts (1997) and in Kurthen, Bergmann, and Erb (1997).

Anti-Defamation League. (1995). *The skinhead international: A worldwide survey of neo-Nazi skinheads*. New York: Author.
Bergmann, W. (1998). Violence as social control: Right-wing youth in Germany. In M. W. Watts (Ed.), *Cross-cultural perspectives on youth and violence* (pp. 99–115). New York: JAI.
Boehnke, K., Hagan, J., & Hefler, G. (1998). On the development of xenophobia in Germany: The adolescent years. *Journal of Social Issues, 3*, 585–602.
Bundesamt für Verfassungsschutz [Federal Office for Protection of the Constitution]. (1996). *Verfassungsschutzbericht* [Online]. Retrieved August 15, 1998, from: http://www.bundesregierung .de/02/0201/innen
Bundesamt für Verfassungsschutz [Federal Office for Protection of the Constitution]. (1997). *Verfassungsschuttbericht* [Online]. Retrieved August 15, 1998, from: http://www.bundesregierung .de/02/0201/innen
Bundesamt für Verfassungsschutz [Federal Office for Protection of the Constitution]. (1998a, March). *Rechtsextremistische Skinheads. Entwicklung, Musik-Szene, Fanzines* [Right-wing extremist skinheads: Development, music scenes, fanzines] [Online]. Retrieved November 1, 1998, from: http://www.verfassungsschutz.de
Bundesamt für Verfassungsschutz [Federal Office for Protection of the Constitution]. (1998b, July). *Right-wing extremism in the Federal Republic of Germany: Situation report* [Online]. Retrieved November 1, 1998, from: http//www.verfassungsschutz.de
Bundesamt für Verfassungsschutz [Federal Office for Protection of the Constitution]. (1998c, March). *Right-wing extremist activities in INTERNET* [Online]. Retrieved November 1, 1998. from: http://www.verfassungsschutz.de
Bundesamt für Verfassungsschutz [Federal Office for Protection of the Constitution]. (1998d). *Verfassungsschutzbericht* [Online]. Retrieved August 15, 1998, from: http://www.bundesregierung .de/02/0201/innen
Finnegan, W. (1997, December 1). The unwanted. *The New Yorker*, 61–78.
Hagan, J., Merkens, H., & Boehnke, K. (1995). Delinquency and disdain: Social capital and the control of right-wing extremism among East and West Berlin youth. *American Journal of Sociology, 100*, 1028–1052.
Hamm, M. (1993). *American skinheads: The criminology and control of hate crime*. Westport, CT: Praeger.
Hasselbach, I. (with Reiss, T.). (1996). *Führer-ex: Memoirs of a former neo-Nazi*. New York: Random House. (Portions excerpted in Hasselbach, I. [with Reiss, T.] (1996, January 6). How Nazis are made. *The New Yorker*, 36–57.
Heitmeyer, W., & Müller, J. (1995). *Fremdenfeindliche Gewalt junger Menschen. Biographische Hintergründe, soziale Situationskontexte und die Bedeutung strafrechtlicher Sanktionen* [Antiforeigner violence of young people: Biographical background, social context and the significance of legal sanctions]. (1995). Bad Godesberg, Germany: Forum.

Kalinowsky, H. H. (1990). *Rechtsextremismus und Strafrechtspflege. Eine Analyse von Strafverfahren wegen mutmaßlicher rechtsextremististischer Aktivitäten und Erscheinungen* [Right-wing extremism and the law: An analysis of legal proceedings of suspected right-extremist activities] (3rd ed.), Bonn, Germany: Bundesministerium der Justiz.

Kurthen, H., Bergmann, W., & Erb, R. (Eds.). (1997). *Antisemitism and xenophobia in Germany after unification.* New York: Oxford University Press.

Landesamt für Verfassungsschutz. (1998). *Landesverfassungsschutzbericht* (Report of the Provincial Office for Protection of the Constitution, Hamburg) [Online]. Retrieved March 29, 1999, from: http://www.hamburg.de/Behoerden/LfV/v-bericht

Levin, J., & McDevitt, J. (1993). *Hate crimes: The rising tide of bigotry and bloodshed.* New York: Plenum.

Mushaben, J. M. (1996). The rise of femi-Nazis? Female participation in right-extremist movements in unified Germany. *German Politics, 5,* 240–261.

Oesterreich, D. (1998). Authoritarianism and aggression: German youth and right-wing extremism. In M. W. Watts (Ed.), *Cross-cultural perspectives on youth and violence* (pp. 39–51). New York: JAI.

Southern Poverty Law Center. (1998, Fall). Chaos to conspiracy: Racist skinhead violence growing more organized. *Intelligence Report,* pp. 23–24.

Warts, M. W. (1997). *Xenophobia in united Germany: Generations, modernization, and ideology.* New York: St. Martin's.

Watts, M. W. (1999). Xenophobia among young Germans in the nineties. In S. Hübner-Funk & M. du Bois-Reymond (Eds.), *Intercultural reconstruction: Trends and challenges* (pp. 117–139). Berlin, Germany: Walter de Gruyter.

Watts, M. W., & Zinnecker, J. (1998). Varieties of violence-proneness among male youth. In M. W. Watts (Ed.), *Cross-cultural perspectives on youth and violence* (pp. 117–145). New York: JAI.

Willems, H. (1995). Development, patterns and causes of violence against foreigners in Germany: Social and biographical characteristics of perpetrators and the process of escalation. *Terrorism and Political Violence, 7,* 162–181.

*Meredith W. Watts is a retired professor of political science at the University of Wisconsin–Milwaukee.

Watts, Meredith W. "Aggressive Youth Cultures and Hate Crime: Skinheads and Xenophobic Youth in Germany." *American Behavioral Scientist* 45, no. 4 (2001): 600–615.

Part 3: Prevention and Intervention

This section will look at the various ways in which state institutions and non-state actors try to prevent young people from developing extreme-right ideas or joining extreme-right groups, as well as try to help them to leave extreme-right organizations. Andreas Beelmann, in "Preventing Right-Wing Extremism," opens with a survey of the international literature on prevention strategies, distinguishing between various strategies and objectives. Ineke van der Valk, in "Youth Engagement in Right-Wing Extremism," draws on comparative literature in her specific study of the Netherlands. She takes a broad approach, focusing both on factors that are important in joining radical movements and those relevant to leaving them. She suggests several intervention policies designed to counter and prevent engagement in extremist activity. Yngve Carlsson, in "Violent Right-Wing Extremism in Norway," also addresses both intervention and prevention, but focuses specifically on Norway. Finally, Cynthia Miller-Idriss, in "Raising the Right Wing," looks at what educators can do. Her study emphasizes the importance of knowledge for both educators and their pupils. Young people are often vulnerable to extreme-right ideas and organizations because of inadequate knowledge about their political and social context, but educators are often limited in their (re-)socialization of young right-wing extremists because of their own stereotypical ideas about the extreme right. In fact, their efforts may increase the appeal of the radical right.

As you read through the articles, think about the following questions:
- Is it more important to prevent young people developing extreme-right attitudes or joining extreme-right groups?
- Are prevention and intervention strategies more successful when they include state institutions?
- Should exit programs be proactive or reactive? In other words, can intervention programs be successful if the right-wing extremist has not reached out first?

Preventing Right-Wing Extremism: European and International Research

by Andreas Beelmann*

I. DELINEATING THE PROBLEM

In many societies, prejudice towards immigrants and other minorities, feelings of being threatened by out-groups, increasing votes for extreme right-wing political parties, discrimination against foreigners, social exclusion in daily life and overt violence towards out-groups seem to have become everyday phenomena (Heitmeyer 2006; Klink and Wagner 1999; Zick and Küpper 2007). This growing problem is emerging during a period that increasingly demands that individuals and social groups co-operate in facing the realities of multicultural societies, growing political integration within Europe and rapidly advancing economic globalization. Against this background, problems such as right-wing extremism and xenophobia become a major challenge for civic society.

These problems are not just limited to adults. Xenophobia and right-wing extremism also seem widespread among children and adolescents. In a major representative survey of more than 10,000 German school pupils aged 13 to 19, Wetzels and Greve (2001) found that 19.2% of these adolescents could be called somewhat xenophobic and 12.2% strongly xenophobic. Still more disconcerting was that two-thirds of them had a propensity or affinity to violence. The total proportion of adolescents both xenophobic *and* with a propensity to violence was about 8%. Almost one-half of this sub-group even had a record of violent offences. Such statistics make it necessary to ask how to provide optimal conditions for young people to successfully become responsible adults and live social lives marked by tolerance. It also raises the question what can be done to counteract or prevent both this affinity to violence and tendency toward xenophobia.

In order to plan effective measures, it is first necessary to have a clear notion of the object to be prevented. Although there are different ideas on how to define right-wing extremism (Zick and Küpper, in press), one is to summarize it as attitudes and behaviours related to political ideologies that express themselves through phenomena such as marked prejudice, racist attitudes and both politically and racially motivated acts of violence. Hence, from a psychological perspective, it is necessary to distinguish between two elements of right-wing extremism: an extremely negative evaluation of, or attitude toward, members of other groups, and deviant and mostly violent behaviour towards these out-groups and their members. The following provides an overview of conceptual issues and the effectiveness of prevention measures that focuses on modifying both negative attitudes (e.g., prejudice) and negative behaviour (e.g., violence, crime) in children and adolescents.

II. THE EVOLUTION OF PREVENTION STRATEGIES

Scientifically-based intervention strategies require both a sound empirical and sound theoretical basis (Beelmann and Raabe 2007). At least three issues are relevant in this context:
- What is the target population?
- Which prevention strategy should be applied?
- What should prevention measures include?

What is the Target Population?

In the beginning, prevention measures have to specify their intended targets. For example, is there one homogeneous group or are there a variety of different problem groups? In the field of right-wing extremism, existing research indicates that the latter is probably the case. In 1993, Willems et al. already distinguished between four sub-groups groups within the right-wing extremist scene: (1) of-fenders motivated by right-wing extremism, (2) violence-prone youths with no political ideology, (3) fellow-travellers and (4) youths whose xenophobia result-ed from vague feelings of disadvantage. It is highly likely that prevention mea-sures will need to be different for each of these groups or distinguish between them, meaning a variety of approaches is required. However, the selection of specific target groups is not limited to features of their problem behaviour. It is also necessary to ask which age groups should be selected; which additional characteristics (such as gender) should be taken into account when planning prevention measures.

Which Prevention Strategy Should be Applied?

Prevention strategies that address *all* members of a defined target group, such as all the students of a particular age cohort, can be distinguished from preven-tion measures targeting *specific groups at risk* of developing right-wing extremist views. Universal strategies have the advantage of reaching all those in a target group who are potentially at risk. However, it is a very costly form of intervention to target a large group such as an entire age cohort. Targeted prevention more readily tailors measures to fit the specific situation of the target group. However, this requires reliable selection criteria (risks) and an ability to handle stigmatisation processes when making such selections (see Beelmann and Raabe 2007).

What Should Prevention Measures Contain?

A sound prevention concept has to take a closer look at the causes of the problems and how they develop over time. Indeed, for preventive measures, such a perspective is indispensable. First, any preventive measure can only be justified with reference to tested assumptions regarding the predicted developmental trajectory (Brandtstädter and von Eye 1982; Beelmann and Raabe 2007). Second, the relevant conditions that are relevant for the problem to emerge, such as causal or risk factors, provide important indicators for what the preventive measure should contain and the optimal time point for its application. For these reasons, we turn to developmental aspects of right-wing extremism.

III. THE DEVELOPMENT OF RIGHT-WING EXTREMISM

The development of xenophobic attitudes has often been studied under the more general rubric of the development of prejudice. This research indicates that processes involving negative judgment and prejudice do not just emerge in youth and young adulthood but are already present at much earlier developmental stages (Aboud 1988; Nesdale 2001). Even preschool children use social categorization processes to structure their social environment. The type and use of the categorizations (stereotypes) becomes increasingly differentiated over time, and by early adolescence is no longer based on simple verbal and visual discrimination (Bar-Tal 1996), but on implicit judgment processes (McGlothlin, Killen and Edmonds 2005).

Hence, to a certain extent, stereotyped attitudes and prejudices must be viewed as normal. Nonetheless, such phenomena are significant for later right-wing extremism. A few longitudinal studies have shown that a high level of prejudice in the early stages of development is systematically related to the development of negative behaviours toward out-groups, the quality of later peer relations, selective peer friendships, and the social exclusion of out-group members (Aboud, Mendelson and Purdy 2003, Killen and Stangor 2001, McGlothin et al. 2005).

Such processes may well favour the development of stable prejudice and discriminatory tendencies and markedly increase the risk of more problematic, longer-term developments. If the goal is to analyse the emergence of right-wing extremism, it is necessary to search for those conditions and causes that are responsible for a significant deviation from a normal developmental trajectory.

A variety of factors have been suggested as possible causes of right-wing extremism. One frequently proposed cause at the *individual level* is low cognitive competence combined with deficits in empathy and socio-cognitive skills. This is accompanied by a strong disposition towards prejudice that favours discriminating against members of out-groups (Aboud 1988; Bigler and Liben 2006). A recent longitudinal study showed a significant relationship between weak basic cognitive abilities, school failure at age eight, and markedly racist attitudes in adolescence (Ihle, Esser Schmidt 2005).

Other explanations focus more strongly on *familial and social determinants.* In their work on the authoritarian personality, Adorno and his colleagues were already analysing the conditions that lead to stable, negative evaluations of strangers (Adorno et al. 1950). They argued that growing up in a rather unemotional family climate in which an authoritarian parenting style prevailed, favours a personality development marked by intolerance and xenophobia. More recent studies show that both a normative-authoritarian family climate and xenophobic attitudes held by the parents are related to marked xenophobic attitudes in the child—particularly when there strong attachment between parent and child (Gniewosz and Noack 2006; Hopf et al. 1995; Ihle et al. 2005; Noack 2001).

Beginning in early adolescence, the *peer group* starts to exert an especially strong role in the development of xenophobic attitudes. A high degree of peer rejection has been correlated with marked prejudice—although only in adolescents with low self-esteem (Kiesner et al. 2003). The attitudes of significant peers also seem to play a decisive role in ideological radicalisation. A retrospective interview study with violent xenophobic offenders (see Frindte et al. 2001) found that an identifiable ideologization started in early adolescence, with the influence coming from friends who were part of racist milieus. In addition, violent offenders had already been conspicuously aggressive in early childhood. Indeed, a significant portion of the adolescents who extremely xenophobic attitudes also have a broad range of behavioural problems (Ihle et al. 2005; Kiesner et al. 2003). Hence, there seems to be a relationship—not yet sufficiently analysed—in some children and adolescents between marked prejudices or racist attitudes and violent behaviour.

Finally, *societal factors* are often thought a cause of right-wing extremism. These include a spatial, temporal, and social destabilization of life circumstances, a lack of social solidarity, increasing individualization and negative experiences with social transformations (in Germany, for example, through re-unification in 1990). They accompanied by experiences of disintegration, discrimination and declassification (Heitmeyer 1995). Such destabilization processes provide the background for individual negative development, and its role should not be underestimated, particularly when we look at the function of negative judgment processes within the framework of social identity formation.

This list of potential influencing factors indicates we probably need to assume multiple causation and complex dynamic processes in the development of stable prejudice patterns and right-wing extremist attitudes. Situation-specific variables also likely contribute to specific expressions in behaviour (Bannenberg, Rössner and Coester, 2006), though such constellations are similar to the ones found in the development of aggressive and violent behaviour in general (Beelmann and Raabe 2007; Lösel and Bender 2003). Longitudinal studies have shown that early antisocial behaviour is relatively stable and linked to a multitude of risk factors and risk processes in the developmental trajectory (Beelmann and Raabe, 2007). However, little is known about how the development of prejudice relates to violent and criminal behaviour towards members of out-groups, even though such research would seem promising (Wagner, van Dick and Zick 2001). The aforementioned study by Frindte et al. (2001) found a relation between early antisocial behaviour, the development of prejudice in adolescence, and later violent behaviour toward members of out-groups. The first xenophobically motivated act of violence was preceded by a roughly 2-year ideologization phase in the peer context.

IV. EXISTING PREVENTION CONCEPTS AND THEIR EFFECTIVENESS

Recent years have seen an increased focus on *hate crimes* and what to do about them (Altschiller 2005; Bannenberg et al. 2006; Steinberg, Brooks and Remtulla 2003). Most research on the phenomenon has taken a political or civic perspective. The German government initiated major political programmes (e.g. ZIVITAS) in response both to isolated but spectacular acts of right-wing violence and to the increasing number of votes given to extreme right-wing political parties. Such programmes aim to reduce the frequency of xenophobia and right-wing violence, and work to increase the dissemination of democratic values and tolerance for diversity (Lynen von Berg, Palloks and Steil 2007; Lynen von Berg and Roth 2003).

The focus was frequently more on right-wing extremist offences and less on preventive strategies in a stricter sense. In addition, most projects initiated in these 'action' programmes did not include evaluations with prospective designs and suitable control groups; instead, they only produced case-specific and descriptive reports that make it hard to generalize based on their outcomes (Lynen von Berg et al. 2007). This lack of systematic evaluation is not restricted to German or European programmes on hate crimes, but seems as pervasive in North American and international research (Steinberg et al. 2003). Therefore, the focus here is only on measures for preventing prejudice, promoting intergroup relations, and findings on preventing violence and crime.

A. Preventing Prejudice and Promoting Intergroup Relations

Negative judgment biases and marked patterns of prejudice foster the development of more serious forms of discrimination, violence and crime towards members of marginal social groups; they are likely to aid in the development of right-wing extremism. Historically, efforts to prevent prejudice from developing and improve intergroup relations can be traced back to efforts to desegregate the U.S. school system (Brown v. Board of Education 1954) and to Allport's (1954) classic work on the effect of contacts between social groups. Both generated a great deal of empirical research (Schofield 1995; Pettigrew and Tropp 2006), particularly in the social context of schools and universities. Table 1 presents an overview of the content and goals of four sets of prevention approaches in this field (for more detail, see Oskamp 2000; Stephan and Stephan 2001; Stephan and Vogt 2004; Wagner, Christ and van Dick 2006).

The available reviews on the effectiveness of these intervention approaches genet report highly positive findings, although not without critiques. Schofield's (1995) analysis of *school desegregation*, for example, produced rather mixed findings revealed, in line with Allport (1954), that contact alone was not a sufficient condition for creating positive effects. Success depended critically on whether the programmes led to personal relationships and friendships between members of different ethnic groups (Aboud and Levy 2000). In addition, more long-term evaluation studies, using sophisticated research designs, seemed to produce lower effects (Stephan and Stephan 2001).

Effects of *cooperative learning methods* have also been studied frequently and intensively. Johnson and Johnson (1989, 2000) integrated more than 180 studies in a meta-analysis, and concluded that cooperative learning methods markedly increase the interpersonal attraction between members of different

Table 1. Overview of Prevention Approaches for Improving Intergroup Relations and Reducing Prejudice

Type of approach	Contents and goals
Integrative classroom teaching/Cooperative learning techniques	Joint classes or non-competitive learning techniques for members of various social groups, the members of which typically come from different ethnic groups. The goal is more frequent contact and friendships; the assumption is that such contact leads to a general improvement in their social relations.
Multicultural education, diversity, and anti-racism programmes	Programmes intended to break down xenophobic attitudes, such as in school classes by providing information about out-groups, discussing democratic or ethical values and the acceptance of diversity, and by direct intergroup contact, such as through excursions or training in intercultural communication techniques.
Cognitive/Socio-cognitive training programmes	Heterogeneous category for approaches whose common goal is to promote cognitive/socio-cognitive competencies that relate systematically to prejudice and discrimination. Major forms of training are: cognitive, taking social perspective and empathy, promoting moral development, and conflict resolution programmes.
Public relations work and media campaigns	Dissemination of information about the out-group through education campaigns with prominent members of the out-group aim at promoting knowledge about the out-group and initiating more intensive contacts with them.
Educational films/ Stories with vicarious contact	Films and stories in which information on contacts (vicarious) with the out-group are presented in child-appropriate formats; assumption is that this will lead to a reduction in prejudice (e.g. contacts between children from different ethnic groups in Sesame Street, extended-contact stories).

ethnic groups in the classroom as compared with individual and competitively-oriented learning strategies. This finding was supported by one of the few German-language studies in this area, one that combined cooperative learning with information about the ethnic out-group (in this case, immigrants of Turkish origins; see Avci-Werning 2004).

Multicultural training, diversity, and anti-racism programmes are variants within a highly heterogeneous group of political education programmes. In an early review, Stephan and Stephan (1984) concluded that the majority of the existing empirical studies showed positive effects on the prejudices of children and adolescents. An updated meta-analysis (Stephan, Renfro and Stephan 2004) produced effect sizes varying from $d = .25$ to $d = .38$ (corresponding to correlations from $r = .13$ to $.19$). After analysing seven studies on the impact of special anti-racism programmes, McGregor (1993) even found an effect size of $d = .48$ ($r = .23$) on the decline in racist attitudes. Wagner, van Dick and Christ (2006) found a similarly positive outcome assessment—at least when attitudes toward different ethnic groups were used as success criteria.

The effects of *cognitive and socio-cognitive* programmes are also basically positive. Empirical evaluations show that a reduction in biased judgment processes and prejudices can be achieved in children and adolescents (Aboud and Levy 2000). Nonetheless, conclusive statements here are difficult, because this label covers a wide variety of different approaches, including programmes to improve cognitive skills (Bigler and Liben 1992), to train social perspective-taking and empathy (e.g. the Blue-Eyes/Brown-Eyes simulation or the bystander intervention experiments; see Stephan and Finlay 1999), to promote moral development (e.g., value confrontation techniques) and to resolve conflicts (Johnson and Johnson, 1996).

Integrative evaluations of measures involving *public relations and media* programmes (e.g. educational campaigns, educational films and television programmes) are also problematic. Analyses of public relations campaigns do not just indicate moderate programme effects but show negative effects as well (i.e., an increasing tendency towards prejudice) due to a higher sensitivity and perceptions of out-group threat (Vrij and Smith 1999). Several aspects need to be considered here to avoid negative effects, and an analysis of the affective processes involved needs to be conducted (Winkel 1997).

Similar problems with empirical evaluation also apply to films and television programmes for children and adolescents, even though most report positive effects (Graves 1999; Persson and Musher-Eizenman 2003). It is unclear to what extent television series such as *Sesame Street* actually led to interethnic contacts. More recent possibilities for improving attitudes towards out-groups that are based on learning materials are provided by *extended-contact stories*. These are particularly applicable in situations in which direct intergroup contacts are not possible owing to low availability. In these programmes, children read adventure stories in which vicarious friendships are described between an in-group and an out-group member. This should break down prejudices and build up positive attitudes in a manner similar to real contacts. Several recent evaluation studies argue that this concept shows promise (Cameron, Rutland and Brown 2007).

In sum, a variety of measures have been applied to improve intergroup relations prevent prejudice in children and adolescents One important prevention element here seems to be contact between different social groups even when this is only vicarious and occur in hypothetical scenarios (Pettigrew and Tropp 2005). However, the necessary features of the contact situation already specified by Allport in 1954 seem to continue to be of central importance: Members of both groups must have equal status, they need to share common goals, and they are in a non-competitive setting in which authorities and institutions provide social support. Finally, in light of the problem with right-wing extremism discussed here, one main limitation is that many studies confine themselves only to assessing attitudes. Direct behavioural measures and long-term effects have hardly ever been assessed, making it nearly impossible to appropriately evaluate their positive effects in preventing right-wing extremism.

B. Prevention of Violence and Crime

A great deal of research is now available on the prevention of violence and crime in children and adolescents (Beelmann and Rabe 2007; Welsh and Farrington 2006). Approaches range from the socio-political (improved education provisions), through police and legal (changes to weapons laws, video monitoring of crime hot spots), to social work and psychological measures (interventions for children and adolescents, services for parents). Those measures that have proven particularly efficacious include: social training programmes for children (Beelmann and Lösel 2006; Lösel and Beelmann 2003), parent training programmes (Lundahl, Risser and Lovejoy 2006), comprehensive school programmes (Beelmann 2008), and family-oriented early intervention (Tremblay and Japel 2003).

Social training programmes focus on learning important social competencies (such as how to make friends) and improving socio-cognitive skills (such as social problem-solving, or self-control and impulse control).These are central features in social information processing and behaviour control leading to social competence, and hence address what have repeatedly been confirmed as risk factors for antisocial development (Beelmann and Raabe 2007). The programmes are generally carried out in groups, as a structured sequence of exercises and role-play based on training manuals. They are relatively easy to convert for use as a universal prevention strategy, such as in preschools and schools, and are relatively inexpensive.

Numerous studies have asserted the effectiveness of such programmes. Lösel and Beelmann (2003) performed a meta-analysis of studies that were explicitly focused on preventing antisocial problems and found an average effect size of

$d = .39$ $(r = .20)$. Nonetheless, the effects on actual problem behaviour (violence, crime) were markedly lower than on success criteria based on specific social skills, such as social problem-solving competence in hypothetical conflict scenarios.

Other programmes focus more on the parents. Such *parent training programmes* are designed to promote positive parenting behavior, thereby intervening in an equally important risk factor for antisocial developmental problems. They are mostly carried out in groups and contain a structured sequence of sessions addressing positive parenting practices (support, acceptance, supervision) and how to impart social rules and tackle problem behaviour in children (e.g., by setting limits). Meta-analyses show that such programmes can have even stronger effects than social training programmes for children. However, they often modify only the target variable that is directly intended (e.g., the specific behaviour of the parents) and have little or no effect on child's criminal behaviour (Lundahl et al. 2006). Parents in high-risk families, in addition, frequently either do not participate in these programmes or drop out. Solutions have yet to be found for these problems (Beelmann 2007).

School prevention concepts have also become much more popular in recent years, since schools provide conditions relatively favourable to implementing programmes (Beelmann 2008). One programme that has received a great deal of international attention, and has been widely implemented, is the Olweus Bullying Prevention Programme (Olweus 1996). In recent years in the U.S., other large-scale prevention projects have proven particularly popular, including the very comprehensive Fast Track Program (see Conduct Problems Prevention Research Group 1992). This concentrates on promoting children in the school context as well as improving communication structures between school and family. However, the findings are mixed regarding their impact on violence and crime: the success rates for the Olweus programme in Norway remain unconfirmed in other countries, and success rates for the Fast Track Program are less than sensational when related to their intensity. Other studies show that long-term successes lasting into adulthood are possible (see the Seattle Social Development Project, Hawkins et al. 1992, 1999), particularly when programmes start when children are first admitted to school.

Family-related early prevention concepts are designed to prevent violence and crime, starting in the preschool years, or even earlier. They belong to a tradition of early intervention and compensatory preschool education developed and promoted in the United States (Tremblay and Japel 2003; Webster-Stratton and Taylor 2001). They include services such as day care, advice on how to rear and feed children, together with general information on child development, promoting children's cognitive abilities, and promoting the parents' own careers and social life. Very comprehensive evaluations exist on the effectiveness of these programmes, with some exceptionally long follow-up intervals in which later delinquency and crime served as outcome criteria. In the High/Scope Perry Preschool Study, for example, the intervention group had a significantly lower incidence of court convictions and incarcerations for criminal offences almost 35 years after the programme was implemented (Schweinhart et al. 2005).

Unfortunately, such favourable outcomes are still rather isolated. Projects with similar content sometimes show much lower or even negative effects (Tremblay and Japel 2003). However, on the whole, comprehensive early prevention programmes seem to be more appropriate as prevention measures for handling chronic risk constellations or groups that already demonstrate problem behaviour than, for example, isolated and short-term child or parent training. However, looking at the costs and the efforts involved in such programmes, it is necessary to ask whether or not these strategies economically viable as universal prevention measures (i.e. as a service for all children and adolescents). Moreover, as in prejudice prevention, it is hard to estimate the effectiveness, and the utility, of all the measures described here for preventing crime and violence in right-wing extremist offences or for preventing hate crimes.

V. Conclusion

There is some evidence that the measures for preventing prejudice and anti-social behaviour presented here might well be promising for preventing right-wing extremism. Nonetheless, hardly any links exist between the two research areas, and our knowledge of how to design effective programs to counter right-wing extremism remains very limited. One reason for this is the continued lack of well-designed longitudinal studies about the development of right-wing extremism and the relevant developmental processes that could serve as a basis for theoretically sound prevention programmes based on developmental models. There is also a lack of long-term evaluations of prevention programmes (Beelmann 2006). This deficit is particularly evident in the area of prejudice prevention, pointing to the need to more systematic evaluations in both, future prevention research, and in 'action' programmes to counter right-wing extremism. Rational strategies based on empirical data are required—not just in order to allocate resources effectively but also, and above all, to prevent serious negative developments in children and adolescents, and provide effective protection to the victims of such developments.

References

Aboud, F. E. 1988 Children and prejudice. Oxford: Blackwell.

Aboud, F. E. and Levy, S. R. 2000 'Interventions to reduce prejudice and discrimination in children and adolescents,' in S. Oskamp (ed.) Reducing prejudice and discrimination, Mahwah: Lawrence Earlbaum Associates.

Aboud, F. E., Mendelson, M. J. and Purdy, K. T. 2003 'Cross-race peer relations and friendship quality,' International Journal of Behavioral Development 27: 165–173.

Adorno, T. W., Frenkel-Brunswik, E., Levinson, D. J. and Sanford, S. R. 1950 The authoritarian personality, New York: Norton.

Allport, G. W. 1954 The nature of prejudice, New York: Doubleday Anchor Books.

Altschiller, D. 2005 Hate crimes, Santa Barbara: ABC-CLIO.

Avci-Werning, M. 2004 Prävention ethnischer Konflikte in der Schule: ein Unterrichtsprogramm zur Verbesserung interkultureller Beziehungen, Münster: Waxmann.

Bannenberg, B., Rössner, D. and Coester, M. 2006 'Hasskriminalität, extremistische Kriminalität, politisch motivierte Kriminalität und ihre Prävention,' in R. Egg (ed.) Extremistische Kriminalität; Kriminologie und Prävention, Wiesbaden: Kriminologische Zentralstelle.

Bar-Tal, D. 1996 'Development of social categories and stereotypes in early childhood: The case of "The Arab" concept formation, stereotype and attitudes by Jewish children in Israel,' International Journal of Intercultural Relations 20: 341–370.

Beelmann, A. 2006 'Wirksamkeit von Präventionsmaßnahmen bei Kindern und Jugendlichen, Ergebnisse und Implikationen der integrativen Erfolgsforschung,' Zeitschrift für Klinische Psychologie und Psychotherapie 35: 151–162.

Beelmann, A. 2007 'Elternberatung und Elterntraining,' in F. Linderkamp and M. Grünke (eds) Lern- und Verhaltensstörungen, Genese, Diagnostik und Intervention, Weinheim: Psychologie Verlags Union.

Beelmann, A. 2008 'Prävention im Schulalter,' in B. Gasteiger-Klicpera, H. Julius and Ch. Klicpera (eds) Sonderpädagogik der sozialen und emotionalen Entwicklung. Handbuch der Sonderpädagogik, Band 3, Göttingen: Hogrefe.

Beelmann, A. and Lösel, F. 2006 'Child social skills training in developmental crime prevention: Effects on antisocial behavior and social competence,' Psicothema, 18: 602–609.

Beelmann, A. and Raabe, T. 2007 Dissoziales Verhalten von Kindern und Jugendlichen. Erscheinungsformen, Entwicklung, Prävention, Intervention, Göttingen: Hogrefe.

Bigler, R. S. and Liben, L. S. 1992 'Cognitive mechanisms in children's gender stereotyping: Theoretical and educational implications of a cognitive based intervention,' Child Development 63: 1351–1363.

Bigler, R. S. and Liben, L. S. 2006 'A developmental intergroup theory of social stereotypes and prejudice,' Advances in Child Development and Behavior 34: 39–89.

Brandstädter, J. and von Eye, A. H. 1982 Psychologische Prävention: Grundlagen, Programme, Methoden, Bern: Huber.

Cameron, L., Rutland, A. and Brown, R. 2007 'Promoting children's positive intergroup attitudes towards stigmatized groups: Extended contact and multiple classification skills training,' International Journal of Behavioral Development 31: 454–466.

Frindte, W., Neumann, J., Hieber, K, Knote, A. and Müller, C. 2001 'Rechtsextremismus = "Ideologie plus Gewalt"—Wie ideologisiert sind rechtsextreme Gewalttäter?,' Zeitschrift für politische Psychologie 9: 81–98.

Gniewosz, B. and Noack, P. 2006 'Inrergenerationale Transmissions- und Projektionsprozesse intoleranter Einstellungen zu Ausländern in der Familie,' Zeitschrift für Entwicklungspsychologie und Pädagogische Psychologie 38: 33–42.

Graves, S. B. 1999 'Television and prejudice reduction: When does television as a vicarious experience make a difference,' Journal of Social Issues 55: 707–727.

Heitmeyer, W. 1995 Gewalt. Schattenseite der Individualisierung bei Jugendlichen aus unterschiedlichen Milieus, Weinheim: Juventa.

Heitmeyer, W. 2006 Deutsche Zustände, Folge 4, Frankfurt a.M.: Suhrkamp.

Hopf, C., Rieker, M., Sanden-Markus, M. and Schmidt, C. 1995 Familie und Rechtsextremismus, Weinheim: Juventa.

Ihle, W., Esser, G. and Schmidt, M. H. 2005 'Aggressiv-dissoziale Störungen und rechtsextreme Einstellungen: Prävalenz, Geschlechtsunterschiede, Verlauf und Risikofaktoren,' Verhaltenstherapie und Verhaltensmedizin 26: 81–101.

Johnson, D. W. and Johnson, R. T. 1989 Cooperation and competition: Theory and research, Edina: Interaction.

Johnson, D. W. and Johnson, R. T. 1996 'Conflict resolution and peer mediation programs in elementary and secondary schools. A review of research,' Review of Educational Research 66: 459–506.

Johnson, D. W. and Johnson, R. T. 2000 'The three Cs of reducing prejudice and discrimination,' in S. Oskamp (ed.) Reducing prejudice and discrimination, Mahwah: Lawrence Earlbaum Associates.

Kiesner, J., Maas, A., Cadinu, M. and Vallese, I. 2003 'Risk factors for ethnic prejudice during early adolescence,' Social Development 12: 288–308.

Killen, M. and Stangor, C. 2001 'Children's social reasoning about inclusion and exclusion in gender and race peer group contexts,' Child Development 72: 174–186.

Klink, A. and Wagner, U. 1999 'Discrimination against ethnic minorities in Germany: Going back to the field,' Journal of Applied Psychology 29: 402–423.

Lösel, F. and Beelmann, A. 2003 'Effects of child skills training in preventing antisocial behavior: A systematic review of randomized evaluations,' Annals of the American Academy of Political and Social Science 587: 84–109.

Lösel, F. and Bender, D. 2003 'Protective factors and resilience,' in D. P. Farrington and J. W. Coie (eds) Early prevention of adult antisocial behavior, Cambridge: Cambridge University Press.

Lundahl, B., Risser, H. J. and Lovejoy, M. C. 2006 'A meta-analysis of parent training: Moderators and follow-up effects,' Clinical Psychology Review 26: 86–104.

Lynen von Berg, H., Palloks, K. and Steil, A. 2007 Interventionsfeld Gemeinwesen. Evaluation zivilgesellschaftlicher Strategien gegen Rechtsextremismus, Weinheim: Juventa.

Lynen von Berg, H. and Roth, R. (eds) 2003 Maßnahmen und Programme gegen Rechtsextremismus wissenschaftlich begleiten. Aufgaben, Konzepte und Erfahrungen, Opladen: Leske+Budrich.

McGlothlin, H., Killen, M. and Edmonds, C. 2005 'Intergroup attitudes about peer relationships,' British Journal of Developmental Psychology 23: 227–249.

McGregor, J. 1993 'Effectiveness of role playing and antiracist teaching in reducing student prejudice,' Journal of Educational Research 86: 215–226.

Nesdale, D. 2001 'Development of prejudice in children,' in M. Augoustinos, and K. J. Reynolds (eds) Understanding prejudice, racism and social conflict, London: Sage.

Noack, P. 2001 'Fremdenfeindliche Einstellungen vor dem Hintergrund familialer und schuslischer Sozialisation,' Zeitschrift für politische Psychologie 9: 67–80.

Olweus, D. 1996 Gewalt in der Schule. Was Lehrer und Eltern wissen sollten—und tun können, Bern: Huber.

Oskamp, S. (ed.) 2000 Reducing prejudice and discrimination, Mahwah: Lawrence Erlbaum Associates.

Persson, A. and Musher-Eizenman, D. R. 2003 'The impact of a prejudice-prevention television program on young children's ideas about race,' Early Childhood Research Quarterly 18: 530–546.

Pettigrew, T. F. and Tropp, L. R. 2006 'A meta-analytic test of intergroup contact theory,' Journal of Personality and Social Psychology 90: 751–783.

Schofield, J. W. 1995 'Review of research on school desegregation's impact on elementary and secondary school students,' in J. A. Banks and C. A. McGee (eds) Handbook of research on multicultural education, New York: MacMillan.

Schweinhart, L. J. et al. 2005 Lifetime effects: The High/Scope Perry Preschool Study through age 40, Ypsilanti: High/Scope Press.

Steinberg, A., Brooks, J. and Remtulla, T. 2003 'Youth hate crimes: Identification, prevention and intervention,' American Journal of Psychiatry 160: 979–989.

Stephan, C. W., Renfro, L. and Stephan, W. G. 2004 'The evaluation of multicultural education programs: Techniques and a meta-analysis,' in W. G. Stephan and W. P. Vogt (eds) Multicultural education programs, New York: Teacher College Press.

Stephan, W. G. and Finlay, K. 1999 'The role of empathy in improving intergroup relations,' Journal of Social Issues 55: 729–743.

Stephan, W. G. and Stephan, C. W. 1984 'The role of ignorance in multicultural education,' in N. Miller and M. B. Brewer (eds) Groups in contact: The psychology of desegregation, New York: Academic Press.

Stephan, W. G. and Stephan, C. W. 2001 Improving intergroup relations, Thousands Oaks: Sage Publications.

Stephan, W. G. and Vogt, W. P. (eds) 2004 Multicultural education programs, New York: Teacher College Press.

Tremblay, R. E. and Japel, C.2003 'Prevention during pregnancy, infancy and the preschool years,' in D. P. Farrington and J. W. Coid (eds) Early prevention of adult antisocial behaviour, Cambridge, UK: Cambridge University Press.

Tremblay, R. E., LeMarquand, D. and Vitaro, F. 1999 'The prevention of oppositional defiant disorder and conduct disorder,' in H. C. Quay and A. E. Hogan (eds) Handbook of disruptive behavior disorders, New York: Kluwer Academic/Plenum.

Vrij, A. and Smith, B. J. 1999 'Reducing ethnic prejudice by public campaigns: An evaluation of a present and a new campaign,' Journal of Community and Applied Social Psychology 9: 195–215.

Wagner, U., Christ, O. and van Dick, R. 2006 'Gutachten: Maßnahmen zur Kriminalitätsprävention im Bereich Hasskriminalitat unter besonderer Berücksichtigung primär präventiver Maßnahmen,' in Bundesministerium der Justiz und Deutsches Forum für Krimimalprävention (ed.) Hasskriminalität—Vorurteilskriminalität. Projekt Primäre Prävention von Gewalt gegen Gruppenangehörige—insbesondere junge Menschen, Band 2, Berlin: Bundesministerium der Justiz.

Wagner, U., van Dick, R. and Zick, A. 2001 'Sozialpsychclogische Analysen und Erklärungen von Fremdenfeindlichkeit in Deutschland,' Zeitschrift für Sozialpsychologie 32: 59–79.

Webster-Stratton, C. and Taylor, T. 2001 'Nipping early risk factors in the bud: Preventing substance abuse, delinquency, and violence in adolescence through interventions targeted at young children (0–8 years),' Prevention Science 2: 165–192.

Welsh, B. C. and Farrington, D. P. (eds) 2006 Preventing crime. What works for children, offenders, victims, and places, Dortrecht: Springer.

Wetzels, P. and Greve, W. 2001 'Fremdenfeindliche Gewalt—Bedingungen und Reaktionen,' Zeitschrift für politische Psychologie 9: 7–22.

Willems, H., Eckert, R.; Würtz, S. and Steinmetz, L. 1993 Fremdenfeindliche Gewalt: Einstellungen, Täter, Konflikteskalation, Opladen: Leske + Budrich.

Winkel, F. W. 1997 'Hate crime and anti-racism campaigning: Testing the approach of portraying stereotypical information-processing,' Issues in Criminological & Legal Psychology 29: 14–19.

Zick, A. and Küpper, B. 2007 'Vorurteile, Diskriminierung und Rechtsextremismus—Phänomene, Ursachen und Hintergründe,' in K. J. Jonas, M. Boos and V. Brandstätter (eds) Zivilcourage trainieren! Theorie und Praxis, Göttingen: Hogrefe.

Zick, A. and Küpper, B. (in print) 'Rechtsextremismus und Rechtspopulismus,' in A. Beelmann and K. J. Jonas (eds) Diskriminierung und Toleranz. Psychologische Grundlagen und Anwendungsperspektiven, Frankfurt a.M.: VS—Verlag für Sozialwissenschaften.

*Andreas Beelmann is professor in the Institute of Psychology of the Friedrich Schiller University in Jena, Germany.

Beelmann, Andreas. "Preventing Right-Wing Extremism: European and International Research." In Right-Wing Extremism in Switzerland: National and International Perspectives, edited by Marcel Alexander Niggli, 252–264. Baden-Baden: Nomos, 2009.

© 2009 Nomos Publishing, Baden-Baden, Germany.

Used by permission.

Youth Engagement in Right-Wing Extremism: Comparative Cases from the Netherlands

by Ineke van der Valk*

INTRODUCTION

In the post-war period the traditional extreme right-wing movement in the Netherlands has for a long time been a rather marginal phenomenon. However, facilitated by greater access to information via the internet and through the focus of specific youth cultures, this movement has increased in prominence over the past two decades. The focus of this chapter is on research results relating to factors determining entry of these youngsters into the far-right extremist scene and factors contributing to their eventual disengagement from this movement. Special attention is given to the role of violence in joining and leaving the movement. Nowadays discrimination of ethnic minorities in the Netherlands is increasingly framed in terms of hostility against the Islamic religion. On the basis of research on radicalization and deradicalization of youngsters and on ongoing research into islamophobic ideologies and practices such as violent attacks on mosques, this chapter argues that the Dutch far-right extremist landscape may be transformed when radical groups are increasingly influenced by an Islamophobic ideology that is gradually gaining momentum. Ideological shifts are already visible in the discourse and practices of several right-wing extremist groups. The chapter also discusses what Islamist extremism and the extreme right wing have in common and in what respect they differ. Insight into factors determining entry and exit of extremist groups and organizations equally offers insight into the possibilities of intervention.

RIGHT-WING EXTREMISM

Defining the concept of right-wing extremism has been a subject of debate among scholars investigating the extreme right for decades (see *inter alia* Backes & Moreau 1994; Betz 2003: 74–93; Eatwell 2003: 47–74; Hainsworth 2000; Husbands 2002: 38–59; Ignazi 2002: 23–37; Jaschke 2001; Kowalsky and Schroeder (eds) 1994; Pfahl-Traughber 1994; Pfahl-Traughber 1995). These continuing discussions are often inherent to the study of complex social phenomena which—by their very nature—are always subject to change. Aside from this, however, there is something else about right-wing extremism that sets it apart from other socially complex phenomena: its emotionally charged history since the Second World War, by which it has come to be associated with mass murder, annihilation and conquest. That association brings with it two complicating aspects that make it more difficult to achieve a shared definition of right-wing extremism:

- Since 1945, right-wing extremist groups have been the object of political and social isolation, together with repressive measures of all kinds. That is why the extreme right has been following a survival strategy for decades that is intended to conceal its ideological views and to present a more moderate message, or one that is modified in some other way. This survival strategy involved divergent efforts of adaptation as well as mainstream and fringe political activity[1] (van Donselaar 1991: 16ff).
- After the Second World War, aside from being used as a concept within political sciences, right-wing extremism also became a label that was used to discredit groups, ideas or personalities.

In this context it should be noted, moreover, that the concept of right-wing extremism, at least in the Netherlands, did not feature in public discourse until after the Second World War.

On the basis of definitions and theories of right-wing extremism in the relevant literature I use the following working definition. Right-wing extremism is a catch-all concept for political opinions situated on the extreme right fringe of the conventional left/right spectrum and, for those formations—political parties, social movements and media—that support and disseminate these opinions. Scholars engaged in the study of right-wing extremism and the ideas and convictions it espouses generally agree on the following common ideological characteristics:

1. A direct or indirect resistance to the principle of fundamental equality of all human beings as it is conceived in human rights treaties. This resistance is primarily expressed by giving primacy and great value in social and political relations to belonging to a 'race,' ethnic group, nation, culture or religion. Human and civic rights in this vision are subordinated to the strife for ethnic homogeneity. A positive orientation to what is considered 'us and ours' and a negative orientation to what is considered 'alien' is a strong characteristic of right-wing extremism: nationalism, ethnocentrism and racism are strongly articulated. Contemporary right-wing extremism defines itself as a movement struggling for the protection of its own national or Western identity in a world that it considers fundamentally hostile to Western values and culture.

2. A direct or indirect resistance to the current political system of parliamentary democracy and the constitutional state, including daily political practices of governments, political parties and judicial authorities. This resistance is expressed by systematic practices of delegitimization of mainstream political practices. These are often combined with a populist claim of representing the common folk.

3. A tendency towards non-democratic, authoritarian and hierarchical forms of organization in which a strong leader dominates.

The extreme right-wing view is not clearly demarcated, theoretically founded and closed. Many variations, accents and different emphases occur. It is a dynamic phenomenon that varies in terms of expressions and changes according to time and social context. It includes social movements and partisan orientations alongside diffuse mentalities that may be found amongst youngsters and practices of signification constructed around everyday experiences of ordinary people. For the post-war period a distinction should be made between classical neo-Nazi parties and hard-line movements on the one hand and post-industrial right-wing radical movements that have developed since the 1980s on the other. The latter are generally more moderate than the former and do not reject the constitutional state as a matter of principle. On the contrary, they are often part and parcel of a political system which they try to delegitimize in the eyes of common people. To mark a clear distinction between different right-wing currents and the boundaries of extremism, the Dutch Intelligence Service AIVD assesses the extent to which political goals are deemed antidemocratic or within the legal order and whether the means and instruments used are undemocratic or democratic (AIVD 2011: 5).

Comparative research has shown that in countries where modern populist radical right parties that operate within legal boundaries are strong, hard-line neo-Nazi right-wing extremist parties tend to be weak (Spöhr and Kolls 2010). This is also the case in the Netherlands. Indeed, a review of the Dutch extreme right-wing movement over the past 15 years reveals some striking patterns in this respect.[2] Compared to other European countries such as France or Germany, 'classic' right-wing extremism in the Netherlands has been weaker (see also Witte in this volume). This was already the case during the inter-war years. Politically organised classical right-wing extremist organizations have become less and less significant, particularly in recent periods. By contrast, by the midpoint of the past decade, expressions of radicalism on the internet, the formation of loosely organised extremist youth groups, as well as the gathering of some tougher, violence-prone neo-Nazi groups (all predominantly composed of adolescents) became all the more important. The number of underage perpetrators of racial violence increased. At the same time other subjects attracted attention: in the new millennium the Western world was brutally confronted with 'new' forms of extremism. Islamist extremists committed terrorist crimes inflicting many casualties. In the Netherlands the brutal killing of one person, the filmmaker Van Gogh, by a jihadi extremist shocked people locally and across the globe. Partially as a reaction to the phenomenon of Islamist extremism, the problem of Islamophobia has grown considerably in the past years, not only in terms of the increased verbal and physical violence directed at the Muslim community but also in terms of the growing tendency to turn a blind eye to crimes of expression and discriminating utterances aimed at them. Expressions that raised indignation some years ago are now passing unnoticed without provoking any public reaction at all. Most importantly, Islamophobia in the Netherlands has now become politically organised. A new phenomenon developed in the first decade of the new millennium: the rise and prospering of a populist Islamophobic party that is strongly supported by international opinion makers that shape Islamophobic viewpoints and consider the Netherlands the frontline in the war against Islam (Car 2005). The remainder of this chapter focuses on the author's research into these issues: radicalization and deradicalization of youngsters; Islamophobia and responses to Islamist extremism.

ENTRY AND EXIT

To gain a deeper understanding of the mechanisms whereby young people become involved in the extreme right wing, a research team at the Anne Frank House initiated a study in which in-depth interviews were held with former extremists who had been hard-line activists of far-right groups and movements. The researchers studied in particular the determinants and phases of involvement and disengagement and the correlation between them. They also looked at the possibilities of effective interventions.[3] The majority of the persons they interviewed were male, as is typical of right extremist organizations. The respondents lived across the country and were between 12- and 18 years-old when they joined the extreme right and between 15 and 24 when they left the movement. Several had committed racist crimes and some of them had been in jail. Family circumstances differed widely: with complete families and single-parent families, working-class and better educated parents; apolitical parents or rightist and leftist voters amongst the parents; some parents had outspoken prejudices about ethnic minorities and others none at all. Most of the interviewees were secondary school students who lived at home with their parents; a few had part-time jobs in addition to school. Despite this varying picture, a common element for many of the respondents was that they experienced problems at home. This might have been a factor that made them vulnerable.

It is impossible to discuss all the findings of this research project, but some particular results are worth mentioning. First of all it is important to note that political ideas did not appear to play a prominent role for any of the respondents as a motivation to engage in the extreme right-wing movement. They felt at most a vague ideological identification. However, it was found that respondents often did have ethnic prejudices that were sometimes prompted by negative experiences with ethnic minority youth.

The experience of unjust treatment by the government and society, a factor contributing to radicalization as identified in Van der Pligt and Koomen (2009), especially with regard to radicalized Islamists, was not found to be a factor in this investigation. The research team did, however, detect a general negative attitude and mistrust towards the government and society. There sometimes was evidence of experiences of unjust treatment from peers, some of them from ethnic minority backgrounds. The interviewees had little trust in the police to protect them from such threats.

A more important motivating factor that was identified, however, was a search for social belonging, a wish to make friends. The youngsters were look-ing for a lifestyle that fitted them and felt a need for excitement, adventure and often violence. There was also an emotional need to rebel, to protest and to discuss social problems. Frustrations and feelings of hatred, sometimes vague and sometimes related to lived experiences, found in extreme right-wing groups an outlet for these emotions, which quite often led to violence. 'The extreme right offers an interpretive framework for these experiences and prejudices that strongly appeals to the experienced group threat of "us versus them"'(Van der Valk and Wagenaar 2010: 72). It is only in a later phase that more ideological elements such as anti-Semitism were introduced to the young recruits by more experienced leaders. It was also in this later phase that the use of violence in-creased and came to occupy a central position.

The study results suggest that young people are active in the movement for shorter or longer periods, and during that time they fulfill varying functional roles such as ideologues, organisers, implementers and followers. Some organ-ise a group, arrange meetings and initiate actions. Others are more managerial and inspirational when it comes to vision and ideological issues. They educate members in right-wing extremist doctrine, dominate formally or informally or-ganised debates and discussion sessions and practise politics. Yet another group, the implementers, is active in daily practices. They take part in secret or open actions and activities.

Sooner or later some of the young members decide to walk out of the group and leave the extreme right-wing movement behind. The study clearly shows that this decision to leave the scene and the implied processes of socio-cognitive deradicalization and physical disengagement do not follow a linear pattern that applies to all respondents. Some begin to doubt the ideology, others are disappointed in the behaviour of other members who, in their eyes, do not even live according to the norms and values of the group. Still others begin to have misgivings about the actions of the group or they are disappointed in the movement as 'a trustworthy social environment' (ibid: 73). Some activists leave but remain loyal to the ideas, but the obverse is also true. An obvious factor that stimulated people to leave the movement, according to the study, was the need for a more conventional, socially integrated existence: in short, work, partner and a house, a wish that was obviously related to their age.

A question that was identified as crucial to the process of leaving the movement is whether there is any perspective of a new social life when the right-extremist milieu is left behind. If not, and if the person is socially isolated from mainstream society and peers, then leaving the right-wing extremist scene turned out to be very hard.

VIOLENCE

The study found that violence played a multifaceted role in relation to both radicalization and deradicalization. Being victim of violence sometimes furthered the radicalization process at the onset but also in later phases. Reports of violence committed by youngsters of other ethnic groups not only stimulated racist prejudices but also the use of violence by the radicalized interviewees themselves. Once the youngsters were completely engaged in the movement, identified with it and had successfully been introduced into its ideology, the use of violence became self-evident: for many of them, to carry weapons became a normal way of life. Pre-organised street violence directed towards ethnic minorities in different cities across the Netherlands became an important activity for some groups, as one respondent described:

> Violence does take place in the streets. A number of people are really good at it. You're walking down the street and feel like a little violence and you start looking for a foreigner to bash. Sometimes it is just a few punches and the person runs away. Sometimes you really lay into the person and leave

him lying on the ground. One of us got into a fight with a nigger once and beat him to pulp. (...) Some people pick a fight with Moroccans and get scared and try to calm things down, whilst they themselves provoked the fight.

Leftist, anti-racist young people who demonstrated against right-wing extremism were also confronted violently (and sometimes responded in kind). The researchers argue that the use of violence clearly enhanced the status of activists in the right-wing extremist milieu. Under pressure from the group people sometimes did what they would not do in a more normal context:

Sometimes it was fun and sometimes it was fucking difficult, especially when you had to hit people you know. I forced myself to do this in order not to let down the group.

In the movements that were examined violence and threats of violence were also used internally as a means of applying pressure and intimidation. Officially, most formal organizations however rejected the use of violence whilst at the same time turning a blind eye when their members were involved in such violent incidents.

Violence was also found to be a factor that plays a role in deradicalization and disengagement processes. It was, however, seldom a decisive factor provoking someone to leave the movement. By contrast, violence may also induce individuals to stay within the movement, when perceived as an attractive characteristic of right-wing extremism. Those who leave may be confronted with yet another expression of violence as a form of revenge and reprisal. One interviewee voiced these concerns:

I am afraid that people get nervous. If I meet them in the street it is the question who runs the fastest (. . .) It is a world of squaring accounts.

Quite often, however, it never goes beyond threats. Various respondents argued that this was different to other countries, where reprisals are more common and leaving the movement is more frequently seen as a betrayal.

Right-wing extremism is a dynamic and fluid phenomenon that is subject to ideological change. Racism towards foreigners and citizens with a migrant background, however, is a durable component. In the current climate in the Netherlands, Muslims, and especially Moroccan Muslim immigrants are the most common targets. This form of targeting has been termed 'Islamophobia' within academic circles and anti-discrimination movements—a concept initially defined as a set of feelings and expression of fear, enmity and hatred towards Islam and Muslims (Runnymede Trust 1997).

ISLAMOPHOBIA

The Netherlands has about 850,000 Muslims out of a total population of 16 million inhabitants. The majority of the Muslim population in the Netherlands can be traced back to the arrival of migrant workers during the 1960s primarily from Morocco and Turkey. Today the Netherlands has 475 registered centres of Islamic worship.

Although Islamophobia is a relatively recent concept, it is not a recent phenomenon. It has strong roots in (colonial) history but has undergone a revival due to international developments, in particular the end of the Cold War, the rise of transnational Islamist violent extremism, expressed so dramatically in the 9/11 attacks on the US, the ensuing war on terror, international migration and the evolution of ethnically diverse societies with related social problems. The Islamophobic discourse targets the Islamic religion—often understood or rather deliberately represented as ideology—as well as Muslim culture. The conception of Islamophobia as an expression of feelings of fear and hatred is too limited, however. It highlights the emotional component whilst underestimating its cognitive aspects. Think, for example, of conscious efforts to discredit certain groups of people in order to raise people's fear. Following theories of racism and the studies of Chris Allen (2010) on Islamophobia, this chapter adopts the following working definition of the concept: Islamophobia is an ideology that is historically and socially determined. It attaches a negative signification to Islam and Muslims with the help of images, symbols, texts, facts and interpretations. The perception, signification, attitudes and conduct of people towards Islam and Muslims thus underscore their exclusion as 'the Other' whilst favouring unequal and discriminatory treatment in the social, political, cultural and economic realm. These processes often also include people who are viewed as Muslims on phenotypic or other grounds such as clothing, but who in fact are non-believers. Islamophobia as a contemporary form of exclusion and discrimination has religious as well as gender and ethnic dimensions. These dimensions are closely intertwined. The complexity of the phenomenon is partly due to this intersectional character. Islamophobia may be considered as a new form of culturally orientated racism that has replaced more biologically orientated forms since the 1980s (Barker 1981).

A rise in Islamophobia within the Dutch context is in particular visible in terms of anti-Islamic discourse on the internet, in the political discourse of the Dutch Populist Party (PVV) which obtained 24 seats in the 2010 parliamentary elections, and in hate speech of extremist organizations. It is visible in widespread opinions that consider the Islamic faith as a backward ideology that hampers human and societal development and threatens civilization by throwing it back to the Middle Ages. It is also visible in negative attitudes in wider sections of the population towards Muslims. Almost seven years have passed since the murder of filmmaker Van Gogh in November 2004. Opinion polls show that high levels of hostility towards Islam have persisted ever since. On average, around 50 per cent of respondents in the Netherlands and Germany have expressed negative attitudes towards Muslims, according to the Pew Research Centre (2005), a far higher degree of animosity than has been detected in, for example, the UK (14 per cent) and the US (22 per cent). These are worrying signs not only from the perspective of equality and human rights but also because resulting polarization may foster radicalization on both sides, a fertile ground for both jihadi and Islamophobic extremism.

Islamophobic viewpoints are central to PVV politics (Fennema 2010; Kuitenbrouwer 2010; Van der Valk 2012; Willemsen 2010). The party characterises Islam as an ideology rather than a religion and no distinction is made between Islam and Islamist extremism. According to this interpretation, Islam is a global force for domination and conquest of the Western world. This vision is expressed in a political program that sets out to counter 'Islamisation' and violate the rights of Muslims. Although the Dutch criminal justice system has not condemned party leader Geert Wilders according to the penal law, judges have described some of his expressions as denigrating, shocking, hurtful, discriminatory and on the border of what could be tolerated. Wilders has made numerous references to Islam as an existential future threat:

> (. . .) I have good intentions. We tolerate something that totally changes our society. Of course I am aware that there will not be an Islamic majority in the next decennia. But it is growing. With aggressive elements, imperialism. Walk on the streets and see where it leads to. One feels that one does not live in one's own country any more. There is a struggle going on and we have to defend ourselves.[4]

> Islam is an ideology that is distinguished by murder and manslaughter and only produces societies that are backward and pauperised.[5]

According to the party leader, the demise of Western society and civilization is immanent due to 'the multicultural elites that fight an all out war against their populations' and protect 'an ideology that has been aiming at our destruction for fourteen centuries.'[6]

Despite the outspoken Islamophobic position of the PVV, the liberal and Christian-democratic coalition that forms the actual government officially cooperates with the PVV, thereby tolerating and legitimizing its anti-Islamic stance, as Witte discusses in this volume.

Traditionally hard-line neo-Nazi right-wing extremist organizations and groups (which are small both in number and size) are rather reluctant to follow the PVV in this respect. They are primarily anti-Semitic and have national socialist sympathies, although this is sometimes publicly denied. Their racism is not based on ethno-religious grounds. These groupings are not interested in Islam and explicitly reject PVV politics, not least because the PVV rejects anti-Semitism and strongly supports Israel. The anti-Semitic dispositions of these traditional neo-Nazi groupings have thus prevented mergers with more recent organizations focusing animosity towards Islam.

Nationalistic and patriotic movements, however, which form another current of traditional extreme right-wing politics distinct from the neo-Nazi elements and increasingly driven by Islamophobia, tend to support Wilders' PVV and have become ever more vocal against Islam and Muslims. This has, for example, been the case for one of the oldest post-war parties, the NVU (Dutch People's Union) since 1973. Close reading of their texts shows a combination of moderate viewpoints promoting collaboration with Muslims as well as vehement rejection of Islamist extremism. The NVU actively disseminates leaflets entitled 'Against the Islamisation of Europe' and was involved in a demonstration against a mosque in Aken in September 2010. In May 2011 German far-right activists joined an NVU-sponsored protest in Enschede near the German border, carrying a banner that read 'Kein Islam in Europe.' In September 2010 NVU party members were advised to vote for the PVV in the next elections.[7]

This development could provoke further growth of Islamophobia in the traditional right-wing extremist movement, spreading this ideology of enmity, hate and fear. In this respect it is also remarkable that some of the youngsters interviewed for the aforementioned Anne Frank House study warned about support for Islamophobia amongst the younger generation of extremists and the Dutch people in general:

> (. . .) If it were now it would have been Wilders. Why? That man says what you think, that is the danger of that man, why he has so many followers. Because there are now an awful lot of people who are against Moroccans or against Muslims more generally. That man says what people think. But those people don't know about politics, they follow blindly. (. . .) I think Wilders is dangerous, I am concerned. I think that Wilders is an obstacle for our beautiful society and that worries me, what will happen if that man comes to power. (. . .) And Wilders says that we have democracy but we can be clear: he presents a dictatorship (. . .).

Different manifestations of Islamophobic radical street groups, however, developed in recent years but have disappeared again following a lack of mobilizing support. This was the case, for instance, of Stop Islamisation of Europe (SIOE NI) that did not succeed in mobilizing more than forty people during 2008 demonstrations. In July 2011 the Dutch Defence League (DDL), related to the English Defence League (EDL), decided to disband too.

VIOLENCE AGAINST MOSQUES

The rise in prominence of Islamophobic discourse within traditional and nascent far-right movements coincided with the proliferation of violent incidents directed against the Muslim community. Some youngsters who were interviewed as part of the study participated in organised actions against Islamic targets. The number of documented cases of Islamophobic violence in the Netherlands has been steadily increasing over the years, peaking in the aftermath of specific contextual events such as the 9/11 attacks and the murder of Van Gogh in November 2004 (Bovenkerk 2006: 95–7; Van der Valk 2012; Van Donselaar and Rodrigues 2002: 23–6). Much of the violence against Islamic targets is directed at centres of worship, mostly mosques as the most visible symbol of Islam. As Lambert observed in this volume within the UK context, violent acts against mosques in the Netherlands mainly consist of arson (or arson attempts), targeted graffiti, vandalism and threats. This author's data on violence against mosques were collected from a variety of sources such as the Dutch National Police Services Agency, the National Anti-Discrimination Agencies, specialized research groups and the media. Despite this variety of sources there are good reasons to assume that the figures are an underestimation of the actual number of incidents of islamophobic violence. Underreporting is rather the rule than the exception: many incidents are not reported to the police or to other institutions. The reason is that victims sometimes do not know whom to report to or lack confidence in the advantages of reporting the attack. Sometimes the administrators of the mosques are asked by the police not to publish the incidents in order to prevent more problems. Most of the perpetrators of racial violence remain unknown. The resolution rate of racial violence cases in general is relatively low in the Netherlands: 12 per cent in, for instance, 2007 (Wagenaar and Van Donselaar 2008). This is also the case for violence against mosques. Almost all the perpetrators in the cases that have actually been resolved are young offenders. It is striking that far more acts of violence against mosques take place in small and medium-size municipalities than in large municipalities and big cities such as Rotterdam, Amsterdam and Utrecht, where of course migrant communities are larger and the number of mosques greater. This is obviously related to the fact that people in large municipalities and big cities have become used to the presence of citizens of ethnic minority backgrounds over the past decade. A review of mosque attacks from 2005 to 2010 reveals that a country as small as the Netherlands witnessed almost three times as many violent incidents against mosques compared to the United States, in terms of reported incidents (data of the American Civil Liberties Union, ACLU 2010): 42 in the US and 117 in the Netherlands. Altogether 239 acts of violence have been committed against Dutch mosques in the last decade (2000 to 2010), 62 of which were arson attacks (or attempts). The zenith was reached after the 9/11 attacks and the Van Gogh murder, with both years concluding with 45 to 50 incidents for each period, including 19 cases of arson for each period.[8]

SIMILARITIES IN EXTREMES

Despite the anti-Islamic slant of these traditional and nascent far-right groups, a number of similarities emerge when far-right and Islamist extremism are compared. To identify but a few comparative factors, on the ideological level, for instance, the rejection of democracy as historically the most acceptable and just system to rule the state is notable. A common practice of violence may equally be identified, or at least an extremely strong resistance against political opponents and a strong tendency to rely on conspiracy theories. Accounts implicating the West in conspiracies against Islam form a prominent feature of the Islamist extremist narrative, whilst the concept of 'Eurabia' is prominent in Islamophobic conspiracy theories.[9] In some cases, anti-Semitism would appear to be a common characteristic between the two forms of extremism, although it does not appear to be a feature of primarily Islamophobic movements. Whilst far-right extremism shows clear preferences for authoritarianism, moreover, Islamist extremist movements appear to rely more on networks bound by a common ideology rather than on structured forms of organization with authoritarian leaders. A network lacks such a formal (hierarchical) structure and has informal and flexible membership and fluctuating leadership, even though a core group might provide coordination (AIVD 2006: 13–18). Experiences have shown that tactics that differentiate between public and informal discourse and political activity—a characteristic of right extremism—also feature within Islamist extremism. But besides the common characteristics that can be identified between Islamist extremism and far-right extremism in terms of common interests, mutual contacts do, surprisingly, also exist [...].

An important reason for studying similarities and differences between divergent forms of extremism is the need to hone possible forms of intervention that can address some of the underlying processes of engagement. This does not necessarily relate to ideological similarities, therefore, but rather similarities that emerge when the people who adhere to these extremist ideologies are compared. As far as young people, adolescents, are concerned the individuals in question would appear to have a number of things in common.

Islamist extremism was long seen as an exclusively imported problem that originated in Islamic world. The reality is quite different. Many violent extremist activists and their supporters were born and raised in European countries or lived their adult lives in Europe. Converts also play an important and sometimes even a leading role. Islamic networks often consist of a complex mixture of actors of various kinds: so-called 'heartland-orientated' actors, working together with 'reborn believers,' and local activists (De Poot and Sonnenschein 2009).

The Islamist networks that have been the subject of research in the Netherlands (ibid) consisted mostly of men, although there were also a few women. They included young and old people, many did not have residence permits and some had criminal records or a history of substance abuse. Converts and second-generation youth were also involved. Only a section of these networks involved what could be regarded as idealistic political activists. Young people especially were rather looking for meaning and social relationships instead of being motivated on ideological grounds. Many second-generation migrants that were involved experienced feelings of alienation. They felt discriminated against and excluded by a majority society that, in their eyes, also oppressed Muslim people in the larger global world (Van der Valk 2010: 89). These youngsters sometimes consider radical-Islamist views as a third way, an alternative to the values of their parents and to the values of the secular society. It serves their interests as they are already publicly positioned, and feel themselves, 'in between two societies': their own community of origin and the European societies in which they were born and raised.

Radicalization processes in different groups and different ideologies in this respect often have much in common and follow similar patterns. The psychological factors that lead to extremism are partly related to reactions of indignation to local situations that are experienced as unjust. Anger and frustration, a vague sentiment of rebellion against society equally emerged as important factors for right extremist radicalization in the aforementioned study on right-wing extremist youth. As we see developmental processes in adolescence work out in different ways, they may find a specific outlet through political radicalization. Adolescent thinking is often black-and-white, without nuances. The youth are often uncertain about themselves, their social identity and their future in a society that is characterised by social polarization along ethnic lines. This makes them particularly vulnerable to group threats, be they symbolic or real. At the same time this form of radicalization is often related to a quest for identity, to a desire for companionship and social belonging and to a drive for revenge or violence, fuelled by propaganda. By joining the radical group they join an 'imagined community' that is shaped by such propaganda and this gives them the sense of belonging that they are missing in their daily lives.[10] In this way different radical youth cultures, Islamist and right-wing extremist, have gradually developed in recent years (Van der Valk 2010; Van der Valk and Wagenaar 2010). The youngsters' radical speech, appearance and conduct, be it extreme right-wing or Islamist, are an attempt to belong and to shape their social identity, and it is in this respect that young Islamist extremists have much in common with young people who organise themselves into extreme right-wing groups.

INTERVENTION POLICIES—SOME SUGGESTIONS

A salient outcome of the Anne Frank House study into determinants of involvement and disengagement were the possibilities of intervention. People disengaging from the right-wing extremist milieu in the Netherlands receive little or no support in the process, although they certainly are in need of it. Even in situations that lend themselves particularly well to such assistance, such as in prison, surprisingly, no such support or help is being made available. The study has shown that interventions are most likely to succeed if they are carried out when the person is still in an early phase of the process of involvement. But the results of this research also suggest that interventions can be successful when subjects begin to question their involvement too. In many cases, right-wing extremists are so isolated from the society around them that finding a way back to society is very hard. This often hampers the termination of a right-wing extremist career. The process of disengagement becomes unnecessarily difficult. Van der Valk and Wagenaar offer an outline for policy interventions to facilitate exit from these movements. Help from outsiders in such cases, they argue, is clearly important, as is a local approach in the communities where the young people live their lives. A helpdesk for formal and informal social support and support groups for parents are considered beneficial in this respect. The researchers also strongly recommend the use of former radicals with hands-on expertise. More than any other actor in the social domain they can contribute positively to the success of interventions.

Several of these former extremists have informed researchers that they feel guilty and consider participating in such a program in order to do something to pay their debt to society. Policies should enable them to do so and give these young people the opportunity to re-integrate into mainstream society.

FINAL REMARKS

This chapter has discussed some of the pathways young activists have followed as they become engaged in extreme right-wing organizations as well as their disengagement from these groups. For these youngsters the role of ideology was often less important than their search for adventure, belonging and friendship, although ethnic prejudices and indignation about the socio-political situation also featured. The new recruits were later introduced to extremist ideologies by more experienced members. Violence turned out to be an important and multifaceted factor in both entry and exit of these groups.

The Dutch cultural and political landscape is rapidly changing and an Islamophobic ideology is gaining ground, facilitated by the possibilities of the internet and the political expression of a populist party that has seen electoral success. This development may well induce a growth of Islamophobia in the traditional extreme right-wing milieu and more nascent extremist movements, leading to further dissemination of this intolerant discourse and heightening the risk of violent extremist attacks being carried out in pursuit of this agenda. Based on a comparison of youth engagement in Islamist and far-right extremism, it was argued that policy development designed to counter and prevent engagement in extremist activity should place attention on what the people who adhere to these extremist dispositions have in common. As far as young people are concerned, this highlights the importance of social needs in particular.

NOTES

1. J. van Donselaar elaborated this pattern in extreme right-wing strategies in *Fout na de oorloq, fascistische en racistische organisaties in Nederland 1950–1990*, Amsterdam: Bert Bakker 1991, p. 16ff. Van Donselaar borrowed the theatrical metaphor from Goffman's analysis of everyday interaction processes.

2. For an overview see the two-yearly reports of the Monitor Racism and Extremism project of the Anne Frank House in cooperation with the University of Leiden. Right-wing extremism in the Netherlands has been the subject of research by this project for 15 years (1996–2011). Otto Frank, Anne's father wanted the Anne Frank House not only to encourage people to visit the secret hiding place and remember the past but also asked them to realise that still today people are persecuted because of their race, religion or political conviction. Against this background the Anne Frank House developed the Monitoring project. English versions of the Monitor reports and related publications may be found on the website of the Anne Frank House: www.Annefrank.org. See also Witte, in this volume.

3. For the full report and the English translation, see Van der Valk, I. and Wagenaar. W., 2010.

4. Rechtbank (Court of Justice) Amsterdam 23 June 2011, LJN BQ9001.

5. G. Wilders, speech at the Court of Justice 7 December 2011, http://drimble. nl/bericht/3466017.

6. Ibid.

7. For more data and analysis of Islamophobia in relation to traditional extreme right-wing and extremist formations see Van der Valk, 2012.

8. For a more detailed overview of violence against mosques in the Netherlands see Van der Valk, 2012.

9. This concept was first developed by Bat Ye'or, a Jewish-Egyptian female writer working in Switzerland, and refers to a process in which Europe is supposedly invaded and subjugated by Arabs and Muslims.

10. The concept of imagined community is from Benedict Anderson, Imagined Communities: Reflections on the origin and spread of nationalism, London: Verso 1991 (rev. edn).

REFERENCES
ACLU 2010—Nationwide Anti-Mosque Activity on the website of the American Civil Liberties Union. (2010). http://www.aclu.org/print/map-nationwide-anti-mosque-activity.
AIVD (General Intelligence and Security Service) (2011). *Right wing extremism and the extreme right in the Netherlands* (p. 5). The Hague: Ministry of the Interior and Kingdom Relations. [www.aivd.nl].
AIVD (General Intelligence and Security Service) (2006). *De gewelddadige jihad in Nederland: actuele trends in de islamitisch-terroristische dreiging* (pp. 13–18). The Hague: Ministry of the Interior and Kingdom Relations. [www.aivd.nl].
Allen, C. (2010). *Islamophobia*. London: Ashgate.
Barker, M. (1981). *The New Racism: Conservatives and the ideology of the tribe*. London: Junction Books.
Backes, U. and Moreau, P. (1994). *Die Extreme Rechte in Deutschland : Geschichte—gegenwärtige Gefahren—Ursachen—Gegenmassnahmen*. München: Akademie-Verlag.
Betz, H-G. (2003). The Growing Threat of the Radical Right in P H. Merkl and L. Weinberg (eds), *Right Wing Extremism in the Twenty-First Century* (pp. 74–93). London/Portland: Frank Cass.
Bovenkerk, F. (2006). Islamofobie in J. van Donselaar and P. Rodrigues, (eds), *Monitor Racisme and Extremisme: Zevende rapportage* (pp. 95–7) Amsterdam: Amsterdam University Press/Anne Frank Stichting/Universiteit Leiden.
Car, M. 'You are now entering Eurabië,' in *Race & Class*, 48 (2006). 1, pp, 1–22. London: Sage Publications. [http://rac.sagepub.com].
Commission on British Muslims and Islamophobia (1997). *Islamophobia: A challenge for us all*, London: Runnymede Trust.
Eatwell, R. (2003). Ten theories of the extreme right in P. H. Merkl and L. Weinberg (eds.). *Right Wing Extremism in the Twenty-First Century* (pp. 47–74). London/Portland: Frank Cass.
Fennema, M. (2010). *Geert Wilders: Tovenaarsleerling*. Amsterdam: Bert Bakker.
Hainsworth, P. (2000). *The Politics of the Extreme Right: From the margins to the mainstream*. London: Pinter.
Husbands, C. (2002). How to tame the dragon, or what goes around comes around: a critical review of some major contemporary attempts to account for extreme-right racist politics in Eastern Europe. In M. Schain, A. Zolberg and P. Hossay (eds), *Shadows over Europe: the development and impact of the extreme right in Western Europe* (pp. 38–59). New York: Palgrave Macmillan.
Ignazi, P. The Extreme Right: Defining the object and assessing the causes. In M. Schain, A. Zolberg and P Hossay (eds), *Shadows over Europe: The development and impact of the extreme right in Western Europe* (pp. 23–37). New York: Palgrave Macmillan.

Jaschke. H-G. (2001). *Rechtsextremismus und Fremdenfeindlichkeit: Begriffe—Positionen—Praxis-felder.* Wiesbaden: Westdeutscher Verlag.
Kowalsky, W. and Schroeder, W. (eds) (1994). *Rechtsextremismus: Einführung und Forschungsbilanz.* Opladen: Westdeutscher Verlag.
Kuitenbrouwer, J. (2010). *De Woorden van Wilders and Hoe ze Werken,* Amsterdam: De Bezige Bij.
Monitor Racism and Extremism (1996–2011). Anne Frank House/University of Leiden. [English translation of reports: www.Annefrank.org].
Pew Research Centre (2005). *Islamic Extremism: Common concern for Muslim and Western publics:* 17-nation Pew global attitudes survey, Washington, DC, [http://pewglobal.org/reports/pdf/248 .pdf].
Pfahl-Traughber, A. (1994). *Volkes Stimme? Rechtspopulismus in Europa.* Bonn: Dietz.
———. (1995). *Rechtsextremismus: Eine kritische Bestandsaufnahme nach der Wiedervereinigung.* Bonn: Bouvier (2., erw. Aufl.).
Poot, de C. and Sonnenschein, A. (2009). *Jihadistisch Terrorisme in Nederland: een beschrijving op basis van afgesloten opsporingsonderzoeken,* Den Haag: Ministerie van Justitie, Wetenschappelijk Onderzoek en Documentatiecentrum. <http://www.wodc.nl/onderzoeksdatabase /inzicht-in-islamitische-terrorismebestrijding-obv-vanrecent-afgesloten-opsporingsonderzoek. aspx> [accessed 13 August 2010].
Spöhr, H. and Kolls, S. (Hrsg.) (2010). Rechtsextremismus in Deutschland und Europa, Actuelle Entwicklungstendenzen im Vergleich, Frankfurt am Main: Peter Lang.
Van Donselaar, J. (1991). *Fout na de oorlog, fascistische en racistische organisaties in Nederland 1950–1990,* (p. 16ff). Amsterdam: Bert Bakker.
Van Donselaar, J. and Rodrigues, P. (eds) (2002). *Monitor Racisme en extreemrechts: vijfde rapport-age,* (pp. 23–26). Amsterdam Anne Frank Stichting/Universiteit Leiden.
Van der Pligt, J. and Koomen, W. (2009). *Achtergronden en determinanten van radicalisering en ter-rorisme.* Amsterdam: Universiteit van Amsterdam, Onderzoeksinstituut psychologie.
Van der Valk, I. (2010). Islamistisch extremisme, in P. Rodrigues and J. van Donselaar (eds). *Monitor Racisme & Extremisme: Negende rapportage.* (pp. 85–108). Amsterdam: Amsterdam University Press/Anne Frank Stichting/Universiteit Leiden. [English version: http://www .annefrank.org/en/Worldwide/Monitor-Homepage/Research/Fifteen-years-of-the-Racism-Extremism-Monitor/]
———. (2012). *Islamofobie en Discriminatie.* Amsterdam: Amsterdam University Press.
Van der Valk, I. and Wagenaar, W. (2010). *Monitor Racisme & Extremisme: In en uit extreemrechts.* Amsterdam: Amsterdam University Press/Anne Frank Stichting/Universiteit Leiden. [English version: http://www.annefrank.org/en/Worldwide/Monitor-Homepage/Research/With-help-rightwing-extremists-pull-out-sooner/].
Wagenaar, W. and van Donselaar, J. (2008). Racitisch en extreemrechts geweld in 2007, in J. van Donselaar & P.R. Rodrigues (eds), *Monitor Racisme & Extremisme: achtste rapportage,* (pp 36) Amsterdam: Amsterdam University Press/Anne Frank Stichting/Universiteit Leiden.
Willemsen, C. (ed.) (2010). *Dossier Wilders: uitspraken van der meest besproken Nederlandse politicus van deze eeuw,* Schelluinen: House of Knowledge.
Ye'or, B. (2005). *Eurabia: The Euro-Arab Axis.* New Jersey: Fairleigh Dickinson University Press.

***Ineke van der Valk** is an independent researcher of racism, extremism, ethnic relations, and diversity in multicultural societies.

Van der Valk, Ineke. "Youth Engagement in Right-Wing Extremism: Comparative Cases from the Netherlands." In *Extreme Right-Wing Political Violence and Terrorism,* edited by Max Taylor, P. M. Currie, and Donald Holbrook, 129–147. London: Bloomsbury, 2013.

Violent Right-Wing Extremism in Norway: Community Based Prevention and Intervention

by Yngve Carlsson*

This article presents strategies and measures for preventing violent right-wing extremism in Norway.[4] The purpose of such a presentation is to inspire and make suggestions as to how this specific problem may be met. It is then up to the readers to find out whether they can include them in their problem-solving repertoire in their respective contexts. One cannot and shall not uncritically transfer problem-solving strategies from one context to another. I will therefore begin by emphasising the situation in Norway regarding violent right-wing extremism. The guiding questions here are: what kind of problems are the described strategies an answer to? And, under which societal conditions both the problem and the problem-solving strategies have been developed? I will then present some key strategies and measures to deal with such problems. In the end I will discuss their results and limitations.

This article focuses on intervention, especially when the problem with violent extreme groups is limited and potentially manageable. There are two reasons for this:

First, one important experience in Norway has been that local communities have been shocked, confused and uncertain as to how to respond when confronted with aggressive and violent right-wing extremism. This has revealed a need for a toolbox of intervention strategies and methods.

Second, it would be a very complex task to present the full range of a nation's strategies of preventing racism, intolerance, undemocratic values, aggressiveness and violence—even if this nation is a small one. Most of the work to prevent whatever is defined as a problem (bad health, drug-abuse, behaviour-problems, racism etc.) is done through kindergartens, schools, the health-service, the child-care system and youth work units in 432 Norwegian municipalities. Because local municipalities enjoy great freedom as to how to organise their preventive work and can thus decide which methods and measures to use, preventive work cannot be described through nation-wide programs. Moreover, preventive work is often hidden in the daily activities of public institutions, and there is probably a wide variety of ways to prevent the kind of problems discussed in this article. It is reasonable to assert that nobody has access to comprehensive and in depth information as to what is being done in this field in Norway. It is also reasonable to believe not only that good preventive work is carried out by municipal units (schools, youth clubs etc.), NGOs like political parties and their youth organisations, anti-racist organisations, sport clubs, and religious organisations etc., but also that some of this work will be superficial and even counterproductive.

It is easier to provide an overview of intervention strategies and measures when an extreme and violent group is about to develop. One reason for this is that interventions in those Norwegian communities that faced the greatest challenges during the last 12–13 years have either been evaluated or at least described (Carlsson, 1994; Carlsson & von der Lippe, 1997; Carlsson & von der Lippe, 1999; Carlsson & Bjørgo, 1999; Bjørgo, Carlsson & Haaland, 2001; Carlsson & Haaland, 2004).

Since the Norwegian welfare state has this municipal structure, I will mainly deal with local strategies and measures to intervene in emerging right-wing extremist groups.

THE SITUATION OF RIGHT-WING EXTREMISM IN NORWAY

Violent right-wing extremist activity has been a minor problem in Norway (4,7 mill. inhabitants) compared to its Scandinavian neighbour Sweden (9,5 mill.). While there are approximately two to three thousand active and well-organized right-wing extremists in Sweden, there are probably not more than 150–200 in Norway.[5] The scene reached its peak in 1995–1996 with about 300 participants. It reached a small peak again in 1999/2000. After that the size of the scene stabilized at a somewhat lower level. Norwegian right-wing extremists have until the last couple of years been poorly organised, and the pool of talent and skill has been limited. Few have had more than a basic education, and many of the participants have a problematic and criminal background (Bjørgo, 1997; Bjørgo, Carlsson & Haaland, 2001).

Though the problem on the national scale has been minor, right-wing groups have been active in a few Norwegian communities, attacking immigrants and threatening political opponents. Immigrant shops and asylum centers have been attacked by arsonists with bombs. Several immigrants have been attacked and injured. The most serious incident was when a 15-year-old boy with black skin-color was stabbed to death in January 2001 by two boys who participated in the neo-Nazi movement in Oslo. Two years earlier a 17-year-boy was chased into a river by two aggressive young men crying "kill the nigger" in the small-town of

Sogndal in the western part of the country. The boy drowned. Both these boys were absolutely innocent, and had not in any ways triggered the violence.

The capital Oslo and Kristiansand on the south-coast have seen violent conflicts between neo-Nazis and youth groups with immigrant background in which people have been injured. Such conflicts always have the potential to result in fatalities.

From the mid 1990's until 2005 approximately 20 Norwegian communities have experienced groups that have been labelled racist, right-wing extremist, or neo-Nazi; but only a handful of these communities have hosted visible violent groups for more than a few years.

During the last couple of years the neo-Nazi movement in Norway has become better organised as a result of inspiration and assistance from Sweden. The Swedish Resistance Movement has a counterpart in the Norwegian Resistance Movement. This movement predominately organizes boys and young men who have already participated in the violent skin-head group Boot Boys. They emphasize physical training, are more ideologically oriented than earlier, and are not as visibly uniformed as some years ago. There is also another organisation called Vigrid—lead by the 62 year old Tore Tvedt who is inspired by William Pierce who is the founder of the National Alliance, the largest and most active neo-Nazi organization in the United States. Vigrid praises old Nordic Gods like Odin, glorifies Adolf Hitler and denies Holocaust. The organisation does not directly encourage violence, but it promotes a racist and violent ideology and opposes the "zionist occupation regime" in Norway. The organization with its old father-like leader actively tries to recruit youth all over Norway. "Blood and Honour" has during the last year also tried to gain a foothold in Norway, so far with limited success.

I have been using the concepts "violent right-wing extremism" and "neo-Nazism." Right-wing extremism is a broader concept than racism, and implies some elements of political ideology and organisation. "Everyday racism" and "racist violence" are commonly used to describe social practices that do not necessarily involve any element of ideology and organisation (Bjørgo, 1997: 21). There are of course more than two hundred Norwegians with racist attitudes. And there are people outside right-wing extremist groups whose violence acts or harassment of people with a minority background are motivated by racism or xenophobia.

Right-wing extremist groups in Norway have during the last years also been labelled "neo-Nazis." This is because some of the groups have adopted a clearer neo-Nazi orientation. They have links to neo-Nazi organisations in Sweden,

Germany and the USA, they to some extent wear nazi symbols, they celebrate the 17 of August (the anniversary of Rudolf Hess's death) and crystal-night, and they have marched in the streets with Nazi-flags and symbols.

Even if the right-wing or neo-Nazi groups in Norway have changed their mode of operation during the last years, the most striking aspects of the situation up till now have been the following:

- The total number of participants in violent right-wing extremist or neo-Nazi groups during the last 10 years has probably not exceeded more than 300, and has been lower than that most of the time.
- Local groups have been few and they have disintegrated after a short period of time in most locations.
- Even in most of the localities in which such groups have been fairly permanent (Bøler in Oslo, Hokksund and Kristiansand), the size of these local groups has decreased. The most visible group in the Kristiansand area (100.000 inhabitants) has shrunk from 40 participants in 2000 to about 10–12 in 2004 (Carlsson & Haaland, 2004).
- So far Norway has not experienced violent football-supporter groups to the same extent as Sweden and Denmark. The by-far biggest supporter group, Vålerenga in Oslo, and the national Norwegian Supporter Alliance, have a clear anti-racist profile.[6]

There are some important contextual explanations for this rather stable and controlled situation in Norway.

THE HISTORICAL, POLITICAL, ECONOMICAL AND GEOGRAPHICAL CONTEXT

The Historical Explanation

Norway suffered a lot from the five year German occupation (1940 to 1945) in collaboration with the Norwegian national-socialist party Nasjonal Samling. The Norwegians took on a very active confrontation with Nazism after the war. Those with nazi-convictions and those who collaborated with the enemy were exposed to both legal sanctions and informal bullying and harassment. There has hardly been anything more stigmatising in Norway, both for individuals and local communities, than to be connected with nazi ideology. The Norwegian population was vaccinated against Nazism. This vaccination is still in effect, but is probably waning among some youth.

The Political Explanation

The immigration of guest workers and refugees from non-European countries into Norway started late, in the late 1960's. Today nearly six percent of the population have non-western origins. In Oslo nearly 20 percent (and 30 percent of the children) have such a background. The process of integrating of immigrants has produced some tensions and problems. And these problems have been very clearly articulated by the Norwegian Progress Party. It is not fair to call it a right-wing extremist party. It is a populist party. But prominent party leaders, both on the local and national level, have during the last 20 years articulated xenophobic views. The party obtained 22 percent of the votes in the election of the Norwegian parliament in September 2005. It is the greatest opposition party to the new "red-green" government. The party's current success is due more to its economic and social policy7, than to its anti-foreign sentiments. Even though the xenophobic rhetoric has been moderated the last few years after having expelled some of the most outspoken party-leaders, the party still has a rooted credibility among people holding xenophobic views. The party has made it acceptable to express xenophobic and even racist views in public debate. While the party has most probably channelled some people with such views into a more "decent" political direction rather than into more extreme groups, such a party may legitimate attitudes that make discrimination and hostility towards immigrants more acceptable in the long run.

The Economic Explanation

Norway is no longer a typical industrial nation. Today only 22 percent of the work force is employed in industry. During an economic recession between 1988 and 1993 when a lot of factories either reduced their staff due to technological improvements or were forced to close down, the national unemployment rate rose to six percent, which was still low compared to the rest of Europe. In typical industrial communities, the unemployment rate was much higher, especially among young people. Young working-class lads whose job-aspiration was to work in the local paper-mill, pulp-factory or sawmill, suddenly faced closed gates. Anti-foreign sentiments grew during this time, as people blamed refugees for their own miserable situation. Both individual refugees and houses for refugees were attacked. Although many of the attacks were clearly motivated by racism, the perpetrators neither had deeply rooted racist convictions nor neo-Nazi-sympathies. However, such communities were visited by leading racists or neo-Nazis trying to exploit the situation and add fuel to the fire (Carlsson, 1994; Carlsson & von der Lippe, 1997; Bjørgo, 1997).

During the last 10 years the Norwegian unemployment rate has stabilised at 3–4 percent (3.3 % in the summer of 2005). The economy is fertilised by some of the oil income, and there is a demand for labour power within the building and construction, health service, trade, logistics and transport sectors. It may still be difficult to get a job, but for young men, even those with little education, the labour-market is probably better in Norway than elsewhere in Europe. The experience from intervention-projects both in Kristiansand and Oslo has been that it is even possible to find jobs for marginalised youth belonging either to the violent right extremist scene or to violent immigrant youth groups8 (Carlsson & Haaland, 2004; Carlsson, 2005).

The Geographical Explanation—"Transparency"

Compared to most European states Norway has huge geographical dimensions. It is about 2800 km by car from Kristiansand in the south to Kirkenes near the Russian border in the north-east. Even though there is a concentration of people in the Oslo-area, most of Norway's 4.7 million population lives in small towns and rural districts scattered all over the country. There are only four cities with more than 100.000 inhabitants (Oslo, Bergen, Trondheim and Stavanger). Except Oslo (520.000 inhabitants in the municipality and 800.000 in the urban area) and maybe Bergen (250.000 inhabitants), all other cities, towns and villages are very transparent. Local individual and group right-wing extremist-activity will normally be detected very rapidly either by the local police, the local branches of the security police, political opponents, youth-workers, or the local media. Since neo-Nazism and violent racism are hot topics for the media, local incidents will normally also reach the national news media, and as a result will incite both local and state action. This small-scale society with its close interpersonal ties among people in different agencies and organisations on the municipal level has a lot of advantages when it comes to prevention and intervention.

This being said, one should not make Norway more exotic than necessary. There are of course many cities, towns and rural districts e.g. in Germany that share many of the characteristics of their counterparts in Norway. Oslo can be compared to cities like Dresden, Hannover, Leipzig and Nürnberg. Kristiansand with its 77.000 inhabitants and Brumunddal with its 8.000 inhabitants are in many ways comparable to numerous European cities and small towns. The most important difference when it comes to geographical conditions is that many German cities and towns are generally integrated into more densely populated areas, entailing short travel distances. This is a fruitful condition for building up extremist groups, organisations and networks. Moreover, the size of the population makes both formal and informal social control much more difficult. Consider that Berlin has 75% of the Norwegian population on 900 km2, and that Nordrhein-Westfalen has an area 10% of Norway's and a population roughly the same as that of Norway, Denmark and Sweden combined.

PROBLEMSOLVING PIT-FALLS

Racist or neo-Nazi groups and their violent acts have received a lot of media-attention in Norway. The threshold for being given attention in the national media in Norway is probably lower than in most other European countries, due to the small size of the country. Since being labelled a "racist-place" or a "Nazi-community" has such a stigmatising effect (Bjørgo & Carlsson, 1999), local municipalities are clearly motivated to neutralise such a reputation. Since most municipalities that meet this problem for the first time lack any experience or a developed strategy, there is a danger that they will fall into one of the following pit-falls:

Denying or Belittling the Problem

In some communities where immigrants have been exposed to violence, local authorities have tried to deny a possible racist motive. When there has not been any clear racist or neo-Nazi ideology behind the acts, it has been easy to interpret the acts within an established scheme for categorising such acts. They have been explained as a result of "drunkenness" or as "boyish pranks." In doing so they have sometimes not been able to recognise that the acts, or the establishment of new groups, may have taken on new and more serious dimensions (Eidheim, 1993).

It is also tempting to belittle or deny a problem more *consciously*, because to do something about the problem implies recognising it. In some communities the local authorities have thus consciously tried to sweep the problem under the carpet. Since small violent groups may dissolve and disappear by themselves, and since there is always a chance that the latest violent act is the last one, such a "sweep-it-under-the carpet-strategy" may sometimes succeed. The danger is of course that the problem may grow when not counteracted by the police, civil society and/or the local municipal authorities.

Inability to Take Action

Recognition of a problem with right-wing extremist activity and violence is of course not a guarantee for adequate action. Those municipalities that meet this problem for the first time will probably neither have the necessary competence to properly analyze the situation, nor the right tools to intervene. The result may be that nothing is done, or that it takes years to do anything. Irresolution may also be the result of disagreement between key actors as to who is responsible. In the small town of Brumunddal in the late 1980s municipal leaders claimed that this was a matter for the police and the police claimed that this was the responsibility of municipal agencies like schools and social services (Carlsson, 1995). In the meantime little action occurred, and the problem grew to a size never before seen in Norway or even in all of Scandinavia so far. In the 1990s Swedish towns like Klippan (Wigerfelt & Wigerfelt, 2001), Karlskrona (Rundquist, 1999) and Trollhättan, Vänersborg and Uddevalla (Blomgren, 1999) experienced right-wing extremist activity that was even more serious than that in Brumunddal.

Moral Panic and Visible Action

The attention in the national media given to violent acts and violent group behaviour in specific communities has caused genuine shock, disgust and moral panic. Moral panic tends to lead to over-reactions or misjudged responses to (alleged) incidents of racist violence or manifestations of neo-Nazism. Strong public reactions against racism may however be of great value in themselves. The problem is that the "diagnosis" may sometimes be misjudged or exaggerated. What on the surface appears to be racism or neo-Nazism may sometimes be an expression of something else—e.g. real conflicts between individuals or groups that happen to be divided along ethnic lines. In such situations, one cannot always assume that the ethnic minority side is an innocent victim and the ethnic majority side by definition racist aggressors. Quick responses may address only symptoms, thereby failing to address the causes that are the real problem. This typically takes the form of symbolic measures that are highly visible without having any effect on the problem itself—e.g. deciding to build a new community-youth house. In wealthy Norway it may be fairly easy to "throw money at a problem" in order to symbolise a willingness to act. Such responses are usually decided upon without an analysis of what actually constitutes the problem. The causes of racist motivated violent acts or the establishment of a neo-Nazi group are normally much more complicated than the lack of a youth house.

KNOWLEDGE SUPPORT—A FOUNDATION FOR COMMUNITY ACTION

One lesson learnt from communities with violent racist or neo-Nazi groups in the 1990s, was that problems of xenophobic violence should be considered as responsibility of the entire community. A second lesson was that it was highly useful to involve experienced advisors competent in dealing with such problems, since almost all municipalities meeting this problem for the first time are uncertain and thus waver. As a consequence, the central government decided in 1996 to establish a pool of experts, "The Interdisciplinary Advisory Service for Local Action against Racism and Xenophobia." This advisory service consists of a dozen researchers and practitioners, including police officers, social workers, pedagogues and conflict mediators. Together, they provide complementary forms of expertise to municipalities and local agencies that have to deal with problems which they do not know how to handle. Usually a team of two advisors will help the municipal agencies develop an adequate analysis of the problem, ascertain the magnitude of the problem and give advice as to which responses might be effective.

BASING JOINT INTERVENTION ON KNOWLEDGE: HOW TO PRODUCE AN ANALYSIS OF THE LOCAL PROBLEM?

Both research and more experience based knowledge of racist and violent youth groups in Norway show that the root causes for the emergence of such groups, and the ways these problems manifest themselves, may be very different in different communities (Bjørgo & Carlsson, 1999). It is therefore important to describe the character, magnitude and seriousness of the problem, and also to try to identify both the manifest and underlying factors that have caused the problem in each community.

It is also advisable that those agencies that have some kind of responsibility to do something with the problem take part in the process of describing and analysing, as well as proposing solutions.

Depending on the model of mapping, participants in this process should include the police, relevant municipal departments, schools, voluntary organisations, and representatives from the youth population.

Three different models for mapping and analyzing a local problem have been used in Norway:
- An inter-agency working group with knowledgeable representatives (5–10 persons) from relevant agencies work together to collect and analyse information, and on this basis produce a report or action plan. They normally also discuss the individuals participating in the group,

their roles, and how to deal with them as individuals. Most Norwegian municipalities are small (half of the 432 municipalities have less than 5.000 inhabitants) and are thus very transparent. Even bigger municipalities like Kristiansand (77.000 inhabitants) are transparent, so that information on individuals is rich. However, sharing information about individuals is not unproblematic because of the confidentiality act in public administration.

• A "mapping seminar" (one or two days) with 20–40 participants representing different agencies and perspectives. It is useful to bring in an external expert who is experienced in running such processes, and a person who has in depth knowledge of racist and neo-Nazi groups and their mode of operation. This is a "quick" method, but may be "good enough" to assess the problem. In some cases the analysis will show that the problem at hand has little to do with racism or extremism, and that it must therefore be dealt with tools from other "tool-bags." In other cases the analysis will reveal a minor or nascent problem that can be addressed with fairly simple measures. In some Norwegian communities such a "mapping seminar" has taken place within a few days after a violent episode where racists motives were suspected or where those involved were part of a racist group. Due to confidentiality rules, however, such seminars are not appropriate for discussing the role of individuals and how to handle them. But this may be done in a more limited group after such a seminar.

• A research project by external researchers providing a description and analysis of the problem. While incorporating their knowledge, the researchers will probably do this from a different perspective than the local agencies. Four municipalities with such problems have received research assistance (Brumunddal, Nordstrand in Oslo, Vennesla and Kristiansand). A fifth community (Bøler in Oslo) received consulting from an experienced researcher for three years, without being subject of a research project.

Such methods may of course also be combined. A "mapping seminar" may be arranged a few days after a serious episode as a foundation for immediate action. This may be followed by a more thorough analysis as a foundation for more long-term prevention and intervention if the problem seems more rooted, complex, or grave.

The goal of such local mapping and analysis is to improve the accuracy of interventions. Asking a lot of questions about what, when, how, how many, and why etc. will reduce the risk of wasting resources on measures that probably will have no effect or, if they do, may even be counterproductive. Two examples: One should use different strategies if the group is well organised, has connection to foreign organisations, and has well educated participants between 20 and 30 years old, compared to a group consisting of aggressive boys age 14–16 mixed up in an on-going fight with a group of aggressive immigrant kids. A local scene with 100 participants must be met in a different way than a scene with only a handful of activist. In most Norwegian communities such groups or scenes will be small. This means that individually oriented measures of intervention will play an important role.

A COMPETENT, EXPERIENCED ADVISORY SERVICE

The Norwegian advisory service was established for the same reasons as the German "Mobile Beratungsteams." Since the problem with racist or neo-Nazi groups is fairly limited in Norway, the advisory service is of course not staffed with permanently employed advisors. They are permanently employed by the police, research institutions, or municipal units, but are willing to assist municipalities when they are in need of expertise.

To establish a team with fully employed members to handle such problems is probably not a good idea. It will most likely be difficult to get those with the most experience and expertise to accept full time employment in such a team. Teams with fully employed members run the risk of not having the necessary competence, thereby raising the risk that they may mislead those they are meant to guide. The team-members in Norway are among the most competent in the particular problems at hand in the country.

In 2000 Denmark established an "emergency team" with permanently employed advisors. The team's function was to advise communities with violent and troublesome youth groups (especially those with a minority background). The team was hardly used, probably because the advisors did not represent any prominent expertise in the field, and it was dissolved after four years. It was an expensive solution to have a full team just sitting there waiting. The Norwegian team has not had many call-outs either (3–4 each year) because the problem has been so limited in Norway. But maintaining this readiness for action does not cost the state any extra money. The costs are only running when some part of the team is in operation.

Norway has avoided using younger and less experienced advisors who may be lead by a strong political interest and who lack the necessary professional distance and awareness required of an advisor. According to Lynen von Berg (2004) this seems to have been a problem with some of the "Advisory Service" in Germany.

A COMBINATION OF SUPPRESSION, SOCIAL CONTROL AND SOCIAL PREVENTION/INTERVENTION

The rich and developed states in Europe and North-America possess an impressive array of means to prevent crime and violence. Community based strategies, methods, projects and programs are continuously being developed to deal with all forms of deviance (Cohen, 1985). This is of course also the case with measures to prevent racist violence and to intervene into violent extremism. In an affluent and well-organised welfare state such problems will not be met by a single measure, but by a combination of many. Such measures mostly fall into two different strategies. One is police suppression and different measures of social control. The aim of this strategy is to deter violence and to signal that ideologies that dehumanise refugees, homosexuals and political opponents, thereby legitimating violence towards them, are unacceptable. The other strategy is social intervention and integration, which is a "constructive approach" aimed at integrating participants in extreme groups and perpetrators back into the community. In plain words—the first strategy uses the stick, the second uses the carrot. Below I shall restrict myself to those measures that have been most directly used against racist violence and right-wing extremist groups in Norway and whose epicentre has been the municipality or community. I will not mention strategies to foster tolerance and a democratic spirit, since such strategies have a much longer time frame and their goals extend beyond preventing right-wing extremism. I also cannot discuss in detail what is done by the Police Security Service since my knowledge of their work is restricted.

POLICE SUPPRESSION AND OTHER FORMS OF SOCIAL CONTROL
Police Intervention

Ideological extremists who threaten political opponents and local political representatives are a matter for the Police Security Service. Extreme right-wing groups are monitored by the police security service both at the national and local level. Since extreme groups are few and Norwegian communities are transparent, the local branches of the security police are well informed.

The local police are responsible for preventing violence through patrolling the streets, intervening in acute situations, investigating illegal action and bringing perpetrators to court. Leading (violent) right-wing extremists are usually closely monitored and thus have little leeway to commit crimes without being caught. In Brumunddal in the early 1990s both the police and court administration gave high priority to the issue of racist violence. Violent acts were quickly investigated and brought to court within a few weeks (Carlsson, 1995). Unfortunately, under normal conditions the Norwegian criminal procedure works very slowly (especially compared to Sweden), and years may pass between a violent act and its perpetrator being sentenced in court and sent to prison. The sluggishness of the process makes it difficult to use quick sentencing and imprisonment as a means to neutralize leaders and detach them from the rest of the group (Carlsson & Haaland, 2004).

The Handbook on Right-Wing Extremism and Racism

The local police in Norway are by and large unfamiliar with right-wing extremism, violent racism and neo-Nazism. To prevent irresolution and inertia among the police, the Norwegian Police Directorate produced in 2001 a Handbook on illegal right extremist activity—in both an open and a restricted version. The handbook contains both information about the phenomenon and detailed guidelines on how to handle local problems and situations. The open version of the handbook contains:

- a presentation of the right-extremist groups and organizations operating in Norway and their characteristics;
- the kind of threats these organizations and groups pose to national security, political opponents and immigrants in general;
- their mode of operation and their activity on the Internet;
- a presentation of the symbols they use and the occasions they mark;
- a discussion of the freedom extremist groups enjoy according to the constitution to speak, gather and demonstrate, and the provisions in the penal code that limit this freedom;
- a presentation of illegal acts that are particularly connected to right-wing extremists groups;
- a presentation of the investigation procedure in cases where racism is suspected;
- the coercive measures the police are entitled to use;
- a presentation of the role of the secret police/the counter-intelligence compared to that of the local police.

Preventive Police Officers and the Empowerment Conversation

Small Norwegian police stations will normally have one or two preventive police officers, bigger stations (covering 50–100.000 people) normally have a small department with 4–10 preventive police officers. Preventive Policing has played a major role in intervening in violent and extreme groups in Norway. One important tool in the preventive police-officer's tool-bag is the empowerment conversation. Both the young person (below 18 years) and his or her parents are obliged to meet at the police-station (warranted by an article in the Police law) if the police are informed that the young person is engaged in unlawful activity or becoming involved with a problematic and criminal youth group. The purpose is partly to warn the youngster and his/her parents about the consequences of committing crime and/or being associated with a destructive group, and partly to discuss what can be done to prevent the youngster from sliding deeper into the group or into a criminal career. If the young boy or girl and his/her parents are motivated towards positive change, the police can also call for assistance from the municipal services to help the young person onto a more positive track.

For some youth this warning and access to help is a sufficient means to get them out of a violent group or scene. But for others the problems are so deeply rooted and complex, that such a conversation is of limited use. Such a cheap and simple measure is of course no panacea.

In 2003 the Police Security Service ran a nationwide campaign against the Vigrid organization. At the time the organization was attracting young people, including young girls, with its mystic rituals (baptism, confirmation-rituals and even marriage in the name of the old Nordic God Odin). In collaboration with the local preventive police, 95 youth known to have contact with the organization were called to the local police station for an empowerment conversation. They were informed about what Vigrid really was, and about the consequences of further involvement in the organization. Half of them expressed an immediate intention to break with the organization.

PUBLIC DEMONSTRATIONS AND INFORMAL SOCIAL CONTROL

Public demonstrations are of course not part of a uniform state strategy, they are more a spontaneous way for communities to react to violent attacks on immigrants or to the presence of local racist and right-wing extremist groups.

In Brumunddal in 1991, 4.000 persons (out of a population of 8.000) attended a public meeting at which a prominent right-wing extremist leader, who wanted to add fuel to a local fire, was going to speak. When he started to speak, they all turned their backs without saying a word; first those in the front directly in front of the speaker's platform, then those in the second row and so on. This demonstration was carefully planned and it was preceded by a massive "mouth-to mouth" mobilization campaign in the community. Oslo's autonomous anti-racist movement had been told to leave the confrontation to the local population, and they complied. As a result, this silent and non-violent protest spread to other parts of Norway, and has since become an important alternative both to protest marches and more militant confrontations.

In 2001, after the racist murder of a 15-year-old boy of mixed African and Norwegian origin, 40.000 persons marched through the streets of Oslo in silent protest against racism and neo-Nazism. Marches were held in other Norwegian cities and towns, and even in Copenhagen where 1.000 persons took part in a local demonstration.

The effects of such demonstrations on youth in the extremist groups are uncertain. Although they may stigmatize and isolate them further, they show that racism and neo-Nazism has little public support, and this may deter those flirting with such groups. In Brumunddal the immigrants expressed that this local demonstration signaled that they had a lot of sympathy and that they were under the protection of the local population (Carlsson, 1995). For some immigrants this demonstration persuaded them not to leave the community.

Soft Informal Control over Contested Terrain

Since the early 1990s probably more than a thousand Scandinavian cities and small towns have parents walking in the city/town center, in the suburbs or in other "hot-spots" on Friday and Saturday night to prevent heavy drinking, drug use, and violence among young people. In a mid-sized town with 25- to 50.000 inhabitants there will probably be three or four groups of five to six parents walking around in visible yellow waistcoats or reflector vests. The "night raven movement," sponsored by the Vesta Insurance Company, organises walkers in about 450 Norwegian communities. These walkers are mostly recruited from parent-organisations in local schools. The Norwegian Red Cross has night-walkers in 120 communities in Norway as part of their "Stop the violence" campaign.

To be a night-walker is a voluntary task and most participants do this not more than once or twice a year. Their mission is just to be visible, thereby bringing a sober adult presence to arenas dominated by youth. By walking around and talk to the youth in a friendly manner they exercise a soft kind of social control. Confronted with violence or difficult situations they are not to interfere directly, but to call their liaison-officer in the local police force. The police will then quickly arrive on the scene.

The neo-Nazis in Norway have not proclaimed "national befreite Zonen" (no-go areas). But in some communities they have been able to mark territory by making it unpleasant and unsafe for immigrants, and even local citizens in general, to pass through. In most of the communities with a visible racist or neo-Nazi group, the "night-walking" has been strengthened for a period of time by mobilizing more parents into the night.

In the late 1990s in the Oslo suburb of Nordstrand, some local neo-Nazis maintained a highly visible presence in the suburban center on weekends. They had out-door parties in the spring and summer that in addition to local youth, also attracted neo-Nazis from other parts of Oslo and its surrounding areas. In groups of 15–20 the night-walkers started to walk through the center and either talk with the youth in the scene or stand silently amongst them. They had police back-up some hundred meters away if the situation should get out of control. This visible presence of adults in their yellow coats made this area less attractive as a rallying ground for both local youth with racist sympathies and more prominent neo-Nazis in the Oslo area. The most active neo-Nazis moved their activity to another Oslo-suburb (Bøler). Most of the local youth did not follow. In this way the core group in the neo-Nazi scene was split from those flirting with the scene.

In communities with emerging violent and visible groups, one of the first measures to think of is to mobilise more parents as night walkers. This tool lies at the top of the tool-box.

SOCIAL INTERVENTION AND INTEGRATION

A fundamental perspective that characterizes Scandinavian crime-prevention policy in general is to combine suppression and formal and informal control with measures aimed at integrating the perpetrators back into society. This perspective has also characterized the intervention into neo-Nazi or racist groups in Norway. Most youth are not violent racists or neo-Nazis once and for all. Their identity is flexible and subject to change, especially if their situation is changed (Fangen, 2001). In the moral panic that may occur after a disgusting episode, it may be easy to forget this constructive perspective (Eidheim, 1993). The result may be that one cuts off all communication with those belonging to the racist and neo-Nazi scene, and that one tries to kick them out of the community with illegal and brutal means. Exclusion, however, tends to make people inaccessible to integrative forces and will probably strengthen their extremist identity.

The lesson learnt from the communities with racist or neo-Nazi groups is that one should try to reintegrate the participants into the community. Such reintegration must proceed step-by-step, through a combination of different measures.

Parents Groups

Parents often feel helpless and perplexed when their children take part in the activities of an extreme group. They suddenly have few people to discuss their situation with because it is so stigmatising to have a child in a neo-Nazi group. In both Oslo and Kristiansand parent groups were established in the late 1990s to support parents faced with this situation when the local problem was at its peak.

The parents in these groups shared information about the situation and then discussed and set reasonable rules for clothing/uniform, music, and out-door activities. One important goal of such groups is to support the parents in not turning their back on their children, even if they have disgusting attitudes and commit violence. If the parents turn their back on their children, they will probably have no other alternative for consideration and care than the extreme group. An evaluation shows that such groups played a major role in the parent's struggle to get their children out of the groups (Olsen, 2001).

Parental groups not only presuppose parental interest in the welfare of their children, but also that parents possess some fundamental qualities, resources, and values.[9] It must, however, be said that not all parents have this. This is one reason why it may be useful to have an outsider facilitate the discussion. In both Oslo and Kristiansand the groups had such a facilitator.

Building Personal Relations as a Stepping-Stone Into Education and Jobs

A study of the neo-Nazi group in Kristiansand (Bjørgo, Carlsson & Haaland, 2001) revealed that some of the most active neo-Nazis had suffered from severe lack of care in the family, some have parents with severe drug- and psychiatric problems, and some had deceased parents. It is useless in such cases to try to use the parents as a "stepping-stone" back into the community, as is the case with adult extremists above 18 to 20 years of age. An alternative "stepping-stone" may be a significant other who is willing to establish ties by listening to them, thereby wining their trust and being able to support them when they are getting tired of being a part of the racist scene or when they start to question the ideology (Aho, 1994).

Sometimes such significant others turn up in the local community. In the small town of Brumunddal it was a prominent local business manager who already knew some of the youth who were involved, and who had a strong wish that they would not end up as local outcasts. He gave some of the boys both care and consideration, and even offered them jobs in his business. According to Eidheim (1993) this business leader played a major role in splitting the racist scene in Brumunddal.

One cannot expect that such significant others will appear in every community. An alternative is the deliberate establishment of projects, units or practices with which to stimulate the building of personal ties to active neo-Nazis, racists or gang-members. In Kristiansand the Church Youth Project (CUP) plays this role (Carlsson & Haaland 2004). This small flexible organisation outside of the huge municipal bureaucracy has been in operation for 15 years. Its three professional social workers and staff of volunteers work with marginalised children and youth in the city. The three professional workers have managed to build personal relations with and acquire the confidence of some of the leading neo-Nazis. They have helped them find housing and work, or they have helped them get an education (this may be as simple as helping them to get a drivers licence which in turn give them access to the labour market).

The intention is that such a positive change in their situation will in the long run either change their attitudes, or at least reduce their willingness to participate in direct violence. It is important that such individuals maintain some ties to the community. This is a completely different strategy than the "kick-them-out" strategy favoured by some members of the anti fascist movement (Fangen, 2001).

There are also examples in which field workers and preventive police officers became the "significant others" discussed above. Some preventive police officers have been very imaginative and successful in helping young people out of the neo-Nazi scene. They have used their networks to find housing, a place at school (e.g. sport schools, county-college), and/or jobs.

Former participants in the neo-Nazi scene who have left the extremist scene, and who possess the necessary personal qualifications, may play an important role getting others out of a violent and extremist scene. Since the neo-Nazi scene in Norway is limited, it has been difficult to find defectors with the necessary personal qualifications and interests to perform such a function. The idea of using defectors to assist people out of the neo-Nazi scene was launched by Tore Bjørgo in 1997. The idea was adopted in Sweden in 1998 with the establishment of an exit-project staffed with defectors from the neo-Nazi scene. These defectors have since helped young people out of the right-wing extremist scene by building personal relationships, and they have thereby built up a network of defectors for defectors (Swedish Crime-prevention Council, 2001). The Swedish exit-project has also provided assistance to Norwegian neo-Nazis wanting to leave the scene. Through presentation in the Stern magazine, this Swedish exit-project has served as an inspiration for similar exit-projects in Germany.

An important argument behind this "inclusion-strategy" is that many participants, including prominent leaders, in extreme groups want to leave. They sometimes feel paranoid, are tired of conflicts with their enemies and fellow members, long for a more normal life, or start to question the ideology. But they do not know how to break the ties with the group since it fulfils a lot of needs for them. They therefore need help both to see alternative ways out of the situation, and to act on preferred alternatives (Bjørgo, 1997). One important means to achieve this is a person who can establish a personal relationship to them.

Small Scale Problems and Simple Logic

The Norwegian strategy towards violent right-wing extremism has been developed in a situation where the problem has been limited. The approach is based on the notion that if one can limit recruitment to a local group or scene and facilitate disengagement, it is possible to bring the group or scene "under a critical mass." A local group or scene with 30–40 participants is becoming a viable group. It is big enough to have interesting parties. Such a group will normally be visible in the community and therefore attract new recruits looking for action. It may also attract visiting "comrades" from other parts of the country or abroad both for parties and training. Before such a group grows too big, it should be possible to dismantle it. This can be done by promoting disengagement through the above mentioned means of inclusion, in combination with sending those who have committed serious crimes through the court-system and into prison. Youth in general may be deterred from flirting with the scene through public demonstrations, and those already flirting with the scene may be deterred from further involvement by empowerment conversations with the preventive police.

In some communities in Norway it has been impossible to dismantle such a group completely. In such cases, however, one may succeed in reducing it to a handful of persons. The group will then no longer be able to make its mark on public space, and the parties will no longer be interesting. In this way it will lose its power to attract new recruits. When the members of such a group grow older, their interest in recruiting new members may also be limited. For adult men between 25–30 it is probably not interesting to bring 14–15 year old boys into the friendship group, unless the men are deeply dedicated ideological activists.

OUTCOME

It is difficult to provide waterproof evidence that these strategies have succeeded. When problems with violent extreme right-wing groups are limited to the extent that they are in Norway, there is of course a possibility that most groups will dismantle without intervention from outside. It is, however, a fact that the anti-nazi-vaccine from World War II is expiring, which may make participation in right-wing extremist groups more legitimate than earlier. Many Norwegian youth have experienced violence at the hands of youth with an immigrant background, especially robberies, which could lead to counter-mobilisation. This change does not seem to have aggravated the situation, which is currently still under control. First, there are no more right-wing extremists in Norway now than there were during the last decade. Second, the local groups in Kristiansand, Hokksund and Bøler (an Oslo suburb) have all been clearly reduced. And finally, almost all new groups have either been dismantled or strongly reduced. It is most likely that this situation is to some extent connected with the action taken to fight the problem.

LIMITATIONS

The presented strategies of course also have their limitations. They do not address the forces that cause racism, intolerance, and a totalitarian world view. To prevent racism and foster tolerance and belief in democratic values is a much more long-term and complex task. Although the school-system plays a major role in this work, the belief in democratic procedures must be trained in a variety of different arenas.

The strategies presented here focus on the community and on intervention. The goal has been to prevent extreme and violent groups from being established, and to dismantle existing groups. Such a community strategy will be of less importance if and when people with a racist and/or neo-Nazi ideology establish networks that transcend community borders. New forms of communication have been established through the use of mobile telephones and the Internet. From every corner in Norway you can communicate with like-minded persons all over the country and all over the world. Instead of belonging to a small and fragile local group, one can join right-wing extremist organisations and networks that administer the feeling of belonging to a wider and more important "mission." Cheaper transportation (especially airplane-fares) and better roads make it easier for right-wing extremists to meet and generate a feeling of unity and togetherness. This mobilisation of individuals into a nation-wide network is one probable reason why the extreme right-wing scene has not been reduced further. Another limitation to this community approach is that it neither addresses the more developed organisation-structures that are being built, nor attacks the music- and culture-industry that support racist and violent subcultures.

The strategies for intervening in violent and extreme groups on the community level are not silver bullets, but they do cover one important problem-solving angle. The community approach will remain important as long as participants in racist or neo-Nazi groups operate in local communities. Since they live most of their lives in such small communities, they will probably continue to do most of their recruiting there. If they are to be included in the wider society, this should be done there where they already belong and have ties, unless they wish to build up a new identity and a new life in another community.

Such local intervention as used in Norway may be seen as a futile extinguishing of small fires. However, since there are no magic means for preventing racist and totalitarian attitudes and violent behaviour once and for all, it will continue to be a rational approach. But it will not be the only one.

NOTES

4. Thanks to Professor Tore Bjørgo at the Norwegian Police University College for valuable comments and contributions to this article.

5. A few years ago the Police Security Service assessed the Norwegian right-extremist scene to consist of 150–200 persons who belong to organisations or groups that encouraged violence. Today they are much more reluctant to provide such numbers, but they claim that the situation has not changed during the last few years. So it is still fair to claim that the number is between 150–200.

6. There are some signs that this violent and racist soccer fan culture is starting to grow in Norway, and these signs are being taken very seriously by the Norwegian Football Association, the Norwegian Supporter Alliance and the police.

7. The party wants to use the enormous Norwegian oil revenues both to lower taxes and to increase public spending especially for the elderly ("those who built this country"). Most economic experts (and the other political parties) claim that this will create huge inflation thereby undermining the Norwegian economy in the long run. The answer from the progress

party to such allegations is that the economic theorists have made so many mistakes in the past that they have no credibility left. A lot of both young and old voters believe this.

8. This does not mean that immigrants in general have easy access to the Norwegian labour market. The unemployment-rate for immigrants was 9.0 % in the summer of 2005 (Source: Statistics Norway: www.ssb.no/innvarbl/) which is nevertheless lower than the over-all unemployment-rate in some other European countries.

9. The discussions in such groups may be very tense if some parents share the racist views of their children. This was a challenge in one of the Norwegian groups until these persons withdrew from the group by themselves.

*Yngve Carlsson is special adviser for the Norwegian Association of Local and Regional Authorities (KS).

References

Aho, James A. (1994): This Thing of Darkness. A Sociology of the Enemy. Seattle and London: University of Washington Press

Bjørgo, Tore (1997): Racist and Right-wing Violence in Scandinavia. Oslo. Tano Aschehoug

Bjørgo Tore & Carlsson, Yngve (1999): Vold, rasisme og ungdomsgjenger. Oslo: Tano

Bjørgo, Tore; Carlsson, Yngve; Haaland Thomas (2001): Generalisert hat—polariserte fellesskap. Oslo: NIBR-pluss 2001: 4

Blomgren, Anna-Maria (1999): Vad gör samhället. Offentlig politikk mot rasistisk och främlingsfiendtlig våld i Vänersborg, Trohättan och Uddevalla. Stockholm: CEIFO

Carlsson, Yngve (1995): Aksjonsplan Brumunddal—ga den resultater. Oslo: NIBR-rapport 1995: 13

Carlsson, Yngve & von der Lippe, Herman (1997): Industribygda og rasismen. Oslo: NIBR-rapport 1997: 17

Carlsson, Yngve & von der Lippe, Herman (1999): Velstandsbydelen og rasismen. Oslo: NIBR-rapport 1999: 9

Carlsson, Yngve & Haaland, Thomas (2004): Voldelige ungdomsgrupper—intervensjon på kommunenivå. Oslo: NIBR-rapport 2004: 20

Carlsson, Yngve (2005): Tett på gjengen. Oslo: NIBR-rapport 2005: 14

Cohen, Stanley (1985): Visions of Social Control, Crime, Punishment and Classification. Cambridge: Polity Press

Eidheim, Frøydis (1993): Hva har skjedd I Brumunddal. Lokalsamfunnet i møte med de fremmede og seg selv. Oslo: NIBR-rapport 1993: 20

Fangen, Kathrine (2001): Demonisering eller ansvarliggjøring. Oslo: Tidsskrift for ungdomsforskning 2001, 1: 26–44

Lynen von Berg, Heinz (2004): Die Evaluierung der Mobilen Beratungsteams des CIVITAS-Programms. Eine kritische Betrachtung ausgewählter Ergebnisse. Teil 2. In: Journal für Konflikt- und Gewaltforschung 2/2004

Olsen, Hilgun (2001): Å være forelder til en nynazist. Oslo: Institutt for kriminologi og rettssosiologi: Hovedoppgave

Rundquist, Mikael (1999): Demokratins Muskler. Kommunpolitikers och lokale myndighetspersoners åtgärder mot nationalsocialismen i Karlskrona. Stockholm: CEIFO

Swedish Crime Prevention Council (BRÅ) (2001): Exit för avhoppara. En uppföljning och utvärdering av verksamheten 1998–2001

Wigerfelt, Anders & Wigerfelt, Berit (2001): Rasismens yttringar. Exemplet Klippan. Lund: Studentlitteratur

Carlsson, Yngve. "Violent Right-Wing Extremism in Norway: Community Based Prevention and Intervention." In *Prevention of Right-Wing Extremism, Xenophobia and Racism in European Perspective*, edited by Peter Rieker, Michaela Glaser, and Silke Schuster, 12–29. Halle: Deutsches Jugendinstitut e.V., 2006.

Raising the Right Wing: Educators' Struggle to Confront the Radical Right

by Cynthia Miller-Idriss*

Generational shifts are also detectable on the fringes of the German political scene, and this is particularly true among the radical right-wing. In the decades after World War II, right-wing extremism was rooted in the remnants of National Socialism, largely supported by former Nazis from the middle and upper classes and consisting, at least in the west, of formal political parties, publications, and cultural organizations (see Kreutzberger 1983, 18–19; Steinmetz 1997). But by the 1980s and 1990s, right-wing extremism had become a phenomenon of young working-class men. The percentage of right-wing violent crimes committed by youth under age twenty was 35 percent in 1986, for example, but had climbed to 70 percent in 1991 (Paul 1995, 40). Suddenly, young people born well after the end of National Socialism began to embrace right-wing subcultures through attendance at extremist music concerts or adherence to the skinhead and neo-Nazi "style" of heavy black boots, shaved heads, and bomber jackets. One late spring afternoon, I met Herr Weiss, a civics teacher in his mid-fifties, at his home in west Berlin. Over coffee and cake, he explained how he has observed a generational shift in the base of right-wing extremism in his own lifetime:

> Well, [my generation] directly confronted the generation who were active participants, who participated in the World War, in the dictator system of the National Socialists, or were themselves in the party or the ss or the army, those were the fathers and grandfathers . . . and that provoked opposition . . . protest, and that was then, that was the 60s, the protest movement. Today, it's totally different of course . . . well . . . perhaps [the teenagers today] are compensating for a sort of underdog consciousness with "Oh, we are a big state again." Well, immediately after unification here was a swell like that . . . "Germany is something again, is stronger and bigger again," and through such a feeling then, the nationalism is newly revived. That's already something different than in my generation. In the younger generation then there were hardly any right-wing radical tendencies: Those were really old Nazis, who founded the NPD and . . .

These shifting patterns of right-wing extremist participation began to receive serious national and international attention in the wake of German unification in 1990 due to a sharp increase in outbreaks of violence against foreigners in both eastern and western Germany, including a series of particularly violent attacks in the early 1990s. In 1991, a man from Mozambique died after he was thrown from a moving train by several skinheads, and several months later, a large group of people attacked two buildings housing asylum-seekers in eastern Germany. The asylum-seekers were evacuated after several days of rioting. In1992, a Turkish woman and two Turkish children died after their west German home was fire-bombed. As right-wing violence declined in the mid–1990s, however, political debates shifted to other issues, such as the status of third-generation guest workers and the reform of German citizenship laws. When right-wing crime rose again sharply in 2000, the topic was forced back onto the national agenda (see, e.g., Krupa 2001; Schwennicke 2001; Tagesspiegel 2001a, c). The German government estimated in 1996, for example, that there were 6,400 violent right-wing extremists in Germany—by 1999, the number had climbed to 9,000 and climbed again to 9,700 in 2000. The total number of right-wing extremists is estimated at about 51,000 people in Germany. Violent acts with right-wing extremist motivation also rose, from 630 in 1999 to 874 in 2000 (as reported by the Verfassungsschutzbericht in Erziehung und Wissenscheft 2000, 10; Krupa 2001).[1] In addition to the statistical increase in violence during the early part of the new century, there are reports that levels of xenophobia and support for the right wing are growing among German young people—in particular, for youth in eastern Germany. One recent study of ninth-grade students in Rostock, a city in northeast Germany, for example, showed that every third student sympathizes with right-wing opinions and every sixth student is prepared to use violence against foreigners, the homeless, or those with alternative lifestyles or opinions (Erziehung und Wissenschaft 2000, 4).

Schools have an explicit mandate to counteract the radical right-wing and in recent years have received increasing attention as a site where right-wing extremism needs to be dealt with more seriously. By the time I began my fieldwork in the fall of 2000, the radical right had emerged as a concern for many of the teachers, administrators, and other educators with whom I came into contact. As I discovered, however, educators' efforts to affect the right wing may inadvertently increase the appeal of the radical right, both as an oppositional subculture and as a space to express national pride, which is otherwise taboo.

DEFINING THE RADICAL RIGHT

The population of students that I studied—primarily male, blue-collar apprentices mostly from the east—is the group of young people deemed most at risk for recruitment into, or participation in, right-wing radical or extremist activities and groups. Despite wide debate about the most significant causes of right-wing extremism, there is some consensus among most German researchers about patterns of xenophobia and the characteristics of typical right-wing radical individuals more generally (see, e.g., Backes and Jesse 1996; Hopf, Silzer, and Wernich 1999; McLaren 1999). Specifically, right-wing radical individuals in Germany are more likely to be employed males in vocational programs or vocational occupations and from families with lower levels of parental education, and levels of xenophobia tend to be higher in the east (Poutrus, Behrends, and Kuck 2000; Rippl and Seipel 1999; Schnabel 1993; Schnabel and Goldschmidt 1997).[2]

The right-wing students I interviewed were the exception, not the rule, among the students I interviewed and interacted with, and the actual number of right-wing radical students in the schools I observed is difficult to estimate. Teachers' estimates about the percentage of right-wing radical students in their classrooms ranged broadly, with some teachers feeling that right-wing radicalism was not a problem at all among their students, while others estimated that the majority of their students sympathized or were involved with the radical right. More important, however, is the fact that the population that teachers feel they need to reach is not limited to students who are active members of right-wing radical or extremist groups. For the purposes of this chapter, include among the "radical right" both students who are active members of right-wing radical or extremist groups as well as students who express right-wing, nationalistic, or xenophobic views in classroom discussions or interviews but may not be active members of groups.

This population of students posed a significant and vocal concern for many teachers I interviewed. Students at all three schools identified themselves to me as current or former participants in right-wing radical scenes, if not active members of organized groups. In one of the schools, students with radical right views or memberships are a presence in most classrooms, and in some classrooms in that school they represent the majority view among their classmates.

Teachers face significant difficulties in trying to identify which of their students are a part of the radical right since many of the usual assumptions about right-wing radicals—that they are young, male, east German, working-class vocational school students—apply to many of their students. Most of the students who identified themselves as right-wing told me that they are not very open about their political views in the classroom (or they complained that if they are open about their opinions, they are silenced). Other students said that they didn't think right-wing students would "show themselves" at school. Moreover, the variety and rapid change of symbols that young people use to identify themselves as right-wing radicals, combined with the popularity of some of the symbols as part of a youth subculture, makes it difficult for parents, teachers, and educators to know and identify who among youth are in fact a part of the radical right. Students may also dress differently in the school setting than in their private lives.

These challenges are not limited to schools—in fact, defining the radical right in the German context more generally is not a simple matter. Contemporary right-wing radicalism in Germany can be understood as a cluster of six elements: 1) biological racism, 2) a social Darwinist belief in the struggle for existence, 3) demands for the exclusion or elimination of "inferior" groups, 4) authoritarianism, 5) acceptance of private vigilante violence against enemies, and 6) hatred of the "left" (Steinmetz 1997, 340).[3] German authorities make a legal distinction between right-wing extremism and right-wing radicalism. Although both categories contain similar elements of nationalism, xenophobia, racism, and authoritarianism, right-wing extremist movements are those considered to be in violation of the German constitution, the Basic Law. Right-wing radicalism, while offensive and troubling, is not illegal (Jaschke 2001, 24–30). The students discussed in this chapter primarily fall into the category of right-wing radicals since it is not always clear whether students' beliefs are directly linked to illegal behavior or not, except in cases where they indicated they had participated in violent or illegal activities.

Finally, it is worth pointing out that part of the difficulty in understanding the right wing and in identifying who is a part of it is the variety of groups that are considered a part of the right wing. While the elements of right-wing extremism identified by Steinmetz (1997) clarify what characterizes a right-wing radical or extremist, the extremists and radicals only represent one aspect of the broader group of young people engaged in the right wing. During my interviews with young Germans, I learned that, not only are there many types of right-wing radicals, but also that these different groups reflect distinct subcultures within right-wing extremism and radicalism. These distinctions become especially important during students' own descriptions of their political opinions since they use the terms to place themselves within or outside of the right-wing radical scene. Each of these groups has multiple further divisions and groupings, but the youth I interviewed described four main groups.

Fascists and *neo-Nazis* comprise two similar groups consisting of politically active right-wing radicals—those who are involved in right-wing parties, plan demonstrations and marches, and organize the right-wing radical movement. They are "fanatically committed to resurrecting national socialism as a political and social order" (Weaver 1995, 145) and are typically involved in formal political parties and fascist organizations. Rene, an information-technology apprentice who identified himself as a skinhead, said that "Nazis want to have the whole country be pure German or only want to have whites and then maybe eventually have control of the world." *Neo-Nazis*, he explained, are the "new Nazis," and *fascists* are more or less the same as Nazis.

Skinheads were described to me as the most likely to be violent and tend to be, as a group, fixated on partying, music, and alcohol. Meredith Watts (2001, 611) describes the skinhead culture as revolving around "music, fanzines (fan magazines), concerts, and other more or less organized symbolic and cultural events." Rene, the IT-apprentice quoted above, said that skinheads "actually just want to have parties and drink on the weekends." They are described as relatively apolitical, fixating on simplistic complaints about foreigners like "they take our jobs away" and are the groups most likely to be responsible for attacking and beating up foreigners on the street at night.[4] They are also sometimes described as followers or "'groupies' of the fascist political groups who search for acceptance from these groups but are not politically motivated" (Weaver 1995, 144). They may attend fascist organizational and political party meetings but are more likely to "serve as security guards at political meetings" and are "usually poorly informed about the tenets of national socialism" (145).

Hooligans are soccer fans and soccer gangs, known for causing riots and damage before, during, and after soccer matches. They are usually characterized as part of the radical right because many of their political views tend to be nationalistic, racist, and xenophobic, but they also tend to be less focused on political issues and more likely to engage in antiforeigner violence as part of pre- and post-soccer-game drunken brawls. In a characterization of violent rightist youths, Weaver (1995, 144) places *hooligans* into the category of youth who are either "nonideological and apolitical," using "violence to gain attention," or "youths from dysfunctional homes who learned violence as a means of communication."

It is important to note that there is overlap among these groups and that some groups actively recruit from other groups. There are significant distinctions within the groups as well. Claudio, a student I interviewed who identified himself as a former *hooligan*, told me that differentcolored shoelaces signify what type of group you belong to and where you stand on certain issues, but said that the colors meant different things in different parts or districts of the city.

In his neighborhood, he said, "white shoelaces means for example that you're ready to fight, you're immediately ready to start hitting." Black or red shoelaces conveyed different messages. All of these distinctions, and the students' explanations of the groups, illustrate the extent to which the right wing has emerged as a set of distinct and complex subcultures among German youth in ways that are often not clearly linked to political opinions or goals. Right-wing extremist groups market products such as CDs, clothing, lighters, jewelry, and perfume and cologne, often using national pride slogans. One right-wing group advertises a perfume called *Walküre*, describing it as "the flowery scent for today's national woman," and promises female customers that "with this perfume you are guaranteed to be attractive to every patriot."[5] Right-wing groups sponsor rock concerts and fund bands that produce right-wing music, with lyrics that are filled with hate and that promote violence against foreigners, Jews, left-wingers, and women who commit "crimes against the German *Volk*" by having relationships with foreigners, among others (see, e.g., Farin and Flad 2001).

The effectiveness of organized radical right-wing groups' efforts to create a youth subculture around music, clothing, and other products should not be underestimated. A year after the original interviews I conducted with young working-class Germans, I returned to Berlin to re-interview several young men who had self-identified as current or former right-wing radicals or had expressed views sympathetic to the right wing during our first interview. The role of youth subcultures in recruiting these young men into the right-wing scene became clear in these interviews. Martin, an information-technology apprentice, reported how he became involved in the right-wing subculture and how he managed to distance himself from it.

"I'VE LEARNED YOU CAN'T GENERALIZE"

Born in 1980 in a small town in East Germany, Martin moved to East Berlin with his family when he was seven. He lives in a rented house in northwest Berlin with his parents and his younger sister. His mother works in a hotel cafeteria, and his father, who used to be a crane-driver, now works in the stock and ordering department of a gourmet food company. His brother, twenty-three, is a professional athlete and now lives in another state with his fiancé, who is of Turkish-German ethnic heritage. After graduating from the middle-level school (*Realschule*), Martin completed an apprenticeship as a sales assistant before he realized that he really wanted to do something technical. He is in the final two months of an apprenticeship to be an information-technology systems electrician, one of four new certified occupations in information technology in Germany.

In his early-to-mid teens Martin became involved with a neighborhood group of right-wing radical young men, whom he describes as a mix of violent skinheads, skinheads, and neo-Nazis with a political perspective. He became involved with the scene through his best friend and doesn't seem to have made a conscious political choice to be a right-wing radical. He listened to the music, cut his hair short, and wore a bomber jacket because he thought it was cool, remarking that "I didn't even know that I was in the scene." All of Martin's other friends also became involved in the scene. As he explains, they had all been friends since kindergarten, and they developed as a group:

> It was two or three of them, who lived that life, who listened to the music, who had this perspective, and since we all knew each other from elementary school, you just hung around with them and then somehow hardly even noticed that you'd gotten involved in the group.

Although he says he heard about violent confrontations between the group and foreigners, he was never involved in any himself. The group would get drunk at night and get into fights and violent confrontations with gangs of Turkish youth in Berlin. "I saw my friend afterward and he was all swollen . . . that's nothing for me." As they got older, he gradually drifted away from the group, and his involvement lasted three to four years total. His brother's new Turkish girlfriend, whom he found very nice and who ultimately became an important confidant and advisor in his life, was one of the main motivations for his departure from the scene. Martin also notes that he came to know a number of foreigners at school who were all very nice. The contradictions between his experiences with foreigners and his participation in a right-wing radical social scene eventually became too much for him.

Although a few of his friends became more involved in the scene, Martin says that it was not difficult to get away from the group—partly because he was younger than the friends who became more involved—and partly because he is a big, strong person. "They couldn't do anything actually," he says. He still sees some of the former friends on the street and greets them, but he said he always finds an excuse why he can't spend time with them. In particular, he distanced himself from his former best friend, who has continued to be involved in the scene, began drinking very heavily, and has been in and out of jail. "As it got more and more extreme," he reports, "you started to think it over . . . no, I didn't really want to do that or he's always starting something with people . . . even if we're just going to the movies, and that's no fun."

According to Martin, his family was not even aware of his involvement in the radical-right scene. Although he listened to right-wing rock music, he did not own any of the music himself and says he always listened to it at a friend's house. His clothes and haircut were simply the style at the time. His parents are not very politically engaged, and while his parents and especially his mother initially had problems with his brother dating a Turkish girl, Martin reports that the girlfriend is now fully accepted by the family. Martin says that his brother's fiancé had the most significant influence on his political opinions and on his life. He believes that friends and the surrounding neighborhood and culture have the biggest influence on young people's involvement in the radical right.

Martin describes himself as someone who likes music, is a loyal and good friend, and is fairly intelligent. He says that was probably part of the problem he had with the right wing: "they were all idiots." Although Martin claims to have distanced himself from the right wing, some of his comments during his first interview illustrated that his views on foreigners were mixed. He said that there are good and bad aspects to immigration—while it brings new ideas, many foreigners engage in criminal activity in Germany. Foreigners should be required to learn to speak German very well, he said, and argued that it should be a condition of German citizenship "that they become German citizens, and not . . . German-Turkish or Turkish." When we discussed his transcript a year later, however, he noted those comments as an area where his opinion had changed significantly. One of his teachers is Turkish, and during a class discussion about foreigners and especially about Turks, "the teacher actually explained it all really well . . . and I somehow just got it. Actually, that they are all also just humans and that there are . . . different cultures and that's it. And there are always a couple of black sheep, but you have them everywhere. And you can't generalize."

While Martin ultimately distanced himself from the right wing as he entered into richer relationships with "non-ethnic" Germans and foreigners, not all young men in the right-wing scene experience such political transformations. Paul, a self-identified right-wing radical who I interviewed three times, is a good example.

"Too Lazy to Be a Neo-Nazi"

Paul was born in 1982 in East Berlin and grew up near the Berlin Wall. In 1989, when the wall fell, his family moved to a district of Berlin that would become renowned for the highly visible right-wing extremist youth who live and hang out among the housing complexes in the neighborhood. He attended a comprehensive school (*Gesamtschule*) in a neighboring district and graduated with an expanded lower school degree (*erweiterte Hauptschulabschluss*). He lives at home with his mother and an older brother, who at the time of our interview was serving in the German army. His father left when Paul was two, and Paul does not know much about him. His mother works for a social service agency in Berlin.

Paul wanted to be an auto mechanic but was not accepted for any apprenticeships in that field. He was fired from a previous apprenticeship (also in construction) because he was late too often. He is now training to be a concrete worker, but wishes he had chosen another occupation because "if you do this job for a long time, you get stupid." Paul leaves home by 5:30 a.m. in order to catch public transportation to his apprenticeship site, arriving by 7 a.m. When he returns home around 5:30 p.m., he usually heads directly to the soccer field, where he spends his evenings with friends. On weekends he goes to professional soccer games and discos, or visits family in northeastern Germany, where they have "good parties." Paul expects to be unemployed after he completes his apprenticeship in a few months. He plans to enroll in the army and hopes to extend his mandatory service to at least four years, and says he would consider being a professional soldier.

Paul is a right-wing radical but is, he observes, "too lazy" to be a neoNazi, whom he characterizes as more active, organizing and marching in demonstrations, which he finds boring. He says that if it's about "We want all the foreigners out completely, then I'm for that of course too . . . but I'm also too lazy to really do anything big about it, to join in with that." He says there are two kinds of right-wing youth: those who talk and those who act (or those who are "partly right" or "completely right"). He describes himself as in the middle, but more on the side of those who talk. Most of his friends are in the partly right-wing group, which means that they don't really show that they are right-wing radicals: "we have the opinion, but we wouldn't act on it. . . . Mostly I don't act on it, but if it, if it really comes to [that], then I do it too." He has been involved in violent fights with foreigners, which he says came about because they attacked his friends. In general, though, Paul supports violence, even if he's not always actively engaged in it, and speaks critically of those who express right-wing views but do not engage in violence, like his brother. His brother, he explains, "would belong to the group who doesn't do anything at all. That thinks that all the foreigners need to get out and so on, for example, but he would never do anything. He's too quiet for that, too lazy." His mother is also antiforeigner, but similarly to his brother, would not engage in violence herself.

Paul believes that one should really have German ancestors in order to be a German. But he does not support the view that Germany should be a space for an "Aryan race," in large part because although he used to think he was Aryan because of his blue eyes and blond hair, he discovered rather recently that his grandfather was Czech, which, he notes, means he (Paul) can't be Aryan. He is lukewarm on the topic, however, remarking that if the Aryan Reich should return again, he "wouldn't have anything against it."

Paul describes himself as stubborn, demanding, headstrong, and helpful. He says (with some pride) that he is "ready to be violent" (*gewaltbereit*). When he was younger, he said, he held back from everything because he was young and weak. Now that he is older and stronger, he does not hold back. He would mostly be violent for personal reasons—such as if a friend was beaten unfairly. "But not if somebody said, for example politicians, 'We have to . . . attack someone,' because . . . then I would say, 'why now?' then I always look for the logic behind it." Paul voted for the PDS in the last election—the former East German communist party. He says that he voted for them because they are "for the east" (*sich für den Osten einsetzt*).

Soccer, family, his health, and friends are the most important things in his life. In general, he thinks that friends and family are equally important in influencing a child's political opinions, but he does not believe that his own family influenced his. Although he describes his mother as being antiforeigner and his brother as having similar opinions, he says that his family is "not at all right-wing." He thinks that his political opinions "just developed," partly through watching the media.

Being German, Paul says, is not important to him. German is not a "philosophy" or a "life approach" (*Lebenseinstellung*) for Paul. He happens to have been born in Germany and "has to live with it." But he is upset by foreigners who come to Germany and take Germans' jobs or create terror. Foreigners who are born in Germany are partly German, he says—but not completely. It depends on how the family raises the child: "If they teach the child German things, then it's normal that the child would at some point become German. . . . For example a Turk, he comes here and instead of German he's taught Turkish. That's, then they should not live in Germany, they should go back to Turkey." If they live in Germany, "they should know German, they should know the German constitution and they should live by German rules, not their rules. Like for example, women have to be all wrapped up and shit like that."

Martin's and Paul's experiences, while only snapshots, are in many ways typical of the experiences of many young men, especially in east Germany. Their peer groups as adolescents—and the pervasive right-wing subculture in their neighborhoods—were particularly important elements in their engagement with the right-wing scene.

ENGAGING THE RIGHT WING

How are teachers engaging with youth like Martin and Paul? As I discovered, they spend much of their time focused on learning how to more accurately identify the right-wing students in their classrooms and crafting argumentation skills to better confront statements that right-wing students make in class (Miller-Idriss 2005). Learning to better identify radical right-wing students, however, is not as easy as it sounds. The symbols that right-wing radical youth use to identify themselves to each other and others—especially the ones that go beyond the more standard and recognizable bomber jackets, high black leather boots, and shaved heads—change, often rapidly, as new symbols are banned by schools or even the government. The German government bans, for example, the display of swastikas and modified swastikas—so young people have come up with new symbols, such as the number "88," which stands for the eighth letter of the alphabet ("HH"), which stands for "Heil Hitler." When schools began banning the number "88," some young people starting wearing T-shirts that had "100–12" (one-hundred minus twelve) on them. Elsewhere, the number "18" is used for "Adolf Hitler" (*Politische Zeitschrift* 2000, 4).[6]

Some of the symbols are subtle and might be easily overlooked by teachers and other adults. Neo-Nazi groups and other right-wing radicals, for example, have taken to wearing T-shirts with the British brand Lonsdale displayed across their chests. The sporty brand was designed for boxers and became popular with a wide range of youth subcultures in Germany (Flad 2001, 106). But neo-Nazi groups find the brand appealing for another reason: when their bomber jackets are zipped halfway up, the shirts show the letters "nsda" within the word "Lonsdale," evoking NSDAP, the initials of the National Socialist Party. More recently, right-wing groups have marketed their own brand, *Consdaple*, which when worn with a half-zipped jacket, displays the full initials of the National Socialist party—NSDAP.[7] Neo-Nazi groups have also marketed other brands that are only available in shops that are part of the right-wing extremist scene. In an examination of right-wing clothing and styles, Flad (2001, 108) observes: "Whoever wears such clothing demonstrates that s/he is a part of the scene or at the very least makes use of contacts in the scene."

The formal state and school curriculum does not provide much assistance to teachers who wish to address the topic of the radical right in their classrooms. The state curricular framework leaves schools with a great deal of flexibility on how they address topics such as the radical right or xenophobia. Teachers "are still often left alone with the growing problem of right-wing extremist attitudes among students," a local newspaper in Berlin reported in December 2000 (Miller

2000). The curriculum framework for social studies for vocational school students recommends that school curriculum include twenty hours (over a three- to four-year period) of instruction on Nazi-Germany and its consequences, part of which includes a discussion of neo-Nazism and the radical right. Xenophobia is also mentioned as a topic that might be included in discussions of human rights or immigration (Senatsverwaltung für Schule, Jugend und Sport 1999). Each school revises its own curriculum plan based on the state's recommendations, and teachers design classroom practice with the school curriculum plan as a guideline. In other words, although both the state curriculum and the school curricula in the schools I studied recommend that teachers spend some time dealing with the issue of neo-Nazism and the radical right, neither provided guidelines for how teachers ought to go about this task.

Many of the teachers with whom I spoke expressed a sense of helplessness about right-wing radicalism among their students. Although they want to address the problem, teachers do not know what to do and feel they need training and help from outside. For some, facing right-wing extremists in their classrooms is something they have dreaded. Frau Cordner, a teacher in her early forties, reports:

When I was at university, that was actually a huge fear that I had. I always thought, "What will happen if one day I find myself sitting across from a Nazi," y'know? And how would I react?

Teachers reported that there were very limited resources available for them when they wanted to confront the issue of the radical right in their classrooms. There is not much support coming from central authorities yet, either. One teacher I interviewed reported that she called the Berlin School Senate (the highest school authority in Berlin) to ask for help dealing with radical-right students in her classroom. Although she called several times, and although there is supposed to be someone at the Senate specifically responsible for such concerns, no one ever returned her phone call. (She eventually went to the teachers' union for help, and they put her in touch with a private organization that deals with the radical right.)

Not all teachers attempt to directly confront right-wing extremism in their classrooms, of course, even when they are aware of it. Teachers may be uncomfortable with the subject in general, may have concerns about tarnishing the school's image, may experience immediate fear of potentially violent students, or simply feel uncertainty about how best to address the situation. But even in the absence of significant resources or training, many of the teachers I observed were making obvious efforts to try to influence students' political views, especially about the radical right and about foreigners, even as they often avoided dealing with the subject of the radical right directly. I found, first of all, that many teachers approach right-wing students with compassion. Frau Cordner, the teacher quoted earlier who said that before she began teaching she was afraid of confronting right-wing students in her classroom, thought she would be angry:

> [I thought that] I would certainly be terribly upset and would feel hatred toward that person. That's not the case . . . There is often frustration, but I always still see the students as students, as people with their limitations too, y'know? And I see that for . . . many of them it is not a, um, well-grounded opinion, rather for many it's a form of provocation, they know that . . . if they say something like that, then it will lead first of all to a half-hour's [class] discussion (laughs) . . . or they repeat it because they've heard it.

In the classroom, the picture that emerges of individual teachers is one of improvisation. Not only are teachers largely unprepared in any formal sense to deal with right-wing extremism in their classrooms, but given the diversity within the right-wing scene and the widespread use of symbols to signify various group memberships and degrees of involvement, teachers often struggle to understand who exactly is a part of the right wing among their students. As a result, teachers often find themselves making split-second interpretations of students' comments and having to decide on the spot how to respond to them in the classroom. Herr Hahn, a teacher in his early fifties, reports: "I personally have the difficulty of having to determine whether . . . [the things that youth say in class] should be categorized, that they have a strong national consciousness, or if the sentence is rather categorized as something that is against foreigners."

In addition to trying to determine the difference between statements that might be patriotic expressions of national identity versus those that indicate exclusionary, xenophobic, or virulently nationalistic sentiments, teachers also sense that some students make right-wing comments to get attention or as part of an oppositional subculture. Herr Hanson, a teacher in his early forties, expressed frustration with the rapid response of schools to what he feels may (merely) be oppositional comments:

> Once in a class here, I had some [students] who noticed, they can provoke a teacher, and they always gave responses that had dual meanings [zwei-deutige Antworten]. And they [school authorities] called a class conference because of National Socialistic incidents. That is, but that was a joke. It was simply . . . there wasn't anything serious behind it, but then there

had to be a meeting with the department chair, two people from the department, the class leader, three teachers from the *Träger* [apprenticeship training body], they came from all directions of the sky. It is something totally dramatic.

Teachers can send students home from school if they display symbols that are legally forbidden, such as a swastika, but in order to do this, they need to understand which symbols are forbidden and which are not, and whether additional restrictions ought to be imposed at the school level. At the construction school, local police conducted a workshop in the spring of 2001 in order to help teachers learn how better to identify right-wing students in their school and classrooms, and earlier that year, the civics department head distributed a handout to civics teachers with a list of banned symbols. At an April 2001 civics faculty meeting, teachers engaged in a lengthy debate about whether to recommend that the school ban bomber jackets and heavy black boots, both of which symbolize right-wing membership among youth but are not legally banned. Identification was also a significant part of the training provided to future vocational school civics teachers at a weekend training seminar offered by the Technical University of Berlin.[8] At the workshop, a representative from the Anti-fascist Press Archive and Educational Center in Berlin[9] led a three-hour presentation reviewing the dress, organization, symbols, music, culture, and subcultures of the right-wing scene.

Argumentation is also a central focus of the resource materials and training offered for teachers by central school authorities and the police (see, e.g., Goether et al. 1999). The intent is to help teachers develop effective responses to xenophobic, racist, or historically false statements made by students, such as "foreigners are taking our jobs away," "the *Neger* come here,[10] seek asylum, and we set a Mercedes in front of their door," or "Hitler himself wasn't so bad, it was really his rear-rank men" (see Hufer 2001, 30–31). Teachers report that learning how to respond to these kinds of comments is an especially important aspect of classroom work, so that they can correct misinformation or misrepresentations put forth by right-wing students. Many of the counterarguments provided for teachers offer facts and data that can be used to challenge misinformation about immigrants, asylum-seekers, the European Union, or unemployment.

Argumentation is also the second stage of training in a local Berlin teacher-training project targeting the radical right. This phase of teacher training is explicitly aimed at helping teachers learn to position themselves against the right, to know the main arguments of the right wing, to learn how to respond effectively, and to be able to create distance. Because many of these teenagers are breaking taboos, such as on issues of national identity, teachers are often unprepared to discuss these issues because the issues have been social taboos for so long, and they need training and help with how to engage these issues in the classroom.[11]

Teachers at the construction school in which I observed classrooms and interviewed students and teachers have not yet reached a consensus on how best to address the problem of the radical right in their classrooms. Among teachers, opinions were divided on the efficacy of focusing on identification and argumentation. Some felt strongly that a ban of right-wing symbols and clothing would be an important symbolic step for the school. Others argued, however, that teachers need to focus less on the symbols and arguments and more on the psychological background of these students. "Otherwise, I'm just a cosmetician, not a doctor," one teacher remarked at a faculty meeting, saying, "We need to talk *with* the students." A workshop for teachers run by the local police (which focused on identification and argumentation) spurred mixed reactions: while some teachers felt supported and were happy to have more information about how to identify and respond to right wing students, others bemoaned the lack of a pedagogical approach. "It wasn't really a workshop for educators," one teacher told me, pointing out that it didn't help him figure out what to do in the classroom with these students.

Moreover, it is clear that right-wing attitudes are not limited to the students who openly display right-wing symbols. Frau Dann, a civics teacher in the construction school, reported that xenophobic attitudes are a problem among most of her students,

> I mean, OK, we saw it during the last class, the xenophobia and so forth. In that respect the other [students] aren't any better, you !know? . . . I mean, [the right-wing student] wears that special outfit, but the others aren't all especially [different] in their opinions, you know?

In sum, I found that teachers' efforts to address directly the radical right focused on improving identification of right-wing radical students and learning how to react to them in the classroom through effective argumentation. I also found, however, that teachers were trying to address the radical right indirectly by attempting to address students' xenophobic tendencies and to influence how young people view the presence of foreigners in Germany. Although many of these efforts were not overtly linked to teachers' efforts to address the radical right, there was a relationship between efforts to address xenophobia and teachers' concerns about the radical right. This is evidenced, at least in part, by the fact that teachers made a more consistent and frequent effort to shape how students view foreigners at the construction school, where teachers also expressed the greatest concern about the presence of right-wing radical students in their classrooms. Some of the teachers also directly referenced the radical right in their arguments about why students should view foreigners or violence against foreigners differently, as the examples below detail.

Efforts to Transform Views of Foreigners

Several teachers made direct efforts to change how students think about foreigners and who belongs in Germany, often during lessons about other topics. Perhaps taking their cues from workshops that have focused on argumentation and argumentative approaches, the teachers I observed favored the use of rational arguments (as opposed, for example, to appeals to emotion or morality) to try to shift students' political opinions about topics related to foreigners or right-wing violence. Some of these efforts were directly linked to arguments about the radical right. For example, Herr Krug tried to shift students' opinions about black market labor by redirecting blame for the problem to Germans, pointing out that German capitalists are at fault for creating the situation: "Those [people] with very short hair say that it [the problem of black market labor] is the fault of the foreigners, but it's not their fault, it's the fault of the employers, who have set up the system." The reference to people with "very short hair" is a direct criticism of the radical right, and his comment was clearly intended to counter right-wing political arguments with factual information, namely, that German employers have set up an employment system which allows foreign laborers to be paid less than German laborers. Prejudice against foreigners, in other words, is often based on problems that originate with Germans and blame should be placed accordingly.

Another teacher, Herr Jaeger, urged students to think through to a logical conclusion what would happen if a radical right-wing party came to power in Germany, using the recent spate of violence against foreigners to illustrate. He pointed out potential repercussions for German firms and the German economy because foreign countries and individuals would boycott German goods, and he referenced the current situation in the state of Brandenburg, where foreign investments had dropped significantly as a result of increased right-wing violence and attacks against foreigners. Tourism had also suffered in the region as a result:

If the NPD came to power . . . Germany would become poorer and poorer . . . Through the activities of these people [the radical right-wing], millions of Deutschmarks have been lost in the state of Brandenburg, for example. No one wants to invest there. What would happen in Germany? Daimler-Benz would go bankrupt.

In focusing on the potential consequences for Germany if a radical right-wing party came to power, Herr Jaeger emphasized that such a situation would be an economic disaster for the country. Like his fellow instructor who mentioned people with "very short hair," Herr Jaeger argues that "these people" are causing financial loss to Germany, referencing the radical right without directly mentioning them.

Teachers also made a concerted effort to shape students' political opinions about foreigners even when the radical right was not part of the discussion. They frequently pointed out the legal and constitutional support for foreigners in Germany, reminding students that in Germany, the rights present in the "Basic Law" are "for everyone living within Germany's borders, not just for Germans." They also tried to encourage students to see foreigners as a more natural part of Germany's history. For example, teachers referenced the influx of guest workers from Turkey, Italy, and other southern European countries after World War II, pointing out that workers were actively recruited by the Germans because there was a shortage of German laborers. Herr Jaeger pointed out to one class that the influx of guest workers during this period was actually part of a pattern of immigration from other countries that had always taken place in periods when Germany needed working men. The need for foreigners in the German economy, in other words, has historically been an issue; waves of immigration over the past several centuries—such as the immigration of Huguenots and Swedes—have coincided with time periods when there were not enough German laborers. In discussing these waves of immigration, Herr Jaeger told students, "So we are all foreigners ourselves, really."

Other teachers tried to place the German experience with foreigners in the European context. One teacher in the information technology school put up an overhead showing that the percentage of asylumseekers Germany had absorbed since the early 1990s, relative to its total population, was actually quite small compared to other European countries. This information appears to have been relatively effective in shaping students' opinions about foreigners, as I learned a few days later, when I interviewed a student from the same class. In a discussion about the number of foreigners in Germany, the student told me that he thought there should be more foreigners, and cited the statistics from the same overhead, explaining that he hadn't been aware that Germany had accepted proportionally fewer asylum-seekers compared to the rest of Europe, and that he now thought Germany should take in more foreigners. This was the only time I heard this argument during a student interview.

One argument I heard frequently—both in and out of schools—concerned the continued population decline in Germany. As a result, Germany needs foreigners as laborers and to support future retirees, by paying into the social welfare system. "Germans are not reproducing enough," Herr Jaeger stated simply during a class in the fall of 2000. He linked the current discussion about retirement in Germany to the issue of immigration, pointing out that Germans are not reproducing at fast enough rates and that in order to keep the population high enough to support future retirees, millions of non-Germans will continue to be needed as part of the German workforce.[12]

There were other efforts to address xenophobia more directly. One teacher, Frau Schwartz, engaged students in a discussion about a demonstration against xenophobia that was to take place in Berlin later that week. The students overwhelmingly thought that demonstrating was meaningless. One student said that politicians only participate in order to gain popularity; another expressed cynicism about ordinary people who participate, saying, "they demonstrate and then by the time they're back in their cars they're acting like [jerks] ... angry at the people in traffic." Another asked, rhetorically, "What good would this demonstration do against people who are right-wing?" Frau Schwartz told students that such a demonstration can show the strength of the opposing side: "It shows that there is another opinion, that there are a lot of people who disagree."

There were times when teachers' efforts to address the right wing seemed rather unfocused. One teacher, Herr Ring, read aloud segments of two autobiographical essays students from another class had written for an assignment. (The students' identities were kept confidential.) He had asked the students to write a story about themselves basing the topic on an important experience from their own development. Both essays that Herr Ring shared in class were written by right-wing radical students. Reading from one student's text, he quoted: "Honestly I am happy if a foreigner dies . . . today I am right-wing, I will stay right-wing, I will defend my fatherland." Herr Ring seemed to be expressing exasperation at the essays, telling the class "and I have to grade these." When the students asked what kind of a grade he gave the essays, however, Herr Ring sidestepped the question, not answering it. He pointed out to the students that although his class could have chosen any topic to write about, several students chose political topics. He then transitioned back to the topic at hand, without engaging students in a lengthier discussion about the content of the other students' essays or why he had deemed it important to bring them up in class. This illustrates some of the teachers' struggle with the challenge of right-wing extremism. Clearly, Herr Ring was disturbed and unsettled by the essays and struggled with how to react to them. By sharing them with another class, he may have wanted to begin a discussion about the issue of the radical right, of the concept of "fatherland," or of violence against foreigners. But he never engaged in this discussion, leaving his intentions unclear.

Like his colleague Herr Ring, Herr Jaeger engaged in a strategy to address issues of xenophobia that may have been somewhat lost on the class. As he began a discussion about how many children Germans need to have in order to keep the population stable, Herr Jaeger commented (in a *very* sarcastic tone), "and by *Germans,* we don't mean everyone that was born here, not the colored people, only the Germans." In response, Dietrich, a right-wing radical student in the back of the room called out emphatically, "Exactly!" Although Herr Jaeger clearly meant the comment sarcastically, the way in which it might have been received by students—especially with no further discussion or explanation—seems very unclear. Instead of directly confronting Dietrich's response or developing his own comment, moreover, Herr Jaeger engaged in another intriguing interaction. He turned toward the entire class and said, "You know, sometimes you can recognize foreigners by their last names, because their names aren't German." Then he turned to Dietrich, the right-wing radical student, who has a "foreign-sounding" last name, and the following dialogue ensued:

Herr Jaeger: Dietrich, are you married?

Dietrich: No, it's my father's name, a Swedish name. Yeah, it's terrible.

Herr Jaeger: (in a friendly and logical tone) Well, why don't you send your father back to where he came from?

Dietrich: He can't.

Herr Jaeger: (in a meaningful way, to Dietrich and the rest of the class) Well then . . .

Again, Herr Jaeger immediately moved on from this discussion back to the topic at hand, without pursuing it further. Despite what were very good intentions on Herr Jaeger's part, if students did not catch the sarcasm in his comments about what "kinds" of Germans need to have children, they could walk away from class having heard an authority figure say that "colored" people are not German.

It is particularly intriguing that most of these discussions of foreigners, immigration, xenophobia, and the radical right stayed within the realm of rational argument or reason. Teachers did not appeal to a sense of morality or to Germany's past when advocating for an inclusive policy toward foreigners or when trying to combat the rise of the radical right, for example. It is also worth point-ing out that although teachers as a rule emphasized rational and argumentative approaches in an apparent effort to convince or teach students about the radical right, there were a few notable exceptions in teaching strategy and pedagogy. The two exceptions I observed involved teachers using hypothetical situations to encourage class discussions about the radical right. In both cases, the teachers appeared to avoid overt attempts to directly influence the kinds of things that students said. In one of these cases, a teacher asked the class to discuss what they would do if they witnessed neo-Nazis attacking a foreigner in a subway station. In the other case, the teacher called on three students with shaved heads and asked them to describe how people would react to them if they walked down the street together wearing bomber jackets and heavy black boots. Both hypo-thetical situations led to lengthy and engaged discussions about the issue of the radical right and xenophobia in Germany and in Berlin.

National Pride and the Radical Right

Expressions of national pride, especially the phrase "I am proud to be a Ger-man," are typically tagged as right-wing extremist expressions in Germany. In part, the linkage of national pride to the right wing results from the increas-ing appropriation of national pride by right-wing extremist groups, whose vocal proclamations that they are "proud to be German" do carry tones of ethnic or racial superiority. Badges with the slogan "I am proud to be a German" are for sale on right-wing party websites (Cohen 2001), and the NPD has handed out stickers with the slogan at information stands (Parade 2001). A 1993 song by Frank Rennicke, one of the best-known right-wing extremist musicians, is titled "Ich bin stolz, ein Deutscher zu sein" (I am proud to be a German).[13] While the lyrics to this song are in and of themselves fairly neutral, the fact that the song was written and performed by a right-wing extremist musician, whose other songs are openly racist and xenophobic, links the concept of national pride more clearly to the right wing. Another right-wing extremist group, Kraftschlag, sings a song "Trotz Verbot nicht Tot" (Not dead despite the ban), which also links the concept of pride to racism and the extreme right: "For the purity of our race we are ready/To take to our weapons/Our time is coming. For Germany and Europe/This time it should be/For the rebirth of the good/Proud, white, and pure!"[14]

There are also attempts by other groups to reclaim German national pride from the right wing, however. For example, the initiative "Germans against rightist violence" launched a campaign in the fall of 2000 with posters and advertisements throughout the country, displaying photographs of multicultural, mostly dark-skinned individuals wearing white T-shirts bearing the phrase, "I am proud to be a German" (Hops 2001; Putz 2000; Schwennicke 2001).

Some of the young people and teachers I observed and interviewed indicated that the attraction of national pride for the right wing results at least in part from the taboo on expressions of national pride. During a civics class discussion about the parliamentary debate on national pride in March 2001, one student argued that if everyone would say that they were proud of being German, then the phrase "wouldn't have any power anymore" for the right-wing extremists. Herr Meyer, a civics teacher in his mid-thirties, observes:

> The problem is that as soon as there is a certain national pride, the media, in part, simply shoves it into the National Socialistic corner . . . which, in my opinion, leads again to extremism. Well, I think, simply, it has to be said that we have to learn from history, and that, we should all also know what happened then and should be conscious of the fact that something like that can happen and also certainly could happen again, but in Germany in the entire educational system, in any case as I see it, from my history, from my development, there is always a guilt conveyed along with it.

Politicians and academics have also suggested that the attractiveness of national pride—and of the right wing—lies in the nature of the taboo itself. In a March 2001 speech at a conference in Leipzig against violence, xenophobia, and right-wing extremism, for example, President Rau argued that young people become involved with right-wing extremism, not based on their convictions, but rather in order "to break taboos" (Oschlies 2001). Others have also pointed out that the radical right-wing has become a site at which to break social taboos and engage in political and social protest. As Weaver (1995, 152) argues, these German youth "know that Nazi symbols are effective in gaining society's attention. Painting a swastika on a school wall or raising a 'Sieg Heil' salute brings the immediate attention of parents and teachers, the press, the government, and the world."

Some of the students I interviewed suggested that there is a link between the development of right-wing extremism and the desire to be proud. Kai, an information-technology apprentice, reported:

> I also think that . . . the hatred of foreigners results from this knowledge, that you know you're not allowed to say it, [that you are proud to be a German] because then you're immediately depicted as evil, but you want to say it somewhere, because you have to feel like you belong somewhere . . . and you also know that if you say it then . . . it [will be] seen negatively and

for that you immediately hate the other nations again, I'd say, because you can't be a German with abandon [*nicht so preisgeben darf Deutscher zu sein*].

According to Kai, xenophobia results in part from a reaction to the internal taboo on national pride as well as from resentment toward other countries for their unwillingness to let Germans express national pride.

Jochen, a cook trainee born in the east, explained why he thinks participation in the radical right is highest among younger east Germans and how it is related to the problem of national pride and national belonging:

> And there was no one who was stronger or richer or anything, it was just a group. And that's simply disappeared and all of the people who lived in that time, who were a part of that, I think there are a lot of people who simply need a group. To have something again that they can be proud of. And back then we could be proud of our . . . that you were a *Thälmanpionier* or a *Jungpionier*, you could be proud of that.[15] I think it's a little bit about the search for something to be proud of and they want to be proud of Germany, but can't be, because, yeah, because they think too many foreigners are there.

According to Jochen, higher participation in the radical right among east Germans is directly linked to their desire to be proud of something. As younger children, they were able to express pride in their *Pionier* groups, but as adults, they are prohibited from expressing a sense of national pride *except* within right-wing radical political circles and groups. Teachers also sensed that participation in the radical right is sometimes linked to a desire for identification with a group. During a discussion about the social disadvantages that many east Germans face today, Herr Metzer, a civics teacher in his early forties, believes that young east Germans who get engaged in the radical right are often seeking to construct a sense of identity. As he noted, "A retro-expression of 'nation' and perhaps also a particularly right-wing extremist expression of 'nation' is an additional point [*Haltepunkt*] with which something like an identity can be constructed, during these overwhelmingly confusing times." Frau Dann, a civics teacher in her mid-fifties, explains:

> National pride, for many students, is the lifeline [*Rettungsanker*]. These right wing radical groups, well especially here at the construction school, where I also see, that they are so . . . this big bald-headed guy [*dicke Glatz-kopf*] is sitting there, you know? Radiant, and he has somehow, imaginarily, his right-wing radical group behind him. You know? He is not sitting here alone. And here, sitting next to him, is the little pipsqueak [*kleine Würst-chen*], who simply admires this man, what kind of self-confidence he has.

You know? (long pause) . . . [Teenagers] want actually to belong somewhere, and over the years their youth centers have been taken from them
and there have been lots of cuts in the youth [policy] area, and in the DDR
the youth were still looked after, the children and youth were looked after,
and that's not the case with us [in unified Germany], and I can understand
really well, that they seek something like that and need it. Many of them
want to define themselves with national pride, and really like to use "I am
a German" as a way of keeping everyone else at a distance, even if they
don't mean it badly at all. But they want to identify positively, and our
society gives [them] too few possibilities to do that.

Other politicians have also argued that the continued insistence of political,
educational, and social leaders on an antinationalist discourse may be pushing
young people further to the right. This was certainly the case for some of the students I interviewed, who suggested that teachers' continuing efforts to delegitimize students' sense of national pride drives students toward the radical right,
which becomes the only space for positive expressions of national identity.

In sum, I found that teachers were struggling with the issue of how best to
address the problems of xenophobia and the radical right in their classrooms.
When they did address it, their efforts were focused on using rational arguments,
such as trying to convince students that foreigners were needed or that the
consequences of the radical right could be devastating for Germany. As I talked
with more and more students, however, I began to suspect that teachers' efforts
might be ineffective.

WHAT SHOULD BE DONE? YOUNG GERMANS' SUGGESTIONS

I asked students whether they thought the radical right was a problem (as
opposed, as some have argued, to something that was merely exaggerated by the
press), and if so, what they thought should be done about it. Most students saw
the right wing as a significant problem, but felt that many of the approaches
to confront the radical right were misdirected. Most of them believed that the
participation of youth in right-wing radicalism or extremism is caused by a lack
of perspective, general dissatisfaction, and a desire to be a part of a group among
young men who do not have much of a sense of a positive future for themselves.
Some students blamed parents, the media, and schools for falsely socializing
young people, and many thought that punishments for right-wing crimes should
be more severe. But by and large, the students overwhelmingly favored social
approaches to reaching out to radical right young people.

The most frequent suggestion from students was to improve educational interventions for right-wing youth or those at risk of becoming right-wing. Martin, for example, a former radical right-wing young man thinks that the government should sponsor more social programs and discussion sessions with young people. It would help if adults talked with these youth, he said, instead of just saying that those teenagers "'are bad, they're good for nothing.'" Adults "brand" such young people, he explained. "They are really driven out of the society and . . . that's not right." Even if the actions of the right wing are reprehensible, Martin seems to suggest, they are still a part of the larger society and can best be reached by addressing them as part of that society, rather than by shutting them out

Mehmet, a Turkish-German hotel trainee, agrees, arguing that putting bans on political parties or on ways of thinking doesn't make any sense. "They need resocialization processes," he said, and suggested that offenders should be made to have a meal with a Turk every day for a week. Another student said that schools should be less segregated and suggested that classrooms be deliberately structured so that all classrooms had a mix of foreigners and Germans. One of the teachers also noted that students need more cultural interaction across different groups, pointing to the lack of interaction and fear of the other among Turkish students from Kreuzberg (a district in Berlin) and students who live in east Berlin.

Carola, a cook apprentice who is the ex-girlfriend of an active right-wing radical youth, suggested that the state create projects to bring right-wing radicals and foreigners together. Because she thinks it would be difficult to force people "off the street" to do this, she suggests starting programs in prisons:

> If for example some skinheads were in prison, you could take them out and lock them up with [foreigners]. Then they should really talk to each other. Then of course they shouldn't take a foreigner who can't speak any German or something, rather that they could really have a good conversation with each other.

Many students felt that the state's closure of youth centers and afterschool clubs, particularly in east Berlin (see Weaver 1995, 147), had caused an increase in right-wing extremism. Young people don't have anything to occupy their time, they observed, and the right wing becomes a social group and an activity base from which they engage in fights or general troublemaking.

Some students said that teachers' approaches were hegemonic and overly narrow. For example, Michael, a construction apprentice, reported:

> I have the feeling that the teachers try to convince us that [right-wing

extremism] is bad . . . and that one shouldn't engage in it if one wants to be a good member of society or do good for the country . . . but you have so few opportunities to learn why they think that . . . you're sort of cornered in to a thought . . . you're just pushed into this societal picture but you can't really see what the other side, what's behind the other side.

Kai, an information-technology apprentice, observed that it would help if schools tried to introduce more intercultural work or teach about international issues or multicultural concerns in a more positive way. It would help, he suggested if

people were taught earlier that the other cultures are worthy, I'd say . . . in school you only learn that the other countries are there and that we harmed all the other countries, that's what you learn in school. But one should also [teach] people . . . I don't know, one should talk more about the positive aspects of countries.

Some of the most insightful comments came from the students I interviewed who identified themselves as having been formerly a part of the right-wing radical scene. During my initial interviews and focus groups, I encountered several young men who told me that they had been a part of the right-wing scene in their early teens, but were no longer involved. While all of the young people I interviewed identified a range of factors they thought influenced youth to engage in the right wing, including schools, family, and peer groups, the young men who told me they were or had been a part of the radical right were more specific about what attracted them. These young men were attracted to the right wing through their exposure to what they perceived as a "cool" right-wing subculture and their personal connections to right-wing radical members, especially close male friends or older siblings. In addition, right-wing rock music played a significant role in many of these young people's experiences. This music is aggressively racist, couching xenophobic, proauthoritarian, fascist lyrics in aggressive heavy metal music that has proven appealing to alienated youth. Claudio, who identifies himself as a former hooligan, says that he got involved in the scene after he started going to professional soccer games with a friend of his:

And you make friends there, and there was also a former friend of mine, he also became right-wing, and then you are a part of a big group and have a bomber jacket and everything . . . and at some point you get really involved, vandalize and loot, getting up in people's faces, getting drunk.

Finally, the explanations offered by former right-wing young people about how they got away from the scene are also informative. One student told me that while he was still an active part of the right wing, he was randomly assigned a seat next to a foreign student (from the former Yugoslavia) in his new vocational school class. As they became friends, he began to recognize the contradictions in his beliefs and was gradually able to pull away from the right wing. Students who had never been involved with the right wing also emphasized the importance of cultural interaction. A student whose family moved from east to west Berlin right after the wall fell, for example, told me that he thinks the reason why he never got involved in the right wing is because he grew up and went to school with so many Turkish youth. His childhood friends from the east, he explains, were socialized into a different scene.

Pride, Desire, and Extremism

In just one generation, a radical transformation in the demographic base of the right wing has meant that popular support for the right wing is largely cemented in working-class youth, rather than in lingering Nazi party members from World War II. The causes for this shift are multiple and complex. In this chapter, I trace an additional mechanism that has been overlooked by scholars who study the German right wing, arguing that a younger generation of Germans' resistance to the taboo on national identity and pride has created a space in which the radical right-wing becomes more appealing. This is particularly true for alienated working-class youth, many of whom are likely to end up unemployed upon completion of their apprenticeships and who see the radical right as a ready site in which to break social taboos and lash out at parents and teachers. And it may be even truer for youth from east Berlin, who sense that national pride—which was encouraged in the east—has been taken away from them in the post-unification era.

This isn't to suggest that young people's desire for pride necessarily leads to participation in the extreme right-wing. But for a small number of youth, their desire to be proud can lead them toward the radical right-wing, whose aggressive marketing with national pride slogans has created virtually the only space in which national pride can be expressed. More broadly, it may be the case that a younger generation's resistance is helping to transform the prevailing narrative about national identity, revealing how nations are continually re-imagined over time.

Educators may be able to help students engage in dialogue about national issues, including national pride, while simultaneously preventing them from latching onto the nation in virulent and violent ways. Whether they are successful depends, at least in part, on what happens in the classroom when topics such as national pride are raised. […]

NOTES

1. There is still some uncertainty, however, as to whether the acts have actually increased in number or are rather simply being counted more accurately (see Homola 2001).

2. Although some studies suggest that unemployed youth are more likely to express xenophobic opinions, crime statistics show that most individuals involved in right-wing criminal acts are employed (see Heitmeyer 1999, 65). A 1991 study by Held et al. also showed that youth with secure employment prospects express greater xenophobia than youth with poor employment prospects (qtd. In Schnabel 1993, 806; also see Steinmetz 1997).

3. Steinmetz cites Heitmeyer (1988) and Heitmeyer et al. (1992).

4. This is my perception based on how students distinguished between the "politically organized" neo-Nazis and the "violent" skinheads. This does not mean, however, that neo-Nazis do not engage in racist violence. Skinheads, however, appear to be more focused on violence and less on political issues.

5. As advertised in the 2003 catalog of the right-wing National Democratic Party of Germany (NPD), *Kampf und Wiedergeburt* (published by the Deutsche Stimme Verlag), p. 127. The group sells fifty milliliter bottles of eau de toilette for 20 Euros. Archival materials accessed on May 26, 2004, at the Antifaschistisches Pressearchiv und Bildungszentrum Berlin e.v. (Antifascist Press Archive and Educational Center in Berlin).

6. I heard about the number "88" several times while in Berlin; the symbol "100–12" was reported by a representative from the Antifaschistisches Pressearchiv und Bildungszentrum Berlin e.v. The number "18" is reported to stand for Adolf Hitler in PZ (Politische Zeitschrift), no. 103, September 2000, 4.

7. According to information provided by a representative from the Antifaschistisches Pressearchiv und Bildungszentrum Berlin e.v.

8. "Aktiv handeln gegen Rechts—Handlungsmöglichkeiten für die Berufsschule" (Addressing the Right Wing Actively—Strategies for Vocational Schools), a weekend seminar from November 30 to December 2, 2001 at the DGB-Jugendbildungsstätte Flecken Zechlin.

9. Antifaschistisches Pressearchiv und Bildungszentrum Berlin.

10. The word *Neger* is translated as "Negro" and has a derogatory connotation.

11. As discussed with a representative from a teacher-training project in Berlin.

12. Current political reforms concerning retirement that were being debated in German parliament at the time of my research were a frequent subject of discussion in the civics classrooms I observed, although not all of the teachers made the link between the need to reform the retirement system and the need to have increased numbers of foreign workers.

13. From the 1993 album *Auslese*. Information in archival materials at the Antifaschistisches Pressearchiv und Bildungszentrum Berlin e.v.

14. Information in archival materials at the Antifaschistisches Pressearchiv und Bildungszentrum Berlin e.v.

15. The Pioneer groups were GDR youth organizations. See Wegner (1996) for further discussion of youth political socialization in the GDR.

*Cynthia Miller-Idriss is associate professor of international education and educational sociology at New York University in the United States.

Miller-Idriss, Cynthia. "Raising the Right Wing: Educators' Struggle to Confront the Radical Right." In *Blood and Culture: Youth, Right-Wing Extremism, and National Belonging in Contemporary Germany*. Durham, NC: Duke University Press, 2009.

Appendix

Of Further Interest

ACADEMIC

Back, Les. 1990. *Racist Name Calling and Developing Anti-Racist Initiatives in Youth Work*. Warwick, UK: Center for Research in Ethnic Relations (Research Paper in Ethnic Relations, No. 14). Available at http://www.warwick.ac.uk/fac/soc/CRER_RC/publications/pdfs/Research%20 Papers%20in%20Ethnic%20Relations/RP%20No.14.pdf.

———. 1991. "Social Context and Racist Name Calling: An Ethnographic Perspective on Racist Talk Within a South London Adolescent Community." *European Journal of Intercultural Studies* 1, no. 3: 19–38.

Bartolomé Gutiérrez, Raquel, and Cristina Rechea Alberola. 2006. "Violent Youth Groups in Spain." *Youth* 19, no. 4: 323–342.

Bjørgo, Tore. 1998. "Entry, Bridge-Burning and Exit Options: What Happens to Young People Who Join Racist Groups—and Want to Leave?" In *Nation and Race: The Developing Euro-American Racist Subculture*, edited by Jeffrey Kaplan and Tore Bjørgo, 231–258. Boston: Northeastern University Press.

———. 2002. *Exit Neo-Nazism: Reducing Recruitment and Promoting Disengagement from Racist Groups*. Oslo: Norwegian Institute of International Affairs.

Boehnke, Klaus, John Hagan, and Hans Merkens. 1998. "Right-Wing Extremism Among German Adolescents: Risk Factors and Protective Factors." *Applied Psychology* 47, no. 1: 109–126.

Can, Kemal. 2000. "Youth, Turkism and the Extreme Right: The 'Idealist Hearts.'" In *Civil Society in the Grip of Nationalism*, edited by Stefanos Yerasimos, Guenter Steufert, and Karin Vonhoff, 335–373. Istanbul: Orient-Institut/IFEA.

Dacombe, Rod, and Momodou Sallah. 2006. "Racism and Young People in the United Kingdom." In *Prevention of Right-Wing Extremism, Xenophobia and Racism in European Perspective*, edited by Peter Rieker, Michaela Glaser, and Silke Schuster, 79–95. Halle: Deutsches Jugendinstitut e.V.

Edelstein, Wolfgang. 2003. "A Culture of Threat: Right-Wing Extremism and Negative Identity Formation in German Youth." *New Directions for Youth Development* 98: 81–97.

Falk, Armin, and Josef Zweimüller. 2005. *Unemployment and Right-Wing Extremist Crime*. London: Centre for Economic Policy Research (CEPR Discussion Paper No. 4997).

Fangen, Katrine. 1998. "Living Out Our Ethnic Instincts: Ideological Beliefs Among Right-Wing Activists in Norway." In *Nation and Race: The Developing Euro-American Racist Subculture*, edited by Jeffrey Kaplan and Tore Bjørgo, 202–230. Boston: Northeastern University Press.

———. 1998. "Right-Wing Skinheads: Nostalgia and Binary Oppositions." *Youth* 6, no. 3: 33–49.

———. 2003. "A Death Mask of Masculinity: The Brotherhood of Norwegian Right-Wing Skinheads." In *Among Men: Moulding Masculinities*, edited by Søren Ervø and Sean Johansson, 184–211. Aldershot, UK: Ashgate.

Grubben, Gé. 2006. "Right-Extremist Sympathies Among Adolescents in the Netherlands." In *Prevention of Right-Wing Extremism, Xenophobia and Racism in European Perspective*, edited by Peter Rieker, Michaela Glaser, and Silke Schuster, 48–66. Halle: Deutsches Jugendinstitut e.V.

Hagan, John, Hans Merkens, and Klaus Boehnke. 1995. "Delinquency and Disdain: Social Capital and the Control of Right-Wing Extremism in East and West Berlin Youth." *American Journal of Sociology* 100, no. 4: 1028–1052.

Hagan, John, Susanne Rippl, Klaus Boehnke, and Hans Merkens. 1999. "The Interest in Evil: Hierarchic Self-Interest and Right-Wing Extremism Among East and West German Youth." *Social Science Research* 28, no. 2: 162–183.

Hartmann, Ulrich, Hans-Peter Steffen, and Sigrid Steffen. 1985. *Rechtsextremismus bei Jugendlichen: Anregungen, der wachsenden Gefahr entgegenzuwirken*. Munich: Kösel.

Heitmeyer, Wilhelm. 1992. *Rechtsextremistische Orientierungen bei Jugendliche. Empirische Ergebnisse und Erklärungsmuster einer Untersuchung zur politischen Sozialisation*. Weinheim: Juventa.

Hicks, Wendy L. 2004. "Skinheads: A Three Nation Comparison." *Journal of Gang Research* 11, no. 2: 51–73.

Hjerm, Mikael. 2005. "What the Future May Bring: Xenophobia Among Swedish Adolescents." *Acta Sociologica* 48, no. 4: 292–307.

Hopf, Christel, et al. 1995. *Familie und Rechtsextremismus: Familiale Sozialisation und rechtsextremistische Orientierungen junger Männer.* Weinheim: Juventa.

Hörschelmann, Kathrin. 2005. "Deviant Masculinities: Representations of Neo-fascist Youth in Eastern Germany." In *Spaces of Masculinities*, edited by Bettina van Hoven and Kathrin Hörschelmann, 128–141. London: Routledge.

Kampf, Herbert A. 1980. "On the Appeals of Extremism to the Youth of Affluent, Democratic Nations." *Studies in Conflict and Terrorism* 4, nos. 1–4: 161–193.

Köttig, Michaela. 2004. *Lebensgeschichten rechtsextrem orientierter Mädchen und junger Frauen- Biographische Verläufe im Kontext der Familien- und Gruppendynamik.* Giessen: Psychosozial-Verlag.

Kürti, László. 1998. "The Emergence of Postcommunist Youth Identities in Eastern Europe: From Communist Youth, to Skinheads, to National Socialists and Beyond." In *Nation and Race: The Developing Euro-American Racist Subculture*, edited by Jeffrey Kaplan and Tore Bjørgo, 175–202. Boston: Northeastern University Press.

Lastouski, Aliaksei. 2008. "Ideas and Practices of the Skinhead Youth Counterculture in Belarus." *Political Sphere* 11:101–113.

Miller-Idriss, Cynthia. 2009. *Blood and Culture: Youth, Right-Wing Extremism, and National Belonging in Contemporary Germany.* Durham, NC: Duke University Press.

Mushaben, Joyce Marie. 1996. "The Rise of Femi-Nazis? Female Participation in Right-Extremist Movements in Unified Germany." *German Politics* 5, no. 2: 240–261.

Niggli, Marcel Alexander, ed. 2009. *Right-Wing Extremism in Switzerland: National and International Perspectives.* Baden-Baden: Nomos.

Perho, Sini. 2000. "The Racist Youth Subculture: The Case of the 'Little Skinheads' of Joensuu." *Youth* 8, no. 3: 17–36.

Pilkington, Hilary. 2010. "No Longer 'On Parade': Style and the Performance of Skinhead in the Russian Far North." *Russian Review* 69, no. 2: 187–209.

Rommelspacher, Birgit. 2006. *Der Hass hat uns geeint. Junge Rechtsextreme und ihr Ausstieg aus der Szene.* Frankfurt: Campus.

Sasada, Hironori. 2006. "Youth and Nationalism in Japan." *SAIS Review* 26, no. 2: 109–122.

Schieber, Martina. 2000. "Extreme Right Attitudes in the Biographies of West German Youth." In *The Turn to Biographical Methods in Social Science: Comparative Issues and Examples*, edited by Prue Chamberlayne, Jaonna Bornat, and Tom Wengraf, 214–228. London: Routledge.

Schubart, Wilfried. 1997. "Xenophobia Among East German Youth." In *Antisemitism and Xenophobia in Germany after Unification*, edited by Hermann Kurthen, Werner Bergmann, and Rainer Erb, 143–158. Oxford: Oxford University Press.

Sela-Shayovitz, Revital. 2011. "Neo-Nazis and Moral Panic: The Emergence of Neo-Nazi Youth Gangs in Israel." *Crime Media Culture* 7, no. 1: 67–82.

Tarasov, Aleksandr. 2001. "Offspring to Reforms—Shaven Heads Are Skinheads: The New Fascist Youth Subculture in Russia." *Russian Politics and Law* 39, no. 1: 43–89.

Virtanen, Timo, ed. 2000. *Youth, Racist Violence and Anti-Racist Responses in the Nordic Countries.* Available at http://www.nuorisotutkimusseura.fi/julkaisuja/virtanen/contents.html.

Watts, Meredith W. 1996. "Political Xenophobia in the Transition from Socialism: Threat, Racism and Ideology Among East German Youth." *Political Psychology* 17, no. 1: 97–126.

Willems, Helmut. 1995. "Right-Wing Extremism, Racism or Youth Violence? Explaining Violence Against Foreigners in Germany." *Journal of Ethnic and Migration Studies* 21, no. 4: 501–523

Young, Kevin, and Laura Craig. 2008. "Beyond White Pride: Identity, Meaning and Contradiction in the Canadian Skinhead Subculture." *Canadian Review of Sociology* 34, no. 2: 175–206.

Yuki, Honda. 2007. "Focusing in on Contemporary Japan's 'Youth' Nationalism." *Social Science Japan Journal* 10, no. 2: 281–286.

BIOGRAPHIES

Collins, Matthew. 2011. *Hate: My Life in the British Far Right*. London: Biteback.

Greason, David. 1994. *I Was a Teenage Fascist*. Ringwood: McPhee Gribble.

Hasselbach, Ingo. 1996. *Führer-Ex: Memoirs of a Former Neo-Nazi*. New York: Random House.

Leyden, T. J. (with M. Bridget Cook). 2008. *Skinhead Confessions: From Hate to Hope*. Springville, UT: Cedar Fort.

Roy, Jody M. 2010. *Autobiography of a Recovering Skinhead: The Frank Meeink Story*. Portland, OR: Hawthorne Books.

DOCUMENTARIES

From Russia with Love (Current TV, 2010)
Available at http://documentaryheaven.com/from-russia-with-hate.
Award-winning Current TV documentary of the skinhead movement in Russia, which speaks with skinhead members and leaders about their strategy of intimidation via Internet videos of beatings of minorities and immigrants. 20 minutes.

Inside American Skinheads (National Geographic, 2007)
Available at https://www.youtube.com/watch?v=0dviaE9t1Zo.
A documentary about modern-day racist American skinheads, which focuses on the use of the Internet for recruitment and critically investigates the attempts to provide a more moderate front. While insightful, it has a very sensationalist tone and lacks a broader perspective. 60 minutes.

Inside Story: Is the Extreme Right on the Rise in Europe? (Al Jazeera, 2011)
Available at http://documentary.net/is-the-extreme-right-on-the-rise-in-europe.
This documentary investigates the rise of extreme-right parties in Europe in the wake of the terrorist attack by Norwegian Anders Breivik in the summer of 2011. It aims to answer the following two questions: Is right-wing ideology really making an impression across Europe? And are governments tackling it, or inadvertently fueling it? 25 minutes.

Thug Politics (SBS Australia, 2013)
Available at http://www.sbs.com.au/dateline/story/watch/id/601692/n/Thug-Politics.
Very insightful documentary about the rise of Golden Dawn (CA) in Greece, which focuses on the group's actions and goals as well as some of the resistance against its rise. 16 minutes.

MOVIES

American History X (United States, 1998)
Derek Vineyard is paroled after serving three years in prison for killing two thugs who tried to break into and steal his truck. Through the narration of his brother, Danny Vineyard, we learn that before going to prison, Derek was a skinhead and the leader of a violent white-supremacist gang that committed racial crimes throughout Los Angeles, and his actions greatly influenced Danny. Reformed and fresh out of prison, Derek severs contact with the gang and becomes determined to keep Danny from going down the same violent path as he did.

Fuehrer Ex (Germany, 2004)
Based on the autobiographical experiences of co-screenwriter and former neo-Nazi leader Ingo Hasselbach, this harrowing drama takes a look at the hate-fueled neo-Nazi movement in Germany. In 1980s Berlin, two best friends conceive a plan to escape the Iron Curtain. Their plan fails, and they are sent to a harsh, Communist prison. Hard hitting and unflinching, *Fuehrer Ex* examines the politics of hate and the values of friendship.

Made in Britain (United Kingdom, 1982)
Trevor is a 16-year-old, violent skinhead with no regard for authority, and would rather spend his time stealing cars than sitting in the detention center to which he is sent. His social worker, Harry Parker, tries to do his best, but Trevor is only interested when there is something that he can get out of it. The authorities within the center try to make Trevor conform to the norms

of society, but he takes no notice, and would rather speak in a torrent of four-letter words and racial abuse.

Romper Stomper (Australia, 1992)

Nazi skinheads in Melbourne take out their anger on local Vietnamese, who are seen as threatening racial purity. Finally the Vietnamese have had enough and face off against the skinheads in an all-out confrontation, sending the skinheads running. A woman who is prone to epileptic seizures joins the skins' merry band and helps them on their run from justice, but is her affliction also a sign of impurity?

This Is England (United Kingdom, 2006)

A story set in 1983 about a troubled boy growing up in England. He comes across a few skinheads on his way home from school, after a fight. They become his new best friends, even like family. Based on the experiences of director Shane Meadows.